Othello

edited by Colin Gray

with additional material by
John Seely and Kathy Gray

Series Editor: John Seely

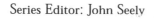

Heinemann

Heinemann Educational Publishers
Halley Court, Jordan Hill, Oxford OX2 8EJ
Part of Harcourt Education
Heinemann is a registered trademark of Harcourt Education Limited

Introduction, notes and activities © Colin Gray, John Seely 2000
Addition material by Kathy Gray
Essay by Joseph Goldsmith

First published in the Heinemann Advanced Shakespeare series 2000

06 05
10 9 8

10-digit: ISBN 0 435193 05 8
13-digit: ISBN 978 0 435193 05 8

Cover design by Miller Craig and Cocking
Cover illustration by Nigel Casseldine
Typeset by TechType
Printed and bound in the United Kingdom by
Biddles Ltd, King's Lynn, Norfolk

CONTENTS

How to use this book

This edition of *Othello* has been prepared to provide
you with several different kinds of information and guidance.

The introduction

Before the text of the play there is:
*   a summary of the plot
*   a brief explanation of Shakespeare's texts.

The text and commentary

On each right-hand page you will find the text of the play. On
the facing left-hand pages there are three types of support
material:
*   a summary of the action
*   detailed explanations of difficult words, phrases and longer
    sections of text
*   suggestions of points you might find it useful to think
    about as you read the play.

End-of-act activities

After each act there is a set of activities. These can be tackled as
you read the play. Many students, however, may want to leave
these until they undertake a second reading. They consist of the
following sections:

Keeping track: straightforward questions directing your
attention to precisely what happens in each act.

Discussion: topics for small-group, or whole-group discussion.

Close study: a detailed exploration of the act, scene by scene and
in some cases, line by line.

Language and imagery: guidance for studying the language
and imagery of the play, and the way they create richness and
significance.

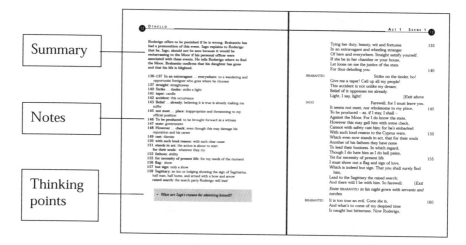

Summary

Notes

Thinking points

Key scene: a focus on an important scene in the act. This section applies the thinking you have done in the CLOSE STUDY to a key scene within the act and encourages you to think about how the scene fits in to the structure of the play as a whole.

Writing: progressive activities throughout the book help you to develop essay-writing skills.

Explorations

At the end of the book there is a variety of different items designed to draw together your thoughts and insights about the play as a whole:

- how to approach thinking about the whole play
- work on character
- work on themes and issues
- advice on essay writing, together with a sample essay written by an A-level student, with comments
- practice essay questions
- glossary of technical terms.

The plot

Act 1

Shakespeare sets the play in Venice when it was one of the most powerful and civilised states of Christian Europe. Othello, a Moor (North African), and, therefore, black, and a professed Christian, is Venice's most trusted and respected general. The Turks, infidels, are threatening to attack areas of the Eastern Mediterranean where Venice holds power, especially the island of Cyprus. (Such a situation arose not long before Shakespeare wrote the play.)

At the start of the play, we learn that Othello has caused great bitterness in his adjutant ('ancient'), Iago, by promoting Cassio, a Florentine, as his lieutenant. He has also shocked a Venetian Senator, Brabantio, by secretly marrying his daughter, Desdemona, to whom many young Venetians have unsuccessfully paid court, particularly Roderigo.

Iago declares his hatred for Othello, and plans to get even with him. He uses Roderigo (who is frustrated at his failure to win Desdemona's love) to inform Brabantio of his daughter's treachery in order to discredit Othello, while keeping to himself the rich presents Roderigo has been asking him to deliver to Desdemona.

News reaches Venice that the Turks are about to attack Cyprus, and the Duke sends for Othello. Before the Duke, Brabantio accuses Othello of seducing his daughter by witchcraft, but Othello tells his version of their love affair, and Desdemona, who has been sent for, backs him up unprompted. Brabantio's complaints are ignored, and Othello prepares to depart for Cyprus immediately, leaving Iago and his wife, Emilia, to escort Desdemona there.

Act 2

A storm destroys the Turkish threat, but the Venetians arrive safely. Iago observes Cassio's elaborate comforting of Desdemona while Othello is still at sea in the storm, and forms his plan to deceive Othello into believing that there is an affair between Desdemona and Cassio. Othello proclaims a night of celebration, and Iago uses it to get Cassio drunk and disgrace himself. He has persuaded Roderigo that Desdemona loves Cassio and that, if Roderigo can discredit Cassio by getting him involved in a street brawl, Cassio will be out of his way. Iago persuades the shamed Cassio to beg Desdemona to plead with Othello for his reinstatement. Meanwhile, he himself will put it in Othello's mind to watch Desdemona with Cassio.

Act 3

Iago's plan works, and Othello, cleverly prompted by Iago, descends rapidly into suspicion and mad jealousy. Iago is further assisted in this by Desdemona's chance dropping of a handkerchief of great sentimental value given to her by Othello (Emilia picks it up). Othello commits himself to revenge, wanting Iago to arrange Cassio's death while he plans to kill Desdemona. Desdemona protests her innocence and Emilia swears the same, but Othello, despite his infatuation with her, cannot be turned from his course.

Act 4

By the series of chances manipulated by Iago, Othello is led to believe that he sees the handkerchief in the hands of Bianca, a whore of Cassio's, and that he hears Cassio talking of Desdemona as if she were a whore who loves him.

Lodovico arrives from Venice with orders for Othello to return, and for Cassio to take command at Cyprus. Desdemona tells Lodovico of the rift between Othello and Cassio. Lodovico is shocked to see Othello strike Desdemona. Iago offers no clear explanation, but hints that Othello has lost control.

Othello orders Desdemona to bed and she asks Emilia to put her wedding sheets on the bed. The two women discuss men and marriage, Desdemona showing that her loyalty to Othello is unfailing.

Act 5

Meanwhile, Iago has set Roderigo (who has claimed that Iago cannot be trusted) to kill Cassio in a night attack. Othello witnesses this and believes Cassio to be dead. In fact, he is only wounded (by Iago); Roderigo is fatally wounded (also by Iago).

Othello, still intoxicated by Desdemona's beauty, smothers her because he believes this is justice. Before Desdemona dies, Emilia hears her say that no one is to blame for her death. Emilia discovers that Othello has killed his wife, convinces him that he was wrong in his suspicions, and is horrified to learn that Iago is behind it all. All Iago's plots are discovered and he wounds Emilia fatally. Othello, tormented by remorse and guilt, kills himself, claiming that he had 'loved not wisely but too well'.

OTHELLO

CHARACTERS

DUKE OF VENICE
BRABANTIO, a Senator, father of Desdemona
GRATIANO, brother of Brabantio
LODOVICO, kinsman of Brabantio
MONTANO, former Governor of Cyprus
OTHELLO, a Moor, general in the service of Venice
CASSIO, his lieutenant
IAGO, his ancient
RODERIGO, a gentleman of Venice
CLOWN, servant of Othello
DESDEMONA, daughter of Brabantio and wife of Othello
EMILIA, wife of Iago
BIANCA, mistress of Cassio

Senators, Gentlemen, Messenger, Sailor, Herald, Musicians,
Officers, Soldiers, Attendants, Servants

Roderigo complains that Iago, who has control of his money, has kept some information from him. Iago denies this. Roderigo reminds Iago that he said he hated an unnamed person. Iago insists that he does, explaining that this person rejected him for the post of deputy and promoted Michael Cassio, whom Iago scorns as a mere administrator. He says that he, Iago, has wide military experience.

2–3 **who ... thine:** who have been using money from my purse as if it were your own
3 **this:** what we have been talking about (the audience doesn't know what this is)
4 **'Sblood ... me:** God's blood! You're just not listening to me
5 **abhor:** shun
8 **great ones:** influential men
9 **In personal suit:** with a personal request
10 **off-capped:** raised their hats
11 **I am worth ... place:** I deserve no lower rank
12 **as ... purposes:** because he is proud and full of his own plans
13 **with a ... circumstance:** with a lot of important-sounding talk
14 **horribly ... war:** bristling with military jargon
16 **nonsuits my mediators:** denies my supporters' request
Certes: certainly
19 **a great arithmetician:** a man who knows about things only in theory
20 **a Florentine:** a man from Florence, a city known for its culture, learning and sophistication
21 **A fellow ... wife:** a man almost certain to sin and be damned every time he sees a beautiful woman who is someone else's wife (i.e. he will have adulterous thoughts)
24 **unless the bookish theoric:** except the theory learned from books
25 **toged consuls:** top civil servants (like Roman consuls in togas)
26–27 **Mere ... soldiership:** all he knows about soldiership is mere talk – he has no experience
27 **had th'election:** was chosen for promotion
28 **of whom:** whose military qualities
29 **Rhodes ... Cyprus:** sites of Venetian campaigns against the Turks

- *What do you sense to be the relationship between Iago and Roderigo?*
- *What is Iago's attitude to Michael Cassio?*

ACT ONE

Scene 1

Enter RODERIGO *and* IAGO

RODERIGO Tush, never tell me, I take it much unkindly
That thou, Iago, who hast had my purse
As if the strings were thine, shouldst know of this.

IAGO 'Sblood, but you will not hear me.
If ever I did dream of such a matter,
Abhor me.

RODERIGO Thou told'st me thou didst hold him in thy hate.

IAGO Despise me if I do not. Three great ones of the city,
In personal suit to make me his lieutenant
Off-capped to him and by the faith of man,   10
I know my price, I am worth no worse a place.
But he, as loving his own pride and purposes,
Evades them with a bombast circumstance
Horribly stuffed with epithets of war,
And in conclusion
Nonsuits my mediators. For 'Certes,' says he,
'I have already chose my officer'.
And what was he?
Forsooth, a great arithmetician,
One Michael Cassio, a Florentine –   20
A fellow almost damned in a fair wife –
That never set a squadron in the field,
Nor the division of a battle knows
More than a spinster, unless the bookish theoric,
Wherein the toged consuls can propose
As masterly as he. Mere prattle without practice
Is all his soldiership. But he, sir, had th'election;
And I – of whom his eyes had seen the proof
At Rhodes, at Cyprus, and on other grounds
Christian and heathen – must be lee'd and calmed   30

Iago says that promotion now stems from favouritism and academic prowess rather than seniority and concludes that he has no reason to love 'the Moor'. Roderigo says he wouldn't follow a master in such circumstances. Iago states that he is ambitious and puts on an act of obedience to serve his own ends while concealing his real feelings.

30–31 be lee'd … creditor: must have the wind taken out of my sails by a mere recorder of losses and profits (i.e. an accountant)

31 counter-caster: counting clerk

33 God bless the mark: God help me
his Moorship's ancient: ensign (personal officer) to the Moor in his great office

36–38 Preferment … first: you gain promotion by academic qualification and favouritism and not by seniority, whereby every deputy is next in line for the top rank

39 I … affined: I am justly, rightly obliged

40 Moor: an African, a black man

42 to serve my turn: get my own back

45 knee-crooking knave: contemptible person who bows and scrapes

46 doting … bondage: obsessed with his creeping and crawling

47 Wears … time: drags out his life

48 provender: food
cashiered: sacked

49 Whip … knaves: I couldn't care less about such dull and honest people

50 trimmed … duty: putting on a careful appearance of correct and dutiful behaviour

51 Keep … themselves: look after themselves first

53 lined their coats: made themselves a good fortune

54 Do themselves homage: give themselves the honours they used to give to their masters
have some soul: have some guts

57 Were … Iago: if I were the Moor, I would not wish to be Iago

58 I … myself: I am looking after my own interests

60 seeming so: putting on an act of love and duty
peculiar: particular and personal

62 The native … heart: my natural desires and character

63 In … extern: in outward behaviour

65 For daws … at: for scavenging birds to peck to pieces

> • *What tones and attitudes do you detect in the way Iago speaks here?*

By debitor and creditor. This counter-caster,
He in good time must his lieutenant be,
And I – God bless the mark – his Moorship's ancient.

RODERIGO   By heaven, I rather would have been his hangman.

IAGO   Why, there's no remedy, 'tis the curse of service,
Preferment goes by letter and affection
And not by old gradation, where each second
Stood heir to the first. Now sir, be judge yourself
Whether I in any just term am affined
To love the Moor.

RODERIGO   I would not follow him then.   40

IAGO   O sir, content you.
I follow him to serve my turn upon him.
We cannot all be masters, nor all masters
Cannot be truly followed. You shall mark
Many a duteous and knee-crooking knave
That doting on his own obsequious bondage,
Wears out his time, much like his master's ass,
For naught but provender, and when he's old cashiered.
Whip me such honest knaves. Others there are
Who, trimmed in forms and visages of duty,   50
Keep yet their hearts attending on themselves;
And throwing but shows of service on their lords,
Do well thrive by them, and when they have lined
        their coats,
Do themselves homage. These fellows have some soul,
And such a one do I profess myself. For sir,
It is as sure as you are Roderigo,
Were I the Moor, I would not be Iago.
In following him, I follow but myself.
Heaven is my judge, not I for love and duty,
But seeming so for my peculiar end;   60
For when my outward action doth demonstrate
The native act and figure of my heart
In compliment extern, 'tis not long after
But I will wear my heart upon my sleeve
For daws to peck at: I am not what I am.

Roderigo reflects bitterly on the Moor's good fortune
(whatever it is) and they arrive at a house which they refer to
as 'her father's'. Iago incites Roderigo to wake up the owner
and destroy his peace. Roderigo does so and Iago joins in
loudly. Brabantio appears above, wanting to know what the
noise is all about. Roderigo suggests that he check whether
his family is all safe. Iago interrupts to tell Brabantio that an
old black man is having sex with his daughter.

66 **full:** good
     thick-lips: an abusive description of a black man
     owe: have or own
67 **carry't:** succeed, carry it off
68 **him:** the Moor
     make after: pursue
69 **Proclaim:** denounce him
71 **Though ... joy:** though his joy is real
72 **changes of vexation:** hints of trouble
73 **lose some colour:** fade
75–77 **Do ... cities:** shout aloud with the same terrible volume
     and tone of fear as is used when a large city is found to be on
     fire at night as a result of negligence
87 **half your soul:** half of what you live for
89 **tupping:** term used to describe a ram mating with a ewe.
90 **snorting:** snoring
91 **devil:** the devil was usually depicted as black; he is referring to
     Othello
93 **reverend:** respected

> • *What knowledge do you have at this point about the Moor,
> the woman and her father (Brabantio)?*

RODERIGO	What a full fortune does the thick-lips owe,
	If he can carry't thus!
IAGO	Call up her father,
	Rouse him, make after him, poison his delight,
	Proclaim him in the streets, incense her kinsmen;
	And though he in a fertile climate dwell,
	Plague him with flies. Though that his joy be joy,
	Yet throw such changes of vexation on't,
	As it may lose some colour.
RODERIGO	Here is her father's house, I'll call aloud.
IAGO	Do, with like timorous accent and dire yell,
	As when, by night and negligence, the fire
	Is spied in populous cities.
RODERIGO	What ho, Brabantio! Signor Brabantio, ho!
IAGO	Awake! What ho, Brabantio! Thieves, thieves!
	Look to your house, your daughter, and your bags!
	Thieves, thieves!

Enter BRABANTIO *above*

BRABANTIO	What is the reason of this terrible summons?
	What is the matter there?
RODERIGO	Signor, is all your family within?
IAGO	Are your doors locked?
BRABANTIO	Why? Wherefore ask you this?
IAGO	Zounds sir, you're robbed; for shame put on your
	gown;
	Your heart is burst, you have lost half your soul.
	Even now, now, very now, an old black ram
	Is tupping your white ewe. Arise, arise;
	Awake the snorting citizens with the bell,
	Or else the devil will make a grandsire of you.
	Arise I say.
BRABANTIO	What, have you lost your wits?
RODERIGO	Most reverend signor, do you know my voice?
BRABANTIO	Not I. What are you?

70

80

90

Roderigo identifies himself and Brabantio orders him to leave because he has told him before that his daughter is not for him. As an influential citizen, he can cause Roderigo trouble. Brabantio dismisses Iago's talk of robbery. Iago continues to confront Brabantio with graphic descriptions of his daughter's sexual activities. When Brabantio reminds Roderigo that he knows him, Roderigo begins to tell him the details of his daughter's escape.

   96   charged: ordered
   99   distempering draughts: drink that has made you wild
100–101 Upon … quiet: you come to disturb my sleep with malicious intent
 103   place: status
 106   grange: isolated farmhouse
 107   In simple … soul: in a direct and honest spirit
 111   covered with: mated with
        Barbary: fine North African breed of horses
 112   coursers: racehorses
        jennets: small Spanish horses
 113   germans: relatives
 114   profane: foul-mouthed
 116   making … backs: having sex
 117   senator: Venice's head of state was the Doge (Duke), but the Great Council had the real power. Every male of twenty-five or over whose family was listed in the Book of Gold was a Councillor. The Councillors chose from among their own number the members of the committees that governed Venice; the senate was the first of these. Iago uses the term 'senator' sarcastically, in response to Brabantio's cry of 'villain'
 119   answer: pay for
 122   odd-even … watch: dreary early hours of the morning

> • *How is Roderigo behaving by comparison with Iago?*
> • *What do we learn about relations between Roderigo and Brabantio?*
> • *What do Iago's motives seem to be in continuing to shout up at Brabantio?*

RODERIGO	My name is Roderigo.
BRABANTIO	The worser welcome.
	I have charged thee not to haunt about my doors.
	In honest plainness thou hast heard me say
	My daughter is not for thee. And now in madness,
	Being full of supper and distempering draughts,
	Upon malicious knavery dost thou come
	To start my quiet.
RODERIGO	Sir, sir, sir –
BRABANTIO	But thou must needs be sure
	My spirit and my place have in them power
	To make this bitter to thee.
RODERIGO	Patience good sir.
BRABANTIO	What tell'st thou me of robbing? This is Venice;
	My house is not a grange.
RODERIGO	Most grave Brabantio,
	In simple and pure soul I come to you.
IAGO	Zounds sir, you are one of those that will not serve God
	if the devil bid you. Because we come to do you service
	and you think we are ruffians, you'll have your daughter
	covered with a Barbary horse; you'll have your nephews
	neigh to you; you'll have coursers for cousins, and jennets
	for germans.
BRABANTIO	What profane wretch art thou?
IAGO	I am one sir, that comes to tell you your daughter and the
	Moor are now making the beast with two backs.
BRABANTIO	Thou art a villain.
IAGO	You are a senator.
BRABANTIO	This thou shalt answer; I know thee Roderigo.
RODERIGO	Sir, I will answer anything. But I beseech you
	If't be your pleasure and most wise consent,
	As partly I find it is, that your fair daughter,
	At this odd-even and dull watch o'th'night,
	Transported with no worse nor better guard

100

110

120

Roderigo offers to be punished if he is wrong. Brabantio has had a premonition of this event. Iago explains to Roderigo that he, Iago, should not be seen because it would be embarrassing to the Moor if his personal officer were associated with these events. He tells Roderigo where to find the Moor.

125 **gross clasps:** foul embraces
lascivious: lecherous, lustful
126 **allowance:** consent, permission
127 **saucy:** cheeky, impertinent
128 **my manners:** my sense of what is fair behaviour
130 **from ... civility:** in contravention of all civilised behaviour
131 **trifle ... reverence:** treat you in a disrespectful way
133 **made ... revolt:** rebelled against you in a disgusting way
135–136 **In an extravagant ... everywhere:** to a wandering and opportunist foreigner who goes where he chooses
136 **Straight:** straightaway
139 **Strike ... tinder:** strike a light
140 **taper:** candle
141 **accident:** this occurrence
142 **Belief ... already:** believing it is true is already making me suffer
144 **not meet ... place:** inappropriate and threatening to my official position
145 **To be produced:** to be brought forward as a witness
146 **state:** government
147 **However ... check:** even though this may damage his reputation and his career
148 **cast:** dismiss
149 **with such loud reason:** with such clear cause
150 **stands in act:** the action is about to start
for their souls: whatever they try
151 **fathom:** ability
154 **for necessity of present life:** for my needs of the moment
155 **flag:** show
156 **but sign:** only a show
157 **Sagittary:** an inn or lodging showing the sign of Sagittarius, half man, half horse, and armed with a bow and arrow
raised search: the search party Roderigo will lead

> • *What impression do you have of Roderigo from the way he speaks to Brabantio?*
> • *What are Iago's reasons for absenting himself?*

But with a knave of common hire, a gondolier,
To the gross clasps of a lascivious Moor –
If this be known to you, and your allowance,
We then have done you bold and saucy wrongs;
But if you know not this, my manners tell me
We have your wrong rebuke. Do not believe
That from the sense of all civility   130
I thus would play and trifle with your reverence.
Your daughter, if you have not given her leave,
I say again, hath made a gross revolt,
Tying her duty, beauty, wit, and fortunes
In an extravagant and wheeling stranger
Of here and everywhere. Straight satisfy yourself.
If she be in her chamber or your house,
Let loose on me the justice of the state
For thus deluding you.

BRABANTIO   Strike on the tinder, ho!
Give me a taper! Call up all my people!   140
This accident is not unlike my dream;
Belief of it oppresses me already.
Light, I say, light!   [*Exit above*

IAGO   Farewell, for I must leave you.
It seems not meet, nor wholesome to my place,
To be produced – as if I stay, I shall –
Against the Moor. For I do know the state,
However this may gall him with some check,
Cannot with safety cast him; for he's embarked
With such loud reason to the Cyprus wars,
Which even now stands in act, that for their souls   150
Another of his fathom they have none,
To lead their business. In which regard,
Though I do hate him as I do hell pains,
Yet for necessity of present life
I must show out a flag and sign of love,
Which is indeed but sign. That you shall surely find
    him,
Lead to the Sagittary the raised search;
And there will I be with him. So farewell.   [*Exit*

Brabantio confirms that his daughter has gone and that his life is blighted. He confirms that Desdemona has fled, feels this is a kind of treason, and begins to wonder whether she has been bewitched. He sets off, armed and with police support, to find his daughter and Othello. He wishes, now, that Roderigo had married her, and promises to reward him for his help.

165   **Past thought:** beyond what can be imagined
168   **treason of the blood:** unnatural rebellion of daughter against father
170   **charms:** magic spells
171   **property:** true nature
174   **O would ... her:** I wish you had married her
175   **Some one ... another:** some of you search in one direction, some in another
180   **I may ... most:** I have influence in most houses
181   **some special ... night:** the night police
182   **I'll ... pains:** I'll make your efforts worthwhile, I'll reward you

> • *Look at Roderigo's lines on this page and consider the different ways in which an actor might play him.*

Enter BRABANTIO *in his night-gown with servants and torches*

BRABANTIO It is too true an evil. Gone she is,
And what's to come of my despised time   160
Is naught but bitterness. Now Roderigo,
Where didst thou see her? – O unhappy girl! –
With the Moor, say'st thou? – Who would be a father! –
How didst thou know 'twas she? – O, she deceives me
Past thought. – What said she to you? – Get more tapers.
Raise all my kindred. – Are they married, think you?

RODERIGO Truly I think they are.

BRABANTIO O heaven! How got she out? O treason of the blood!
Fathers, from hence trust not your daughters' minds
By what you see them act. Is there not charms   170
By which the property of youth and maidhood
May be abused? Have you not read, Roderigo,
Of some such thing?

RODERIGO   Yes sir, I have indeed.

BRABANTIO Call up my brother – O would you had had her! –
Some one way, some another. Do you know
Where we may apprehend her and the Moor?

RODERIGO I think I can discover him, if you please
To get good guard, and go along with me.

BRABANTIO Pray you lead on. At every house I'll call –
I may command at most. – Get weapons, ho!   180
And raise some special officers of night.
On, good Roderigo, I'll deserve your pains.
                                    [*Exeunt*

Iago appears with Othello and tells him that Roderigo has been spreading foul reports of Othello's behaviour – so foul that Iago could barely restrain himself from killing him. Othello says it is as well that Iago didn't. Although Iago points out that Brabantio is very powerful and could have Othello dismissed, Othello is confident that his own past services will speak louder than Brabantio's complaints. Othello states emphatically that he would not risk his freedom except for the fact that he loves Desdemona.

1   **in the trade of war:** in the course of doing my job as a soldier
2   **very … conscience:** an unbreakable principle
3   **contrived:** planned
3–4   **I lack … service:** I lack the evil necessary to advance myself
5   **yerked:** stabbed
      him: Roderigo
6   **prated:** talked on and on
7   **scurvy:** disparaging
10   **full … him:** with great difficulty stopped myself from killing him
11   **fast:** definitely
12   **magnifico:** great man (i.e. Brabantio)
13–14 **hath … Duke's:** has an influence which is powerful as the Duke's
15   **grievance:** trouble
16–17 **The law … cable:** the law, with all his power to put into action, will allow him
18   **signory:** government of senators
19   **out-tongue:** speak over the top of
      'Tis yet to know: it is yet to be made public
21   **promulgate:** make public
      fetch: derive
22   **siege:** rank
      demerits: merits
23   **unbonneted:** on equal terms. In Shakespeare's day, to 'bonnet' meant to remove one's hat as a mark of respect; 'unbonneted', therefore, might mean without showing deference.
25   **But that I:** if I did not
26   **unhoused free condition:** free and unrestrained way of life
27   **Put … confine:** restrict and imprison
28   **For the sea's worth:** even in return for the power and freedom of the sea

- *What is your first impression of Othello?*
- *How do you react to Iago's reports of Roderigo?*

Scene 2

Enter OTHELLO, IAGO, *and* ATTENDANTS *with torches*

IAGO   Though in the trade of war I have slain men,
                    Yet do I hold it very stuff o'th'conscience
                    To do no contrived murder: I lack iniquity
                    Sometimes to do me service. Nine or ten times
                    I had thought t'have yerked him here under the ribs.

OTHELLO   'Tis better as it is.

IAGO   Nay but he prated
                    And spoke such scurvy and provoking terms
                    Against your honour,
                    That with the little godliness I have
                    I did full hard forbear him. But I pray you sir,   10
                    Are you fast married? For be assured of this,
                    That the magnifico is much beloved,
                    And hath in his effect a voice potential
                    As double as the Duke's. He will divorce you,
                    Or put upon you what restraint and grievance
                    The law, with all his might to enforce it on,
                    Will give him cable.

OTHELLO   Let him do his spite:
                    My services which I have done the signory,
                    Shall out-tongue his complaints. 'Tis yet to know –
                    Which, when I know that boasting is an honour,   20
                    I shall promulgate – I fetch my life and being
                    From men of royal siege; and my demerits
                    May speak unbonneted to as proud a fortune
                    As this that I have reached. For know, Iago,
                    But that I love the gentle Desdemona,
                    I would not my unhoused free condition
                    Put into circumscription and confine
                    For the sea's worth. But look, what lights come yond?

Enter CASSIO *and* OFFICERS *with torches*

Iago thinks Brabantio is arriving but Othello refuses to leave – rather, he says he wants to be found and believes his fine qualities will speak for him. Cassio arrives with a message that there is an emergency in Cyprus and Othello is needed in council. While Othello is indoors, Iago tells Cassio about Othello's marriage, but before he can reveal who Othello's wife is, Othello returns.

31 **parts:** personal qualities
33 **Janus:** Roman god who faced both ways
37 **haste-post-haste:** immediate, as quickly as possible
39 **divine:** understand, interpret
40 **heat:** urgency
41 **sequent:** one after the other
44 **hotly:** urgently
46 **three several quests:** search parties in three different directions
50 **boarded a land carrack:** captured and boarded a treasure ship – by which Iago means that Othello has got himself a very rich woman (Iago uses the image of the carrack to describe Desdemona and the profit she brings to Othello as her husband)
51 **lawful prize:** legally confirmed winnings, i.e. a legal marriage

> • *What is the effect of Othello's words when he believes Brabantio is coming (lines 30–32)?*

IAGO	Those are the raised father and his friends.
	You were best go in.
OTHELLO	Not I; I must be found. 30
	My parts, my title, and my perfect soul
	Shall manifest me rightly. Is it they?
IAGO	By Janus, I think no.
OTHELLO	The servants of the Duke? And my lieutenant?
	The goodness of the night upon you, friends.
	What is the news?
CASSIO	The Duke does greet you, General,
	And he requires your haste-post-haste appearance
	Even on the instant.
OTHELLO	What is the matter, think you?
CASSIO	Something from Cyprus, as I may divine;
	It is a business of some heat. The galleys 40
	Have sent a dozen sequent messengers
	This very night at one another's heels;
	And many of the consuls, raised and met,
	Are at the Duke's already. You have been hotly called
	for;
	When being not at your lodging to be found,
	The senate hath sent about three several quests
	To search you out.
OTHELLO	'Tis well I am found by you.
	I will but spend a word here in the house,
	And go with you. [*Exit*
CASSIO	Ancient, what makes he here?
IAGO	Faith, he tonight hath boarded a land carrack. 50
	If it prove lawful prize, he's made for ever.
CASSIO	I do not understand.
IAGO	He's married.
CASSIO	To who?

Enter OTHELLO

IAGO	Marry, to – Come Captain, will you go?

Brabantio and his men arrive. Othello tries to take command but Brabantio is so angry that swords are drawn. Iago challenges Roderigo to fight. Othello does not arm himself and orders everyone to stop, suggesting that Brabantio's seniority is more influential than his sword. Brabantio accuses Othello of stealing his daughter. He believes Desdemona could not have gone with Othello willingly (after rejecting eligible Venetians) if she hadn't been bewitched. He calls on his men to arrest Othello.

53 **Have with you:** I'll come with you
58 **I am for you:** I'm ready to fight you
60 **with years:** because of your seniority and wisdom
62 **stowed:** hidden
63 **enchanted:** put a spell on her
64 **I'll refer ... sense:** I am confident that by any standard of common sense
67 **opposite:** opposed
68 **wealthy ... nation:** the rich young noblemen with their fashionable curled hair
69 **t'incur ... mock:** with the threat of becoming a public laughing-stock
70 **her guardage:** the protection of her family
72 **Judge me the world:** I call the world to judge
    gross in sense: blatant
73 **practised on:** tricked, deceived
74 **abused:** exploited
    minerals: poisons
75 **weakens motion:** weaken her spirit of resistance
    disputed on: legally debated
76 **palpable to thinking:** very obvious when you think about it
77 **apprehend:** take hold of
    attach: arrest
78 **abuser of the world:** corrupter of respectable society
78–79 **practiser ... warrant:** one who practises forbidden arts (i.e. magic, witchcraft)
81 **at his peril:** or he will suffer

- *Apart from appearing loyal to Othello, why does Iago challenge Roderigo (line 58)? What might Roderigo's reaction be?*
- *What do you learn about the way Brabantio sees his daughter?*

OTHELLO	Have with you.
CASSIO	Here comes another troop to seek for you.

Enter BRABANTIO, RODERIGO, *and* OFFICERS *with torches and weapons*

IAGO	It is Brabantio. General, be advised; He comes to bad intent.
OTHELLO	Holla, stand there.
RODERIGO	Signor, it is the Moor.
BRABANTIO:	Down with him, thief!

[*They draw on both sides*

IAGO	You, Roderigo? Come sir, I am for you.	
OTHELLO	Keep up your bright swords, for the dew will rust them.	
	Good signor, you shall more command with years	60
	Than with your weapons.	
BRABANTIO	O thou foul thief, where hast thou stowed my daughter?	
	Damned as thou art, thou hast enchanted her;	
	For I'll refer me to all things of sense,	
	If she in chains of magic were not bound,	
	Whether a maid so tender, fair, and happy,	
	So opposite to marriage that she shunned	
	The wealthy curled darlings of our nation,	
	Would ever have – t'incur a general mock –	
	Run from her guardage to the sooty bosom	70
	Of such a thing as thou; to fear, not to delight.	
	Judge me the world, if 'tis not gross in sense	
	That thou hast practised on her with foul charms,	
	Abused her delicate youth with drugs or minerals	
	That weakens motion. I'll have't disputed on;	
	'Tis probable, and palpable to thinking.	
	I therefore apprehend, and do attach thee	
	For an abuser of the world, a practiser	
	Of arts inhibited and out of warrant.	
	Lay hold upon him; if he do resist,	80
	Subdue him, at his peril.	

Othello recognises that it is not a time for fighting and agrees to go with Brabantio to answer the charge, but points out that he is on his way to respond to the Duke's appeal for help in a national emergency. Brabantio agrees to go with Othello to the Duke. He feels that there he will get support from like-minded people. He sees dire consequences for Venetian society if Othello gets away with stealing his daughter.

82 **of my inclining:** who are loyal to me
86 **course of direct session:** procedure of immediate trial
90 **present:** immediate
95 **idle cause:** trivial claim
97 **as 'twere:** as if it were
99 **Bondslaves and pagans:** slaves and heathens

> • *What do lines 98–99 show us about Brabantio's view of Othello?*

The Duke and other Senators are receiving varying reports as to the size of the Turkish fleet.

1 **composition:** coherence, clear sense
2 **gives them credit:** makes them believable
   disproportioned: incoherent

OTHELLO	Hold your hands,

Both you of my inclining, and the rest.
Were it my cue to fight, I should have known it
Without a prompter. Where will you that I go
To answer this your charge?

BRABANTIO   To prison, till fit time
Of law and course of direct session
Call thee to answer.

OTHELLO   What if I do obey?
How may the Duke be therewith satisfied,
Whose messengers are here about my side,
Upon some present business of the state   90
To bring me to him.

OFFICER   'Tis true, most worthy signor;
The Duke's in council, and your noble self
I am sure is sent for.

BRABANTIO   How? The Duke in council?
In this time of the night? Bring him away;
Mine's not an idle cause. The Duke himself,
Or any of my brothers of the state,
Cannot but feel this wrong as 'twere their own
For if such actions may have passage free,
Bondslaves and pagans shall our statesmen be.

[*Exeunt*

Scene 3

The DUKE *and* SENATORS *at a table; with lights and*
ATTENDANTS

DUKE   There is no composition in these news
That gives them credit.

1ST SENATOR   Indeed they are disproportioned.

However, all the reports confirm the fact that the Turkish fleet is heading for Cyprus. A sailor arrives with more news that the Turks are now heading for Rhodes, but the Venetians suspect this is a decoy move because Cyprus is a more important and easier target for them.

5   **jump ... account:** do not agree a precise number
6   **the aim reports:** the report is based on an informed guess
7   **with difference:** with variations
8   **bearing up:** heading
9   **possible ... judgment:** credible to anyone applying logic
10   **I do not ... error:** I do not feel confident because the reports differ about the details
11   **main article:** the essence of the report
12   **In fearful sense:** with a sense of fear
15   **The Turkish ... makes for:** the Turks are targeting their forces on
18   **How ... change?:** how do you interpret this change of target?
18–19 **This cannot ... reason:** this is extremely unlikely by any test of reason
19   **pageant:** show, decoy
20   **in false gaze:** looking in the wrong direction
21   **importancy:** importance
22   **let ... understand:** let us remind ourselves
23   **as it ... the Turk:** as Cyprus is of more concern to the Turks
24   **So ... it:** so may the Turks win Cyprus by easier means
25   **For that:** because
     stands ... brace: it is not so formidably prepared for war
26   **th'abilities:** ability to defend itself
27   **is dressed in:** is prepared with
     If we ... this: if we remember this
28   **so unskilful:** so tactically stupid
29   **latest:** till last
30   **Neglecting ... gain:** ignoring an opportunity to make an easy gain
31   **To ... profitless:** to provoke a situation which will bring great risk and little profit
32   **in all confidence:** I am certain

> • *What impression do you have of the Venetians' control of the situation with the Turks?*

	My letters say a hundred and seven galleys.
DUKE	And mine a hundred and forty.
2ND SENATOR	And mine two hundred.

But though they jump not on a just account –
As in these cases where the aim reports,
'Tis oft with difference – yet do they all confirm
A Turkish fleet, and bearing up to Cyprus.

DUKE Nay, it is possible enough to judgment.
I do not so secure me in the error,   10
But the main article I do approve
In fearful sense.

SAILOR [*Within*] What ho, what ho, what ho!

OFFICER A messenger from the galleys.

Enter SAILOR

DUKE   Now, what's the business?

SAILOR The Turkish preparation makes for Rhodes;
So was I bid report here to the state
By Signor Angelo.

DUKE How say you by this change?

1ST SENATOR   This cannot be,
By no assay of reason. 'Tis a pageant
To keep us in false gaze. When we consider   20
Th'importancy of Cyprus to the Turk,
And let ourselves again but understand,
That as it more concerns the Turk than Rhodes,
So may he with more facile question bear it,
For that it stands not in such warlike brace,
But altogether lacks th'abilities
That Rhodes is dressed in. If we make thought of this,
We must not think the Turk is so unskilful
To leave that latest which concerns him first,
Neglecting an attempt of ease and gain,   30
To wake and wage a danger profitless.

DUKE Nay, in all confidence, he's not for Rhodes.

It transpires that they have only gone to join another fleet and are again heading for Cyprus. This is confirmed by Montano (who, we will learn, is the commander in Cyprus). The Duke is making plans when Othello and Brabantio arrive. He greets Othello hurriedly and tells him that the state needs his services against the Turks. He then welcomes Brabantio and says that he has missed his advice. Brabantio replies that he has not come for any reason of state.

34 **Ottomites:** Turks
    reverend and gracious: (addressed to the Duke)
36 **injointed ... fleet:** joined up with a fleet sent after them
38–39 **re-stem ... course:** turn back on to their original course
39–40 **bearing ... Cyprus:** making their intentions to attack Cyprus absolutely plain
41 **servitor:** servant
42 **With his ... thus:** advises you out of loyal duty that this is true
49 **straight:** immediately
50 **general:** public
    Ottoman: Turkish
52 **lacked your counsel:** missed your advice
53–54 **pardon me ... business:** I beg your pardon that neither my official position nor any news of public affairs ...
55 **general care:** public concern
56 **particular:** personal
57–59 **Is of ... still itself:** overwhelms me in such a flood that it engulfs and swallows up any other sorrow, and yet continues always the same itself

> • *The Duke's first words to Brabantio are 'I did not see you'. How do you interpret this?*

OFFICER | Here is more news.

Enter MESSENGER

MESSENGER | The Ottomites, reverend and gracious,
Steering with due course towards the isle of Rhodes,
Have there injointed them with an after fleet.

1ST SENATOR | Ay, so I thought. How many, as you guess?

MESSENGER | Of thirty sail. And now they do re-stem
Their backward course, bearing with frank
   appearance
Their purposes toward Cyprus. Signor Montano,   40
Your trusty and most valiant servitor,
With his free duty recommends you thus,
And prays you to believe him.

DUKE | 'Tis certain then for Cyprus.
Marcus Luccicos, is not he in town?

1ST SENATOR | He's now in Florence.

DUKE | Write from us to him; post-post-haste dispatch.

1ST SENATOR | Here comes Brabantio and the valiant Moor.

Enter BRABANTIO, OTHELLO, CASSIO, IAGO, RODERIGO,
and OFFICERS

DUKE | Valiant Othello, we must straight employ you
Against the general enemy Ottoman.   50
[*To* BRABANTIO] I did not see you; welcome, gentle
   signor,
We lacked your counsel and your help tonight.

BRABANTIO | So did I yours. Good your grace, pardon me,
Neither my place, nor aught I heard of business,
Hath raised me from my bed; nor doth the general
   care
Take hold on me; for my particular grief
Is of so flood-gate and o'erbearing nature
That it engluts and swallows other sorrows,
And yet is still itself.

DUKE | Why, what's the matter?

Brabantio goes on to explain that he is overwhelmed because his daughter has been stolen from him by witchcraft. The Duke promises Brabantio that whoever has corrupted his daughter will pay whatever penalty Brabantio chooses. Brabantio accuses Othello, whom the Duke then asks to put his side of the case. Othello admits only that he has married Desdemona. He explains that he has led a rough military life and cannot explain himself in sophisticated language.

62 **mountebanks:** quack doctors
63 **For … err:** for nature to go against itself so outrageously
64 **deficient:** corrupt
   lame of sense: intellectually defective
65 **Sans witchcraft could not:** could not have happened without witchcraft
66 **in this foul proceeding:** by this foul means
67 **beguiled … herself:** lured your daughter away, contrary to her own nature
68 **bloody:** deadly
69–70 **read in … sense:** read every bitter letter and word of condemnation as you interpret it
70 **our proper:** my own
71 **Stood … action:** faced your accusation
73 **mandate:** command
77 **potent:** powerful
81–82 **head … more:** the height and breadth of my assault is no more than this ('head' and 'front' are military terms concerning assaults)
82 **Rude:** rough, simple, uneducated
84 **pith:** strength
85 **nine moons wasted:** nine months past
85–86 **they have … field:** their most valued use has been in military campaigning
88 **pertains to:** concerns
   broil: fighting
89 **grace my cause:** improve my case

> • *The general reaction to Brabantio's accusation is sorrow. The Duke gives Othello a chance to explain himself. How might an audience be affected by this situation?*

BRABANTIO   My daughter! O my daughter!

DUKE *and* SENATORS   Dead?

BRABANTIO   Ay, to me.   60
She is abused, stolen from me, and corrupted
By spells and medicines bought of mountebanks;
For nature so preposterously to err,
Being not deficient, blind, or lame of sense,
Sans witchcraft could not.

DUKE   Whoe'er he be that in this foul proceeding
Hath thus beguiled your daughter of herself,
And you of her, the bloody book of law
You shall yourself read in the bitter letter
After your own sense; yea, though our proper son   70
Stood in your action.

BRABANTIO   Humbly I thank your grace.
Here is the man; this Moor, whom now it seems
Your special mandate for the state affairs
Hath hither brought.

ALL   We are very sorry for't.

DUKE   [*To* OTHELLO]

What in your own part can you say to this?

BRABANTIO   Nothing, but this is so.

OTHELLO   Most potent, grave, and reverend signors,
My very noble and approved good masters,
That I have ta'en away this old man's daughter,
It is most true; true I have married her;   80
The very head and front of my offending
Hath this extent, no more. Rude am I in my speech
And little blessed with the soft phrase of peace;
For since these arms of mine had seven years' pith
Till now some nine moons wasted, they have used
Their dearest action in the tented field;
And little of this great world can I speak
More than pertains to feats of broil and battle,
And therefore little shall I grace my cause

Othello promises to tell the whole story in simple terms. He denies the use of magic to win Desdemona. Brabantio insists that Othello could have won such a well-bred girl only by foul means. The Duke asks Othello to reply to the accusations. Othello suggests they send for Desdemona to give her view and says he will abide by the consequences. The Duke sends for Desdemona.

90 **by your gracious patience:** if you will have the grace to be patient with me
91 **round:** plain, straightforward
unvarnished: unexaggerated
92 **charms:** magic spells
93 **conjuration:** use of spells
96–97 **her motion … herself:** she was shy about her own passions
97 **nature:** natural character
98 **credit:** reputation
100–102 **It is … nature:** only a person of defective judgement could think that a perfect girl like Desdemona could voluntarily break all of nature's laws
102–104 **and must be … should be:** a sound judge must conclude that witchcraft was responsible
104 **vouch:** assert
105 **mixtures:** potions
106 **dram … effect:** potion compounded for this purpose
107 **wrought upon:** put a spell on
To vouch … proof: to assert this does not constitute proof
108 **overt:** open
109–110 **thin habits … seeming:** superficial instances and unlikely examples of fashionable theories
110 **prefer:** bring forward
112 **indirect … courses:** devious and enforced means
114 **fair question:** open discussion
115 **As soul … affordeth:** as one soul opens itself to another

> • *For what reasons does Brabantio find it impossible to believe that Desdemona could have fallen naturally for Othello?*

In speaking for myself. Yet, by your gracious patience,   90
I will a round unvarnished tale deliver
Of my whole course of love; what drugs, what charms,
What conjuration and what mighty magic –
For such proceedings I am charged withal –
I won his daughter.

BRABANTIO   A maiden never bold;
Of spirit so still and quiet, that her motion
Blushed at herself, and she, in spite of nature,
Of years, of country, credit, everything,
To fall in love with what she feared to look on.
It is a judgment maimed and most imperfect   100
That will confess perfection so could err
Against all rules of nature, and must be driven
To find out practices of cunning hell
Why this should be. I therefore vouch again
That with some mixtures powerful o'er the blood
Or with some dram conjured to this effect,
He wrought upon her.

DUKE   To vouch this is no proof,
Without more wider and more overt test
Than these thin habits and poor likelihoods
Of modern seeming do prefer against him.   110

1ST SENATOR But Othello, speak.
Did you by indirect and forced courses
Subdue and poison this young maid's affections?
Or came it by request, and such fair question
As soul to soul affordeth?

OTHELLO   I do beseech you,
Send for the lady to the Sagittary,
And let her speak of me before her father.
If you do find me foul in her report,
The trust, the office I do hold of you
Not only take away, but let your sentence   120
Even fall upon my life.

DUKE   Fetch Desdemona hither.

Othello sends Iago to show the Duke's men where to find
Desdemona. While they are gone, Othello undertakes to tell
as truthfully as if he were making his confession how he
wooed Desdemona. He says that Brabantio loved him and
often invited him to talk about his strange and dangerous
life. As he did so, Desdemona became infatuated, tearing
herself away from her household duties to hear more. And so
he took his chance, and drew from her an earnest request for
him to tell his tale in full.

129 **Still:** continually
132 **ran it through:** told it all in detail
134 **chances:** chance happenings
135 **moving accidents … field:** stirring events on sea and land
136 **scapes:** escapes
     i'th'imminent deadly breach: at the dangerous moment
     when an attacking force breaks through fortifications
137 **insolent:** presumptuous
138 **redemption:** release by payment
139 **portance:** conduct, demeanor
140 **antres:** caves
     idle: empty
142 **process:** my story
144 **Anthropophagi:** eaters of human flesh (i.e. cannibals)
146 **seriously incline:** lean forward to listen earnestly
147 **still:** always
     house affairs: household duties
148 **ever as:** whenever
     dispatch: deal with
150 **discourse:** talk
151 **pliant:** convenient, suitable
152 **a prayer of earnest heart:** a request from the bottom of
     her heart
153 **all my pilgrimage dilate:** recount in full all my travels
154 **by parcels:** in bits and pieces
155 **intentively:** with full attention

> • *How do you respond to Othello's reference to his confession*
> *(lines 123–124), considering the way Brabantio thinks of*
> *him?*

OTHELLO   Ancient, conduct them: you best know the place.

                                    [*Exit* IAGO *with* ATTENDANTS

            And till she come, as truly as to heaven
            I do confess the vices of my blood,
            So justly to your grave ears I'll present
            How I did thrive in this fair lady's love,
            And she in mine.

DUKE   Say it Othello.

OTHELLO   Her father loved me, oft invited me,
            Still questioned me the story of my life
            From year to year – the battles, sieges, fortunes,   130
            That I have passed.
            I ran it through even from my boyish days
            To th'very moment that he bade me tell it;
            Wherein I spake of most disastrous chances,
            Of moving accidents by flood and field,
            Of hair-breadth scapes i' the imminent deadly breach,
            Of being taken by the insolent foe,
            And sold to slavery; of my redemption thence,
            And portance in my travels' history;
            Wherein of antres vast and deserts idle,   140
            Rough quarries, rocks, and hills whose heads touch
                heaven,
            It was my hint to speak – such was the process;
            And of the Cannibals that each other eat,
            The Anthropophagi, and men whose heads
            Do grow beneath their shoulders. This to hear
            Would Desdemona seriously incline;
            But still the house affairs would draw her thence,
            Which ever as she could with haste dispatch,
            She'd come again, and with a greedy ear
            Devour up my discourse; which I observing   150
            Took once a pliant hour, and found good means
            To draw from her a prayer of earnest heart
            That I would all my pilgrimage dilate
            Whereof by parcels she had something heard,
            But not intentively. I did consent,

Desdemona was often moved to tears by his story, and
wished for a man of such experience. Othello took the hint
and told her of his love. Desdemona arrives. The Duke says
that such a tale would have moved his own daughter, and
that Brabantio should make the best of his situation.
Brabantio says he will deserve punishment for condemning
Othello if Desdemona confesses an equal share in the
wooing. He asks her to whom she owes most obedience.
Desdemona explains that she had a duty to her father but,
now that she is married, this duty has passed to her husband.

156 **beguile her of her tears:** charm tears from her
157 **stroke:** blow
159 **pains:** sufferings
160 **passing:** very
161 **wondrous:** wonderfully
163 **had made her such a man:** created such a husband for her
167 **passed:** gone through
173 **take up this mangled matter at the best:** make the best of
    this confused affair
174–175 **Men do ... hands:** men do better to make the best of
    what little they have than to throw everything away
176 **half the wooer:** had an equal share in the wooing
177 **Destruction on my head:** I will accept that I deserve
    punishment
178 **Light on:** fall on (alight on)
182 **education:** upbringing
183 **learn:** teach
185 **hitherto:** till now

> • *Can you tell who first declared love – Othello or*
> *Desdemona – according to Othello's account?*

And often did beguile her of her tears
When I did speak of some distressful stroke
That my youth suffered. My story being done,
She gave me for my pains a world of sighs.
She swore, in faith 'twas strange, 'twas passing
    strange,   160
'Twas pitiful, 'twas wondrous pitiful.
She wished she had not heard it, yet she wished
That heaven had made her such a man. She thanked
    me,
And bade me, if I had a friend that loved her,
I should but teach him how to tell my story,
And that would woo her. Upon this hint I spake.
She loved me for the dangers I had passed,
And I loved her, that she did pity them.
This only is the witchcraft I have used.
Here comes the lady; let her witness it.   170

Enter DESDEMONA, IAGO, *and* ATTENDANTS

DUKE   I think this tale would win my daughter too.
Good Brabantio,
Take up this mangled matter at the best.
Men do their broken weapons rather use
Than their bare hands.

BRABANTIO   I pray you, hear her speak.
If she confess that she was half the wooer,
Destruction on my head, if my bad blame
Light on the man. Come hither gentle mistress.
Do you perceive in all this noble company
Where most you owe obedience?

DESDEMONA   My noble father,   180
I do perceive here a divided duty.
To you I am bound for life and education;
My life and education both do learn me
How to respect you; you are lord of all my duty,
I am hitherto your daughter. But here's my husband,
And so much duty as my mother showed
To you, preferring you before her father,

Brabantio gives in, saying he'd rather adopt a child than have his own, and bitterly gives Desdemona away. The Duke tries to comfort him with platitudes. Brabantio is bitter. The Duke says that Othello knows the state of Cyprus's defences.

188 **challenge:** claim
189 **God bu'y:** God be with you
190 **Please it:** may it please
     on to: to go on to
191 **get:** beget, father
194 **but thou hast already:** if it weren't for the fact that you have her already
196 **at soul:** to the bottom of my heart
197 **tyranny:** to be a tyrant
198 **To hang clogs on them:** to tie heavy blocks of wood to their legs to stop them escaping
199 **like yourself:** like the wise counsellor you are
     lay a sentence: give a carefully judged opinion
200 **grise:** a first move
202 **remedies are past:** the chances of mending the situation are gone
203 **seeing the worst:** facing the worst of the situation
     late: recently
     on hopes depended: continued to rely on hope
205 **next:** quickest
206 **fortune takes:** fate takes it away
207 **Patience ... makes:** being patient makes the sense of injury look silly
208 **The robbed ... thief:** the person who has been robbed yet smiles about it takes something from the thief
209 **bootless:** pointless
210 **beguile:** cheat
212–213 **He bears ... hears:** a man takes a harsh decision well if all he hears is the comforting advice that follows it
215 **That ... borrow:** who, to endure his grief, must draw on his poor reserves of patience
216 **sentences:** fine-sounding words
     to sugar or to gall: to sweeten or to embitter
217 **Being ... equivocal:** having influence in both directions, of equal value and therefore of no value
219 **bruised ... ear:** heart which is hurt is never comforted by words
221 **preparation:** force ready for battle
222 **fortitude:** strength of the defences

- *What are the effects of the Duke's and Barabantio's rhyming speeches (lines 204 – 210 and 211 – 220)?*

So much I challenge that I may profess
Due to the Moor my lord.

BRABANTIO   God bu'y, I have done.
Please it your grace, on to the state affairs.   190
I had rather to adopt a child than get it.
Come hither Moor;
I here do give thee that with all my heart
Which but thou hast already with all my heart
I would keep from thee. For your sake, jewel,
I am glad at soul I have no other child;
For thy escape would teach me tyranny
To hang clogs on them. I have done, my lord.

DUKE   Let me speak like yourself, and lay a sentence,
Which as a grise or step may help these lovers   200
Into your favour.
When remedies are past, the griefs are ended
By seeing the worst, which late on hopes depended.
To mourn a mischief that is past and gone
Is the next way to draw new mischief on.
What cannot be preserved when fortune takes,
Patience her injury a mockery makes.
The robbed that smiles steals something from the thief;
He robs himself that spends a bootless grief.

BRABANTIO   So let the Turk of Cyprus us beguile,   210
We lose it not so long as we can smile.
He bears the sentence well that nothing bears
But the free comfort which from thence he hears;
But he bears both the sentence and the sorrow
That to pay grief must of poor patience borrow.
These sentences, to sugar or to gall
Being strong on both sides, are equivocal.
But words are words; I never yet did hear
That the bruised heart was pierced through the ear.
I humbly beseech you, proceed to th'affairs of state.   220

DUKE   The Turk with a most mighty preparation makes for
Cyprus. Othello, the fortitude of the place is best
known to you; and though we have there a substitute

The Duke puts Othello in command of Cyprus. He must
forego his present joy. He says he is more used to the rigours
of war than to soft beds, but insists that proper
arrangements be made for Desdemona. The Duke suggests
that she should stay with her father. Brabantio and Othello
reject the Duke's proposal. Desdemona explains that her
passion led her to want to live with Othello.

223–224 **a substitute … sufficiency:** a deputy with a reputation
    for competence
224–226 **yet opinion … you:** yet the general opinion, which is
    decisive in these matters, is that the task will be most
    securely performed in your hands
226 **slubber:** spoil, pass roughly over
227 **more stubborn:** more demanding and unavoidable
228 **boisterous:** violent
231 **thrice-driven:** softest
231–233 **I do agnize … hardness:** I recognise that I have an
    instinctive readiness to act in harsh situations
234 **Ottomites:** Turks
235 **bending to your state:** respecting your position
236 **fit disposition:** appropriate arrangements
237 **Due … exhibition:** treatment appropriate to her position
    with suitable financial allowance
238 **besort:** serving staff
239 **As levels … breeding:** as is appropriate to one of her
    family's status
243 **in his eye:** in his sight
244 **my unfolding:** my plea
    lend … ear: listen favourably
245 **charter:** dispensation, authority
246 **simpleness:** lack of worldly experience
247–249 **That I did … world:** the urgency and speed of my
    marriage proclaims to the world that I loved the Moor
    enough to want to live with him
250 **the very quality of my lord:** all aspects of my husband's
    nature and profession
251 **visage:** face
252 **parts:** qualities
253 **consecrate:** dedicate with sacred vows
255 **a moth of peace:** delicate and fragile

> • *From Othello's speech (lines 229–239), what do you learn*
> *of his sense of his own security and power?*

of most allowed sufficiency, yet opinion, a more
sovereign mistress of effects, throws a more safer voice
on you. You must therefore be content to slubber the
gloss of your new fortunes with this more stubborn
and boisterous expedition.

OTHELLO   The tyrant, custom, most grave senators,
              Hath made the flinty and steel couch of war   230
              My thrice-driven bed of down. I do agnize
              A natural and prompt alacrity
              I find in hardness; and do undertake
              This present war against the Ottomites.
              Most humbly, therefore, bending to your state,
              I crave fit disposition for my wife,
              Due reference of place and exhibition,
              With such accommodation and besort
              As levels with her breeding.

DUKE   If you please,
              Bo't at her father's.

BRABANTIO   I'll not have it so.   240

OTHELLO   Nor I.

DESDEMONA   Nor I. I would not there reside
              To put my father in impatient thoughts
              By being in his eye. Most gracious Duke,
              To my unfolding lend your prosperous ear,
              And let me find a charter in your voice
              T'assist my simpleness.

DUKE   What would you Desdemona?

DESDEMONA   That I did love the Moor to live with him,
              My downright violence and storm of fortunes
              May trumpet to the world; my heart's subdued
              Even to the very quality of my lord.   250
              I saw Othello's visage in his mind,
              And to his honours and his valiant parts
              Did I my soul and fortunes consecrate.
              So that, dear lords, if I be left behind,
              A moth of peace, and he go to the war,

Desdemona asks to go with Othello. Othello supports her
request, not so that he can enjoy his wedding night, but
because he wants to respect her wishes. He is past the
urgency of youthful sexual passions. He promises that
passion will not cloud his military judgement. The Duke tells
them to make their own arrangements and orders Othello to
prepare to depart immediately. Othello commits Desdemona
to Iago's care for the journey to Cyprus.

256 **rites:** duties and pleasures of marriage
  bereft: taken from
257 **a heavy interim:** a difficult interlude
  support: suffer
259 **voice:** agreement
260 **Vouch ... heaven:** heaven be my witness
261 **palate of my appetite:** my sexual tastes
262 **to comply with heat:** to satisfy my passion
262–263 **the young ... defunct:** the urgent feelings of youth
  being dead for me
264 **But ... mind:** but to respond openly and generously to her
  wishes
265 **And ... that:** God forbid that
266 **scant:** carry out carelessly
267 **light-winged toys:** flighty distractions
268 **Cupid:** love
268–269 **seel ... instruments:** cloud my eyes, which should be
  dutifully alert, with sexual abandon
270 **That ... business:** so that my pursuit of pleasure corrupts
  and tarnishes my ability to do my job
271 **skillet:** saucepan
272 **indign:** unworthy
273 **Make ... estimation:** attack and destroy my reputation
275–276 **Th'affair ... answer it:** the military situation demands
  urgent attention, and we must respond at full speed
280 **commission:** orders
281 **of quality and respect:** of importance and relevance
282 **import:** concern
284 **conveyance:** care

- *What insight into Desdemona's love for Othello do you get
  from lines 249–258?*

The rites for which I love him are bereft me,
And I a heavy interim shall support
By his dear absence. Let me go with him.

OTHELLO   Let her have your voice.
Vouch with me, heaven, I therefore beg it not   260
To please the palate of my appetite,
Nor to comply with heat the young affects
In me defunct and proper satisfaction;
But to be free and bounteous to her mind.
And heaven defend your good souls that you think
I will your serious and great business scant
For she is with me. No, when light-winged toys
Of feathered Cupid seel with wanton dullness
My speculative and officed instruments,
That my disports corrupt and taint my business,   270
Let housewives make a skillet of my helm,
And all indign and base adversities
Make head against my estimation.

DUKE   Be it as you shall privately determine,
Either for her stay or going. Th'affair cries haste,
And speed must answer it. You must hence tonight.

DESDEMONA   Tonight, my lord?

DUKE   This night.

OTHELLO   With all my heart.

DUKE   At nine i'th'morning, here we'll meet again.
Othello, leave some officer behind,
And he shall our commission bring to you,   280
With such things else of quality and respect
As doth import you.

OTHELLO   So please your grace, my ancient;
A man he is of honesty and trust.
To his conveyance I assign my wife,
With what else needful your good grace shall think
To be sent after me.

DUKE   Let it be so.

The Duke commends Othello's virtue to Brabantio, who
replies by warning Othello about Desdemona's deceitfulness.
Othello asserts his absolute faith in her, and asks Iago to
allow his wife to attend Desdemona. Othello leaves with
Desdemona saying that they have only an hour together. Iago
is left with Roderigo, who is in despair because Desdemona
is clearly interested only in Othello. He is threatening
suicide. Iago mocks him for thinking in this way over a mere
woman.

288 **If virtue … lack:** if virtue is in itself charming and beautiful
293 **My life upon her faith:** I would stake my life upon her
      faithfulness
296 **in the best advantage:** at the most favourable time
298 **direction:** giving instructions
299 **obey the time:** act according to the situation
304 **incontinently:** without any delay
308 **prescription:** doctor's diagnosis
311 **since I could:** since I was old enough to
313 **Ere:** before
314 **guinea-hen:** (1) domestic fowl, (2) woman
317 **fond:** foolish
      virtue: power, ability

> • *What are the implications of the Duke's and Brabantio's*
>   *rhyming couplets (288–289 and 291–292)? How do they*
>   *complement each other?*
> • *What is the effect of the change from verse to prose when*
>   *Othello and Desdemona leave and Iago and Roderigo are*
>   *left alone?*

Good night to everyone. [*To* BRABANTIO] And noble
    signor,
If virtue no delighted beauty lack,
Your son-in-law is far more fair than black.

SENATOR   Adieu, brave Moor; use Desdemona well.   290

BRABANTIO   Look to her, Moor, if thou hast eyes to see
             She has deceived her father, and may thee.

                          [*Exeunt* DUKE, SENATORS, OFFICERS

OTHELLO   My life upon her faith. Honest Iago,
             My Desdemona must I leave to thee.
             I prithee let thy wife attend on her,
             And bring them after in the best advantage.
             Come Desdemona, I have but an hour
             Of love, of worldly matters and direction,
             To spend with thee. We must obey the time.

                          [*Exeunt* OTHELLO *and* DESDEMONA

RODERIGO   Iago.   300

IAGO   What say'st thou, noble heart?

RODERIGO   What will I do, think'st thou?

IAGO   Why, go to bed and sleep.

RODERIGO   I will incontinently drown myself.

IAGO   If thou dost, I shall never love thee after. Why, thou
             silly gentleman!

RODERIGO   It is silliness to live, when to live is torment; and
             then have we a prescription to die, when death is our
             physician.

IAGO   O villainous! I have looked upon the world for four   310
             times seven years; and since I could distinguish
             betwixt a benefit and an injury, I never found a man
             that knew how to love himself. Ere I would say, I
             would drown myself for the love of a guinea-hen, I
             would change my humanity with a baboon.

RODERIGO   What should I do? I confess it is my shame to be so
             fond, but it is not in my virtue to amend it.

Iago explains that human beings should not be slaves to
morality but follow their own wills. Iago says that it is reason
that prevents us giving in to self-destructive passions. He
believes Roderigo's love is a passing infatuation. Roderigo
denies this but Iago insists and dismisses the idea of suicide,
saying that he will be Roderigo's faithful helper. Roderigo must
raise all his money, travel to Cyprus and trust that Desdemona
will soon tire of Othello and seek a younger lover.

318 **Virtue? A fig:** Morality? I wouldn't give a fig for it
     (i.e. worthless)
321 **set:** plant
     hyssop: a herb
322 **gender:** species
     distract: vary
324 **industry:** hard work, exercise
325 **corrigible authority:** the authority which is able to correct
326 **beam:** balance
     scale: weighing-pan (on a set of scales)
327 **poise:** counterbalance
     blood: passion
329 **preposterous conclusions:** ridiculous results
330 **motions:** desires, emotions
     carnal stings: desires of the flesh
331 **unbitted:** unrestrained
332 **sect or scion:** cutting or offshoot
334–335 **a permission of the will:** a passion which your will has
     allowed free rein
337 **knit:** bound
338 **perdurable:** everlasting
339 **stead:** support
340 **defeat thy favour:** disguise your face
     usurped: assumed, put on
343–344 **It was a violent commencement in her:** she began the
     affair impulsively; her love began suddenly
345 **answerable sequestration:** corresponding withdrawal
348 **locusts:** sweet fruit, carob
349 **coloquintida:** bitter fruit
     change for youth: exchange her husband for a younger man
350 **sated:** fully satisfied
352 **damn thyself:** destroy your soul
354 **sanctimony:** religious obedience
     a frail vow: a weak marriage vow
355 **erring:** wandering or mistaken
     supersubtle: extremely sophisticated

> • *Why does Iago repeatedly encourage Roderigo to make all
> the money he can?*

IAGO   Virtue? A fig. 'Tis in ourselves that we are thus or
           thus. Our bodies are our gardens, to the which our
           wills are gardeners. So that if we will plant nettles,   320
           or sow lettuce; set hyssop and weed up thyme;
           supply it with one gender of herbs, or distract it
           with many; either to have it sterile with idleness, or
           manured with industry; why the power and
           corrigible authority of this lies in our wills. If the
           beam of our lives had not one scale of reason to
           poise another of sensuality, the blood and baseness
           of our natures would conduct us to most
           preposterous conclusions. But we have reason to
           cool our raging motions, our carnal stings, our   330
           unbitted lusts; whereof I take this, that you call
           love, to be a sect or scion.

RODERIGO   It cannot be.

IAGO   It is merely a lust of the blood and a permission of
           the will. Come, be a man. Drown thyself? Drown
           cats and blind puppies. I have professed me thy
           friend, and I confess me knit to thy deserving with
           cables of perdurable toughness. I could never better
           stead thee than now. Put money in thy purse. Follow
           thou these wars; defeat thy favour with an usurped   340
           beard. I say, put money in thy purse. It cannot be
           that Desdemona should long continue her love to the
           Moor – put money in thy purse – nor he his to her. It
           was a violent commencement in her, and thou shalt
           see an answerable sequestration – put but money in
           thy purse. These Moors are changeable in their wills
           – fill thy purse with money – the food that to him
           now is as luscious as locusts, shall be to him shortly
           as bitter as coloquintida. She must change for youth;
           when she is sated with his body, she will find the   350
           error of her choice. Therefore put money in thy
           purse. If thou wilt needs damn thyself, do it a more
           delicate way than drowning. Make all the money
           thou canst. If sanctimony and a frail vow betwixt an
           erring barbarian and a supersubtle Venetian be not

Iago has persuaded Roderigo to abandon the idea of killing himself. Roderigo puts his trust in Iago and undertakes to sell all his land. He leaves, and Iago reveals to the audience that he always uses fools as a source of funds. He repeats his hatred for 'the Moor', and says that it is commonly thought that Othello has had an affair with his wife. He is not sure if this is true, but says he will act as though it is. He knows Othello rates him highly and this will help his plotting.

356　**all the tribe of hell:** devils, demons
358　**enjoy:** have sex with
357–358　**A pox ... thyself:** forget drowning yourself
358　**clean out of the way:** absolutely out of the question
359　**compassing:** obtaining
361　**fast:** faithful
365　**hearted:** deeply felt
366　**be conjunctive:** combine, be allies, unite
367　**cuckold him:** turn him into a husband whose wife is unfaithful
370　**Traverse:** off you go
374　**betimes:** early
378　**changed:** a changed man
381　**ever:** always
382　**own gained knowledge:** experience
　　　profane: disgracefully deny
383　**expend:** waste
　　　snipe: (a small bird), fool
385　**thought abroad:** widely believed
385-386　**'twixt ... office:** been to bed with my wife
387　**for mere ... kind:** only out of suspicion that some such thing has happened
388　**Will ... surety:** will act as if it were certainly true
　　　holds me well: has a good opinion of me

> • *Why do you think Roderigo believes what Iago says?*

too hard for my wits and all the tribe of hell, thou
shalt enjoy her – therefore make money. A pox of
drowning thyself, it is clean out of the way. Seek
thou rather to be hanged in compassing thy joy than
to be drowned and go without her.   360

RODERIGO Wilt thou be fast to my hopes, if I depend on the
issue?

IAGO Thou art sure of me. Go make money. I have told
thee often, and I re-tell thee again and again,
I hate the Moor. My cause is hearted: thine hath no
less reason. Let us be conjunctive in our revenge
against him. If thou canst cuckold him, thou dost
thyself a pleasure, me a sport. There are many events
in the womb of time, which will be delivered.
Traverse; go, provide thy money. We will have more   370
of this tomorrow. Adieu.

RODERIGO Where shall we meet i'th'morning?

IAGO At my lodging.

RODERIGO I'll be with thee betimes.

IAGO Go to, farewell. Do you hear, Roderigo?

RODERIGO What say you?

IAGO No more of drowning, do you hear?

RODERIGO I am changed.

IAGO Go to, farewell. Put money enough in your purse.

RODERIGO I'll sell all my land.   [*Exit*   380

IAGO Thus do I ever make my fool my purse;
For I mine own gained knowledge should profane,
If I would time expend with such a snipe,
But for my sport and profit. I hate the Moor,
And it is thought abroad that 'twixt my sheets
He's done my office. I know not if't be true
But I, for mere suspicion in that kind,
Will do as if for surety. He holds me well;
The better shall my purpose work on him.

Iago begins to plot how to replace Cassio as Othello's deputy and arouse suspicion in Othello about Desdemona's faithfulness. He knows that Cassio is credible as Desdemona's lover, and decides to plant this idea in Othello's mind. He knows that Othello is a trusting person, has a high respect for him and is likely to believe him. Iago's hellish plan is conceived.

390 **proper:** handsome
391 **place:** position, post (i.e. Othello's lieutenant)
391–392 **to plume ... knavery:** to inspire myself to commit a double crime with a real flourish
393 **abuse:** deceive, mislead
394 **he:** Cassio
395 **person:** figure, body
  dispose: manner
396 **To be suspected:** which could easily arouse suspicion
  framed: just the type
398 **but:** only
401 **engendered:** conceived

> • *What do you think are Iago's strengths as a maker of plots on the evidence of this speech?*

Cassio's a proper man; let me see now;   390
To get his place, and to plume up my will
In double knavery – How? How? Let's see –
After some time, to abuse Othello's ear
That he is too familiar with his wife.
He hath a person and a smooth dispose
To be suspected, framed to make women false.
The Moor is of a free and open nature,
That thinks men honest that but seem to be so,
And will as tenderly be led by th'nose
As asses are.   400
I have't. It is engendered. Hell and night
Must bring this monstrous birth to the world's light.
                                                    [*Exit*

CTIVITIES

Keeping track

Scene 1

1 What do we find out about the character and intentions of Roderigo and Iago in this scene?
2 What has happened to Brabantio's daughter, and how does he react?
3 What impressions of the Moor have emerged from this scene? What is their effect?

Scene 2

1 What situation does Iago warn Othello about, and how does he respond?
2 What news does Cassio bring? How does he react to Iago's information about what Othello has done?
3 How is a street brawl prevented and what is the outcome?
4 What assumptions does Brabantio make about the way that Othello has won Desdemona?

Scene 3

1 When the scene begins, it focuses on the Duke and his senators preparing for war against the Turks. How does the focus of the scene change and what causes this?
2 When Brabantio complains that his daughter has been lured from him by deception and magic, the Duke promises the full force of the law on Brabantio's side. What actually is the outcome and why?
3 Why, according to Othello, did Desdemona fall in love with him?
4 Why does Desdemona wish to accompany Othello on his campaign to Cyprus?
5 What are Iago's motives for persuading Roderigo not to commit suicide? How does he do it?
6 What does Iago reveal about his own plans for Othello, Desdemona and Cassio? What are his motives?

Discussion

Scene 1

1 Look carefully at lines 1–11 of the scene which open the play.
   • What questions do they raise about Roderigo and Iago and the situation they are in?

- What would an audience understand and not understand about this situation?
2 Do Iago's words in the section from 8–65 help to clarify things? How?
- What further questions do they raise?
3 Consider all the possibilities of Iago's words 'I am not what I am' (line 65).
4 How would you play Brabantio and Roderigo and their reactions to each other?
5 What is the dramatic effect of holding back the entry of Brabantio's daughter and the Moor, and not even naming them?
6 How do you understand Roderigo's words in lines 66–67?

Scene 2

1 This is Othello's first appearance in the play. How do you respond to him from the way he speaks? What aspects of his speech do you think an actor might focus on to help portray this character? (For example, look at the way he begins many of his speeches.)
2 Consider the implications of Iago's words (line 33) 'By Janus, I think no'. How does it help you to see Iago? What connections can you make between his words and actions so far in the play?
3 What clues are there for an actor wanting to play Brabantio as father and Venetian citizen?

Scene 3

1 Brabantio does not appear again in the play, and we hear near the end that he has died. Discuss what you think is the impact of his role in the play and whether you think he should be played as a character who deserves sympathy.
2 This scene really has three sections: news about the Turkish threat; the problem of Brabantio, Desdemona and Othello; Iago's duping of Roderigo. Discuss how they are interconnected but also how they differ in tone.
3 Discuss whether on the evidence so far you think there are aspects of Othello which make him vulnerable. Do you think he should be played as a sympathetic character?
4 Do you think the relationship between Roderigo and Iago is a simple case of a fool being taken for a ride by a clever and unprincipled exploiter?

Close study

Scene 1

1 What does the language of lines 1–7 reveal about the moods and attitudes of Roderigo and Iago?
2 Look at Iago's language in lines 8–65.
- What does he reveal about himself by what he says and the tone and style he adopts? How does he reveal his attitude to the Moor? To Michael Cassio? Which passages do you think might be the most helpful for an actor in conveying this character to the audience?
- How do you think Shakespeare might want us to react to him at first?

3   How are Iago's words in lines 67–77 a response to Roderigo's
    preceding remarks? How do they affect the impact of the play at this
    point? What is Iago's advice? What are his tone and attitude?
4   Lines 74–81. Roderigo says he'll 'call aloud'. What is Iago's advice
    about how to do this, and its implications? Why do you think Iago
    joins in?
5   Lines 82–118.
    • Does Brabantio know there are two people shouting?
    • What is the difference between Roderigo's and Iago's approach
      to rousing Brabantio?
    • What can you tell of Iago's attitudes and intentions from the
      language and imagery he uses to describe the Moor and
      Brabantio's daughter and their activities? How do you respond to
      them?
    • What responses to this situation does Brabantio show during the
      passage?
6   Lines 119–139. What approach does Roderigo adopt to answering
    Brabantio? What language and imagery does he use to describe the
    Moor, Brabantio's daughter and their activities? How do you think
    Roderigo's approach might affect Brabantio?
7   Lines 139–143. What is the impact of this reaction of a father to his
    daughter's 'revolt'?
8   Lines 143–158.
    • Why might Shakespeare have decided to have Brabantio exit at
      this point?
    • How does Iago's explanation of his departure affect our view of
      him?
    • What do we learn about the Moor here?
9   Lines 159–182. What does Shakespeare reveal about the state of
    Brabantio's mind here? How does he do it? What do you think are
    Brabantio's most significant thoughts about his daughter and the
    Moor? How is he reacting to her absence? What is the attitude to
    Roderigo by the end of the scene?

Scene 2

1   Look at Iago's first words in the scene (lines 1–5). What is he
    saying? Why is he saying it? How do you react to him? How is
    Shakespeare developing his portrayal of him? Consider key
    expressions such as 'trade of war' and 'slain', 'very stuff o' the
    conscience' and 'contrived wonder', 'service'. What help is there for
    an actor in the expression 'yerked him here'?
2   What is the impact of Othello's first speech – only five words – after
    Iago's speech?

3   In line 3 Iago says he lacks 'iniquity'. In line 9, he speaks of the 'little godliness' he has. Why does he speak like this?

4   Look at Othello's words in lines 17–28. On what does he base his confidence that he will allow Brabantio to 'do his spite'? How does he reveal that loving Desdemona is a new experience for him? What is the impact of his saying that he would not give up his freedom 'for the sea's worth'?

5   How does Othello's line (30) 'Not I; I must be found' contrast with some of Iago's statements about himself? What are the implications of this contrast?

6   Does Cassio seem to be anything more than a messenger in his first two speeches beginning at lines 36 and 39?

7   How do you react to Iago's description of Othello's marriage at lines 50–51? How does his imagery carry different implications from that which he uses to Brabantio in Scene 1? What does this imply about Iago?

8   In lines 59–61, Othello prevents a street brawl. How does his language achieve this effect? What is its tone?

9   Look at Brabantio's language about Othello and his wooing of Desdemona. Collect as many expressions as you can that convey his attitudes.

10 Line 82–end of scene. Does Othello remain confident of his security? On what do you base your ideas? What expressions are crucial to understanding his sense of himself?

Scene 3

1   Lines 1–47.
   • How does Shakespeare create the impression of a war operations room? Consider the way he uses the two anonymous senators, the sailor, the officer and the messenger.
   • What impression is gained of the Venetian leadership? Why do you think it is important to see this before Brabantio and Othello arrive?

2   Lines 48–170.
   • In lines 53–59, Brabantio explains that he has not come to the senate concerned about 'the general case' but about his 'particular grief'. Consider the imagery he uses to describe his experience. What does it suggest about his feelings?
   • In lines 60–65, Brabantio asserts that his daughter leaving him must be unnatural. Look at the language he uses in this speech to describe what has happened and why. What is its impact? Follow the study up in his speech in lines 95–107.
   • During his speech in lines 77–95, Othello claims that he is 'rude' in speech. Study the speech in detail and consider your response to his claim. What seems to be his style and tone in addressing the senators? What might his intentions be?
   • Study Othello's speech from line 128–170. Does he seem 'rude' in his speech? Up to line 145, he outlines the story of his life that he told to Brabantio and which Desdemona heard in snatches. What aspects of his life does he recount?

How does he describe them? From line 145 to the end, he speaks of Desdemona's interest and how he wooed her and how they fell in love. How does he talk about this process? How does he remember his wooing? How does he understand Desdemona? What seems to be his view of his story?

3　Lines 171–299.

- How, in lines 167–180, does Shakespeare prepare for the impact of Desdemona's first words (180ff)?
- What attitudes of Brabantio's are revealed in the way he questions Desdemona (175–80)?
- In lines 180–189, Desdemona has her first words, in a very challenging situation. What kind of person do you imagine her to be from these words? In what tone does she respond to her father? What clues are there in his response to her (189)?
- What indications are there of Brabantio's feelings in 190–198? Why does he call Desdemona 'jewel'?
- How, in lines 200–228, does Shakespeare show the Duke trying to change the mood of the situation? Considering the way the scene continues, does the Duke succeed?
- What language does Othello use in lines 229–234 to indicate his readiness for war? What is its impact?
- It is agreed by all that the Duke's suggestion that Desdemona stay with Brabantio while Othello is away is a bad idea. How does Desdemona handle the situation (241–246), and explain her wish to accompany Othello to Cyprus (247–258)? Consider especially what is revealed in the 'love'/'live' balance (247) and the language of 247–250. How does she speak of her feelings for Othello? What is the impact of the 'moth of peace' image (255)?
- Othello (259) wishes Desdemona to have her way. Why does he feel the need to go on? What does he reveal about how he thinks he may be viewed by the Duke and senators? Look at the language he uses for sexual pleasure – what does it indicate about his thoughts? (Consider especially 260–267). Is he 'rude' in speech?
- What is ironic about Othello's comments on Iago (283–284), Brabantio's final words in the play (291–292), and Othello's 'my life upon her faith' (293)?
- What does Othello mean by 'the time' (299)? What aspect of 'the time' has he not obeyed?

4　Lines 300–402.

- In what state do you imagine Roderigo to be after he has witnessed the events of the scene so far? How does his language in lines 304 and 307–309 indicate his feelings?
- Iago addresses Roderigo as 'noble heart' (301) and 'thou silly gentleman' (306). What does this reveal about his attitude to Roderigo?

- What is Iago saying to Roderigo and indicating about his own attitudes in 310–315, especially through his references to 'guinea-hen' and 'baboon'?
- In 318–332 Iago explains that human beings should govern themselves by their wills. Explore his image of the garden and the gardener – what are its implications? How does the image of the scales (326–329) follow this up? What does Iago think is the role of reason?
- How does Iago speak of Roderigo's love in 329–332 and 334–335? What would you suggest is his motive for so doing, considering the way the speech continues?
- In 336–339 Iago insists on his good faith to Roderigo. What is the impact of 'put money in thy purse'?
- What is Iago's attitude in 334–360 to the feelings of Desdemona and Othello for each other and of Roderigo for Desdemona? How does he express them and in what tone?
- What is the impact of Iago's choice of language in 354–357? How might his 'wits' and 'all the tribe of hell' be connected?
- By the time we get to lines 361–362, what has Iago done with Roderigo's idea of suicide?
- How do you react to Iago's words 'I hate … reason' (365–366) in the light of what he has been saying so far?
- What is the significance of Iago's choice of 'pleasure' and 'sport' in line 368?
- What are the implications of Iago's prophecy about 'the womb of time' (368–369)? Compare this to Othello's reference to obeying 'the time' in line 299.
- How should Iago's manner change at 381? Why? From what to what?
- What indications are there in this speech (381–402) that Iago follows his previous advice to Roderigo about using his will and reason? Are there contrary indications?
- How do you react to Iago's explanation of his hatred for Othello?
- In 388–400, what understanding does Iago show of Othello and Cassio? What language especially reveals his attitudes? What is the impact of the image in 399–400? How does Iago view himself here?
- With what image does Iago conclude the first act (401–402)? What is its style and impact?

Imagery

Poetic language and imagery in a drama of this sort are used not only to enrich description and convey feeling, but also to reveal the attitude of the speaker and to embody themes in the play in ways which engage the audience's imagination. Imagery is often developed and made more complex through more than one character.

As you study *Othello*, you will notice the language and imagery which are developed throughout the play and focus on:

- civilisation and barbarism
- Christianity and heathenism
- heaven and hell
- order and chaos
- love and animal lust
- the sea, both literally and as a metaphor for the power of passionate feelings

Not all of these are strongly present in Act 1, but you will certainly find some of them. Look at the following references to develop your understanding:

- Brabantio's images of the eligible young Venetian young men that Desdemona has declined to marry, and the conviction he expresses that Othello must have used some kind of black magic to have won her, e.g. Act 1 Scene 2 62–81, or Scene 3 95–107.
- Brabantio's expression of shock that such rowdy behaviour as Roderigo's could occur in such an orderly and civilised place as Venice – 'This is Venice;/My house is not a grange.' (Act 1 Scene 1 105–106).
- Iago's descriptions of sex between Othello and Desdemona (e.g., Act 1 Scene 1 86–91) contrasted with Othello's own description of how he and Desdemona fell in love (Act 1 Scene 3 128–170). What other images have you noticed?

Key scene

After each Act you will be asked to think about one scene or part of a scene that is particularly important in our understanding of the play. The questions and comments in KEY SCENE assume that you have at least worked through the CLOSE STUDY questions relating to that scene. You will find it useful to make notes on your thoughts, ideas and questions as you study each key scene.

Scene 3, lines 49–290
This passage highlights central conflicts in the play. Venice, a bastion of European Christian civilisation, is threatened by a Turkish assault on her outpost of Cyprus. A very senior Venetian statesman, Brabantio, assumes that Othello, the black general whom Venice trusts to defend it against the infidel Turks, must have used witchcraft to put an evil spell on his daughter to win her love. In this passage, we hear Othello and Desdemona describe their 'course of love' and learn that Othello is a Christian; we also see the Duke of Venice put matters of state first, leaving private matters aside. Finally, we see Othello affirm his trust in Iago and entrust his wife's safety to him.

Reread this passage carefully to develop your understanding of the situation as Othello, Desdemona, Iago and Cassio depart for Cyprus. Consider:
- how Shakespeare has pointed to problems to come;
- how he has given the impression that Othello feels secure.

Writing

1 EITHER Write a brief speech for each of the following characters in which you give his/her view of and attitude to the relationship between Othello and Desdemona:
   - Iago
   - Roderigo
   - Brabantio.
   OR Write a brief essay on the different ways in which the relationship between Othello and Desdemona is seen.

2 What ideas about Venice and Venetian society do you gain in Act 1? Consider:
   - Brabantio's status and attitudes towards his daughter and Othello
   - Othello's view of himself and his status in Venice
   - Iago's attitude towards Othello and Cassio
   - The Duke's attitude towards Othello.

3 Show how Shakespeare sets out the contrasting characters of Othello and Iago. What possibilities does this contrast offer for the development of the plot?

4 Explain your interpretation of Iago's character and role in the play so far. Consider:
   - his relationship with the audience
   - his motives
   - the way he deals with other characters.
   (In thinking about this it may be helpful to consider various opinions of Iago as a 'stage villain', 'evil genius', 'embittered officer', 'jealous husband', and 'amateur philosopher'.)

Montano and two gentlemen describe the massive storm now raging on and around the island of Cyprus. None of them has ever seen a storm as violent. They cannot see any signs of ships, and assume that the Turkish fleet is scattered. No ship, unless it could shelter in a bay, could survive this storm. A third gentleman says that a Venetian ship has arrived, having witnessed the wreck of the Turkish fleet.

2 high-wrought flood: violent tempest of the sea
3 main: sea
4 Descry: make out, spot
6 fuller: more powerful
7 ruffianed so: blown so violently
8 ribs of oak: ship's timbers
   mountains: mountainous waves
9 hold the mortise: keep their joints together
10 segregation: scattering
11 For do but: all you have to do is
12 chidden billow: the waves, tormented by the wind
13 main: might, power
14 burning Bear: constellation of the Little Bear
15 guards: two bright stars in the Little Bear, used for navigation
   Pole: pole star
16 like molestation: a disturbance like this
17 enchafed flood: enraged sea
18 ensheltered and embayed: sheltering in a bay
19 bear it out: survive it
21 banged: battered
22 designment halts: attack of Cyprus is stopped
23 sufferance: suffering

• *How do the speakers here convey their experience of the storm?*

ACT TWO

Scene

Enter MONTANO *and two* GENTLEMEN

MONTANO   What from the cape can you discern at sea?

1ST GENTLEMAN Nothing at all; it is a high-wrought flood.
      I cannot 'twixt the heaven and the main
      Descry a sail.

MONTANO   Methinks the wind does speak aloud at land;
      A fuller blast ne'er shook our battlements.
      If it hath ruffianed so upon the sea,
      What ribs of oak, when mountains melt on them,
      Can hold the mortise? What shall we hear of this?

2ND GENTLEMAN A segregation of the Turkish fleet.   10
      For do but stand upon the foaming shore,
      The chidden billow seems to pelt the clouds;
      The wind-shaked surge, with high and monstrous
        main,
      Seems to cast water on the burning Bear,
      And quench the guards of th'ever-fixed Pole.
      I never did like molestation view
      On the enchafed flood.

MONTANO   If that the Turkish fleet
      Be not ensheltered and embayed, they are drowned;
      It is impossible they bear it out.

Enter THIRD GENTLEMAN

3RD GENTLEMAN News lads! Our wars are done.   20
      The desperate tempest hath so banged the Turks,
      That their designment halts. A noble ship of Venice
      Hath seen a grievous wreck and sufferance
      On most part of their fleet.

The gentleman goes on to say that the ship is at Cassio's and that he has come ashore. He also reports that Cassio is anxious about Othello's safety, and Montano echoes this concern, saying that Othello is a great commander. They have just decided to keep a look-out for Othello when Cassio enters, having heard their praise of Othello. Cassio hopes that Othello will survive the storm because his ship is strong.

26 **A Veronesa:** a ship of Verona (a city in the Venetian state)
29 **in full commission:** with the highest authority
32 **touching:** concerning
   sadly: anxious
36 **a full soldier:** a model of military virtue
38 **throw out our eyes:** scan the horizon
39–40 **Even ... regard:** until we blur the distinction between sea and sky
41–42 **For every ... arrivance:** For we expect more arrivals every minute
44 **approve:** praise
47 **Is he well shipped?:** Is he sailing in a well-built ship?
48 **bark:** ship
49 **approved allowance:** highly credited reputation
50 **not ... death:** not overwhelmed by fears of death
51 **Stand in bold cure:** we are confident of a successful outcome

> • *Montano says Othello will be a 'worthy governor' and 'commands/Like a full soldier'. Montano is currently governor of Cyprus. What does this tell you about him?*

MONTANO   How? Is this true?

3RD GENTLEMAN   The ship is here put in,
                  A Veronesa; Michael Cassio,
                  Lieutenant to the warlike Moor Othello,
                  Is come on shore; the Moor himself at sea,
                  And is in full commission here for Cyprus.

MONTANO   I am glad on't; 'tis a worthy governor.   30

3RD GENTLEMAN But this same Cassio, though he speak of comfort
                  Touching the Turkish loss, yet he looks sadly,
                  And prays the Moor be safe; for they were parted
                  With foul and violent tempest.

MONTANO   Pray heaven he be;
                  For I have served him, and the man commands
                  Like a full soldier. Let's to the seaside, ho!
                  As well to see the vessel that's come in,
                  As to throw out our eyes for brave Othello,
                  Even till we make the main and the aerial blue
                  An indistinct regard.

3RD GENTLEMAN   Come, let's do so;   40
                  For every minute is expectancy
                  Of more arrivance.

                  Enter CASSIO

CASSIO   Thanks, you the valiant of this warlike isle,
                  That so approve the Moor. O let the heavens
                  Give him defence against the elements,
                  For I have lost him on a dangerous sea.

MONTANO   Is he well shipped?

CASSIO   His bark is stoutly timbered, and his pilot
                  Of very expert and approved allowance;
                  Therefore my hopes, not surfeited to death,   50
                  Stand in bold cure.

                  [*Cry within* 'A sail, a sail, a sail!']

                  Enter a FOURTH GENTLEMAN

                  What noise?

The fourth gentleman announces the arrival of another ship and Cassio hopes it is the governor, Othello. He tells Montano that Othello has married an outstandingly beautiful woman. The news comes that it is Iago who has arrived safely. Cassio announces the arrival of Desdemona, miraculously unscathed, as if she were a goddess.

53 **brow:** shore
55 **My ... him for:** I hope it is
56 **courtesy:** formal greeting, salute
57 **Our ... least:** the ship is definitely a friendly one
58 **give us truth:** confirm
60 **wived:** married
61 **achieved:** wooed and won
62 **paragons ... fame:** outstrips description and wild rumour
63 **excels ... pens:** surpasses the elaborate creations of exaggerating writers
64 **th'essential vesture of creation:** the purest beauty of creation
65 **Does ... ingener:** exhausts the imagination of the artist
69 **guttered:** furrowed
    congregated sands: sandbanks
70 **Traitors ... keel:** treacherously submerged to snare the unwary keel
71 **As ... beauty:** as if they were aware of human beauty
71–72 **do omit ... natures:** leave off their deadliness
76 **footing:** coming ashore
76–77 **anticipates ... speed:** is a week earlier than we expected
81 **extincted:** deflated, nearly extinguished

> • *What impact does the announcement of Iago's arrival have, immediately after Cassio's description of Desdemona?*

4TH GENTLEMAN The town is empty; on the brow o' the sea
        Stand ranks of people, and they cry 'A sail!'

CASSIO My hopes do shape him for the governor.

                                                      [*A shot*

2ND GENTLEMAN They do discharge their shot of courtesy;
        Our friends at least.

CASSIO   I pray you sir, go forth,
        And give us truth who 'tis that is arrived.

2ND GENTLEMAN I shall.   [*Exit*

MONTANO But, good lieutenant, is your general wived?   60

CASSIO Most fortunately. He hath achieved a maid
        That paragons description and wild fame;
        One that excels the quirks of blazoning pens,
        And in th'essential vesture of creation
        Does tire the ingener.

        Enter SECOND GENTLEMAN

                         How now? Who has put in?

2ND GENTLEMAN 'Tis one Iago, ancient to the general.

CASSIO He's had most favourable and happy speed.
        Tempests themselves, high seas, and howling winds,
        The guttered rocks and congregated sands,
        Traitors ensteeped to clog the guiltless keel,   70
        As having sense of beauty, do omit
        Their mortal natures, letting go safely by
        The divine Desdemona.

MONTANO   What is she?

CASSIO She that I spake of, our great captain's captain
        Left in the conduct of the bold Iago,
        Whose footing here anticipates our thoughts
        A se'nnight's speed. Great Jove, Othello guard,
        And swell his sail with thine own powerful breath,
        That he may bless this bay with his tall ship,
        Make love's quick pants in Desdemona's arms,   80
        Give renewed fire to our extincted spirits,

Cassio says all must kneel before Desdemona. Desdemona thanks Cassio, but is more concerned about Othello's safety and asks Cassio how they were parted. He begins to explain just as a sail is spotted. Cassio greets Iago and Emilia, and explains to Iago that his courtly greeting of Emilia is a matter of breeding. Iago returns that he's more used to scolding than kissing from Emilia. Desdemona defends her as a quiet person.

84	**let ... knees:** kneel down before her
87	**Enwheel thee round:** surround you
89	**aught:** anything
90	**But that:** except that
92	**contention:** clash (i.e. of the storm)
94	**They ... citadel:** The shots are from the ship giving greeting to the island's citadel
95	**See ... news:** Go and find out what the news is
97	**gall your patience:** irritate you
98	**extend my manners:** greet (your wife) in courtly fashion **breeding:** upbringing
100–102	**would ... enough:** if she were to kiss you as freely as she gives me the sharp edge of her tongue you would be well satisfied

> • *What do you think about Cassio's welcome of Desdemona? How does his way of talking about – and treatment of – her compare with the reactions to her we have already seen in the play?*

And bring all Cyprus comfort.

Enter DESDEMONA, EMILIA, IAGO, RODERIGO, *and*
ATTENDANTS

                    O behold,
The riches of the ship is come on shore!
You men of Cyprus, let her have your knees.
Hail to thee lady! And the grace of heaven,
Before, behind thee, and on every hand,
Enwheel thee round.

DESDEMONA   I thank you valiant Cassio.
What tidings can you tell me of my lord?

CASSIO   He is not yet arrived, nor know I aught
But that he's well, and will be shortly here.   90

DESDEMONA O, but I fear . . . How lost you company?

CASSIO   The great contention of the sea and skies
Parted our fellowship.

(*Within* 'A sail, a sail!' *A shot*)

                  But hark, a sail.
2ND GENTLEMAN   They give their greeting to the citadel
This likewise is a friend.

CASSIO: See for the news.

                 [*Exit* GENTLEMAN

Good ancient, you are welcome. [*To* EMILIA]
  Welcome mistress.
Let it not gall your patience, good Iago,
That I extend my manners. 'Tis my breeding
That gives me this bold show of courtesy.

                 [*Kisses* EMILIA

IAGO   Sir, would she give you so much of her lips   100
As of her tongue she oft bestows on me,
You would have enough.

DESDEMONA Alas, she has no speech.

IAGO   In faith too much.

Iago concedes that some of Emilia's scolding is only done inside her head. He jokes that women's pleasant side is only for polite show. Emilia doesn't want Iago writing her description if this is how he thinks. Desdemona asks him how he would praise her. Iago rises – he pretends reluctantly – to Desdemona's challenge, warning that he is very critical. Desdemona explains that she is not really happy but is trying to hide her anxiety about Othello's safety. Iago makes a series of witty comments about women's beauty and brains.

104   **still:** always
105   **Marry:** For sure
        before your ladyship: in your ladyship's presence
105-107 **I grant ... thinking:** I admit she keeps some of her
        words in her heart and scolds me in her thoughts
108   **pictures:** silent images of beauty
109   **bells:** jangling, noisy
110   **saints ... injuries:** you put on a saintly act when you're
        hurting people
        players: actors, deceivers
111   **housewifery/housewives:** play on two meanings:
        housekeeping, and being a 'hussy' or harlot (Iago implies
        that women are only acting when they do housework, and
        really go to work in bed)
113   **Turk:** barbarian (i.e. an insult)
117   **put me to't:** give me such a challenge
119   **assay:** try
121-122 **beguile ... am:** distract myself from the mood I am in
124   **invention:** creativity, imagination
125   **pate:** head, brain
        as birdlime ... frieze: with as much difficulty as it takes to
        pull sticky birdlime off woollen cloth
126   **muse labours:** inspiration struggles to give birth
127   **is delivered:** gives birth
130   **black:** dark-haired
132   **white:** pun on wight = person, man

> • *What view of the relationship between Iago and Emilia
> emerges here?*

I find it still when I have list to sleep.
Marry before your ladyship, I grant
She puts her tongue a little in her heart
And chides with thinking.

EMILIA   You have little cause to say so.

IAGO   Come on, come on; you are pictures out of doors,
bells in your parlours, wild-cats in your kitchens,
saints in your injuries, devils being offended, players   110
in your housewifery, and housewives in your beds.

DESDEMONA   O fie upon thee, slanderer!

IAGO   Nay, it is true, or else I am a Turk.
You rise to play, and go to bed to work.

EMILIA   You shall not write my praise.

IAGO   No, let me not.

DESDEMONA   What wouldst thou write of me, if thou shouldst
praise me?

IAGO   O gentle lady, do not put me to't;
For I am nothing if not critical.

DESDEMONA   Come on, assay. There's one gone to the harbour?

IAGO   Ay, madam.   120

DESDEMONA   I am not merry, but I do beguile
The thing I am by seeming otherwise.
Come, how wouldst thou praise me?

IAGO   I am about it, but indeed my invention
Comes from my pate as birdlime does from frieze –
It plucks out brains and all – but my muse labours,
And thus she is delivered.
If she be fair and wise, fairness and wit,
The one's for use, the other useth it.

DESDEMONA   Well praised. How if she be black and witty?   130

IAGO   If she be black, and thereto have a wit,
She'll find a white that shall her blackness fit.

DESDEMONA   Worse and worse.

Desdemona dismisses Iago's remarks as old bar-room jokes. In answer to Desdemona's challenge to praise the deserving woman, Iago describes a perfect woman and then says she's destined only to be mother and housekeeper. Desdemona is frustrated at this, but Cassio says there is truth in it. Iago comments to the audience on Cassio's courtly behaviour to Desdemona, and threatens to use it against him.

135 **folly:** carelessness (over men)
136 **fond paradoxes:** foolish jokes
139 **thereunto:** as well
143 **authority of her merit:** strength of her desert
144 **did justly … itself:** deservedly gained the approval even of those who are the most ill-intentioned
146 **had … will:** spoke her mind freely
147 **gay:** gaudily dressed
148 **Fled … wish:** denied herself her desires
149 **her revenge being nigh:** her opportunity for revenge being near
150 **Bade … stay:** controlled her sense of injustice
 fly: fly away
151 **She … frail:** she who was never so weak-minded
152 **To change … tail:** as to exhange an ugly lover for a handsome one ('cod' and 'tail' were both terms for the penis)
155 **wight:** person
157 **suckle:** breastfeed
 chronicle … beer: keep trivial household accounts
158 **impotent:** witless, feeble
161 **profane … counsellor:** unholy and immoral adviser
162 **home:** to the heart of the matter
 relish: appreciate
164 **well said:** well done
167 **gyve:** entangle
 courtship: courtly behaviour

> • *Is the dialogue here merely witty banter to pass the time before Othello's arrival or does it have other significance?*

EMILIA	How if fair and foolish?
IAGO	She never yet was foolish that was fair, For even her folly helped her to an heir.
DESDEMONA	These are old fond paradoxes to make fools laugh i'th'alehouse. What miserable praise hast thou for her that's foul and foolish?
IAGO	There's none so foul and foolish thereunto, But does foul pranks which fair and wise ones do. 140
DESDEMONA	O heavy ignorance; thou praisest the worst best. But what praise couldst thou bestow on a deserving woman indeed, one that in the authority of her merit did justly put on the vouch of very malice itself?
IAGO	She that was ever fair and never proud, Had tongue at will, and yet was never loud, Never lacked gold, and yet went never gay, Fled from her wish, and yet said 'Now I may', She that being angered, her revenge being nigh, Bade her wrong stay, and her displeasure fly, 150 She that in wisdom never was so frail To change the cod's head for the salmon's tail; She that could think and ne'er disclose her mind, See suitors following, and not look behind, She was a wight, if ever such wight were –
DESDEMONA	To do what?
IAGO	To suckle fools and chronicle small beer.
DESDEMONA	O, most lame and impotent conclusion! Do not learn of him, Emilia, though he be thy husband. How say you Cassio, is he not a most 160 profane and liberal counsellor?
CASSIO	He speaks home madam; you may relish him more in the soldier than in the scholar.
IAGO	[*Aside*] He takes her by the palm. Ay, well said, whisper. With as little a web as this will I ensnare as great a fly as Cassio. Ay, smile upon her, do. I will gyve thee in thine own courtship. You say true, 'tis

Iago concludes his commentary on Cassio's attentions to Desdemona with a crude comparison. Othello's arrival is heralded, and he and Desdemona are immediately in their own world of love and joy. Othello fears this may be the happiest moment they will have, but Desdemona prays that their love will increase.

168 **tricks:** behaviour
168–169 **strip ... lieutenantry:** strip you of your rank as Othello's lieutenant
169 **it had:** it would have been
170 **kissed ... fingers:** a courtly gesture
171 **to play the sir in:** to put on the behaviour of a courtly gentleman
174 **clyster-pipes:** tubes for injecting an enema
175 **I ... trumpet:** I recognise his personal trumpet call
182 **labouring bark:** struggling ship
183 **Olympus-high:** as high as Mount Olympus (home of the Greek gods)
184 **hell's:** hell is
If ... die: if it were now my time to die
186 **content so absolute:** such complete happiness
188 **succeeds ... fate:** is yet to come in my unknown destiny
188–189 **The heavens ... increase:** let the heavens forbid everything except that our love and comfort should grow
190 **Even ... grow:** as long as our lives last
192 **It ... here:** I am so overwhelmed by feeling that I cannot breathe

---

- *What is Cassio doing while Iago speaks to the audience?*
- *What are Iago's thoughts about Cassio's behaviour?*
- *What is the effect of Othello's greeting of Desdemona as 'my fair warrior'?*

so indeed. If such tricks as these strip you out of
your lieutenantry, it had been better you had not
kissed your three fingers so oft, which now again   170
you are most apt to play the sir in. Very good; well
kissed, an excellent courtesy. 'Tis so indeed. Yet
again your fingers to your lips? Would they were
clyster-pipes for your sake!

[*Trumpet within*

The Moor! I know his trumpet.

CASSIO   'Tis truly so.

DESDEMONA   Let's meet him and receive him.

CASSIO   Lo, where he comes.

Enter OTHELLO *and* ATTENDANTS

OTHELLO   O my fair warrior!

DESDEMONA   My dear Othello.

OTHELLO   It gives me wonder great as my content
To see you here before me. O my soul's joy!
If after every tempest come such calms,   180
May the winds blow till they have wakened death
And let the labouring bark climb hills of seas
Olympus-high, and duck again as low
As hell's from heaven. If it were now to die,
'Twere now to be most happy; for I fear
My soul hath her content so absolute
That not another comfort like to this
Succeeds in unknown fate.

DESDEMONA   The heavens forbid
But that our loves and comforts should increase,
Even as our days do grow.

OTHELLO   Amen to that, sweet powers!   190
I cannot speak enough of this content;
It stops me here; it is too much of joy.

[*Kisses her*

Iago listens to Othello and Desdemona, and comments cynically
to the audience. As Iago concludes his malicious aside with a
plan to ruin the harmony between Othello and Desdemona,
Othello expresses his multiple joys – he is meeting old friends of
Cyprus again, the Turks are destroyed and he is reunited with
his love. Iago tells Roderigo that Desdemona loves Cassio. He
explains that she fell for Othello only because of his boasting
and will tire of his lovemaking.

193 **And this, and this:** he is referring to his kisses
194 **well tuned:** in harmony with each other
195 **set down the pegs:** loosen the strings by unscrewing the pegs
    and so produce a discord
198 **my old acquaintance:** my old friends
199 **well desired:** warmly greeted
201 **prattle out of fashion:** I'm gabbling all over the place
201–202 **dote … comforts:** talk wildly and obsessively in my
    happiness
204 **master:** ship's captain
206 **challenge:** demand
208 **presently:** straightaway
211–212 **native to them:** in their nature
212 **list:** listen to
213 **court of guard:** area where the guards go on watch
214 **directly:** certainly
    him: Cassio
216 **Lay … this:** put your finger to your lips, keep quiet
218 **but for:** merely for
    bragging: boasting
    fantastical: far-fetched
219 **still:** always
    prating: blowing his own trumpet
219–220 **discreet heart:** common sense
220 **eye:** lust
    delight: pleasure
221 **devil:** he is referring to Othello, whose blackness is paralleled
    with the Devil's
222 **dull:** bored
    act of sport: sex
223 **satiety:** repletion, satisfaction
224 **favour:** physical appearance
    sympathy in years, manners: similarity in age and culture

> • *In what manner does Iago address Roderigo? Is there a*
> *change in his approach?*

And this, and this, the greatest discords be
That e'er our hearts shall make.

IAGO [*Aside*]   O you are well tuned now!
But I'll set down the pegs that make this music,
As honest as I am.

OTHELLO   Come, let us to the castle.
News, friends; our wars are done; the Turks are
    drowned.
How does my old acquaintance of this isle?
Honey, you shall be well desired in Cyprus;
I have found great love amongst them. O my sweet,   200
I prattle out of fashion, and I dote
In mine own comforts. I prithee good Iago,
Go to the bay and disembark my coffers.
Bring thou the master to the citadel;
He is a good one, and his worthiness
Does challenge much respect. Come Desdemona,
Once more well met at Cyprus!

                [*Exeunt all but* IAGO *and* RODERIGO

IAGO [*To* ATTENDANT] Do you meet me presently at the
harbour. [*To* RODERIGO] Come hither. If thou be'st
valiant – as they say base men being in love have   210
then a nobility in their natures more than is native to
them – list me. The lieutenant tonight watches on the
court of guard. First, I must tell thee this,
Desdemona is directly in love with him.

RODERIGO With him? Why, 'tis not possible!

IAGO Lay thy finger thus, and let thy soul be instructed.
Mark me with what violence she first loved the
Moor, but for bragging, and telling her fantastical
lies. Love him still for prating? Let not thy discreet
heart think it. Her eye must be fed; and what delight   220
shall she have to look on the devil? When the blood
is made dull with the act of sport, there should be,
again to inflame it and give satiety a fresh appetite,
loveliness in favour, sympathy in years, manners and

Iago tells Roderigo that Othello lacks all the qualities to keep Desdemona. She will be sure to seek a lover. Iago points out Cassio's civilised subtleties and his lust, and that Desdemona has already discovered him. Roderigo cannot believe this, but Iago bluntly says that if Desdemona were saintly she would never have fallen for Othello. He asks if Roderigo saw the flirtation between Cassio and Desdemona. Roderigo insists it was merely good manners. Iago concludes by insisting that Desdemona and Cassio will have sex soon. He tells Roderigo to watch Cassio this night.

226 **conveniences:** fitting attributes
227–228 **heave the gorge:** throw up
228 **disrelish and abhor:** lose her taste for and be disgusted by
 very nature: her instincts
230–231 **most ... position:** a very obvious and natural interpretation
231–232 **who ... fortune:** who is placed as highly to benefit from this good fortune
232–233 **knave very voluble:** a very smooth-talking rogue
233 **no further conscionable:** with no more conscience
234 **seeming:** outward appearance
235 **compassing** achieving
235–236 **salt ... affection:** lustful and very secret immoral desires
236 **slipper:** devious, slimy
237 **finder of occasions:** opportunist
237–238 **has an eye ... advantages:** has an eye for creating opportunities
241 **folly and green:** foolish and naïve
 look after: are taken in by
249 **paddle with:** fondle
251 **courtesy:** good manners
252–253 **an index ... prologue:** a list of contents and a secret introduction
253 **history:** story
256 **mutualities:** shared intimacies
 marshal: lead
257 **incorporate:** bodily, i.e. sexual
259 **Watch you:** keep on the lookout
259–260 **for ... you:** I'll give you your orders

> • *How many times does Iago refer to Cassio as 'knave' here?*
> *What does he imply?*

beauties: all which the Moor is defective in. Now for
want of these required conveniences, her delicate
tenderness will find itself abused, begin to heave the
gorge, disrelish and abhor the Moor; very nature will
instruct her in it; and compel her to some second
choice. Now sir, this granted – as it is a most pregnant 230
and unforced position – who stands so eminent in the
degree of this fortune as Cassio does, a knave very
voluble, no further conscionable than in putting on the
mere form of civil and humane seeming, for the better
compassing of his salt and most hidden loose
affection? Why, none; why, none. A slipper and subtle
knave, a finder of occasions; that has an eye can stamp
and counterfeit advantages, though true advantage
never present itself; a devilish knave. Besides, the
knave is handsome, young, and hath all those   240
requisites in him that folly and green minds look after.
A pestilent complete knave; and the woman hath
found him already.

RODERIGO   I cannot believe that in her; she's full of most blessed
            condition.

IAGO   Blessed fig's end! The wine she drinks is made of
            grapes. If she had been blessed, she would never have
            loved the Moor. Blessed pudding! Didst thou not see
            her paddle with the palm of his hand? Didst not mark
            that?   250

RODERIGO   Yes, that I did: but that was but courtesy.

IAGO   Lechery, by this hand: an index and obscure
            prologue to the history of lust and foul thoughts. They
            met so near with their lips that their breaths embraced
            together. Villainous thoughts, Roderigo. When these
            mutualities so marshal the way, hard at hand comes
            the master and main exercise, th'incorporate
            conclusion. Pish! But sir, be you ruled by me. I have
            brought you from Venice. Watch you tonight; for the
            command, I'll lay't upon you. Cassio knows you not. 260
            I'll not be far from you. Do you find some occasion to

Iago tells Roderigo to provoke Cassio's temper – an easy
task. Iago will use this to cause the citizens of Cyprus to
complain and have Cassio dismissed. This will then leave the
way to Desdemona clear for Roderigo, and the way clear for
Iago's promotion. Roderigo agrees and leaves. Iago says he
believes an affair between Cassio and Desdemona is perfectly
feasible. He explains that he loves Desdemona out of lust,
but also to feed his revenge on Othello whom he suspects of
adultery with Emilia. He will not rest until he has revenge –
or until he has made Othello incurably jealous.

262–263 **tainting his discipline:** casting aspersions on his
ability to command
264 **minister:** supply
266 **sudden in choler:** quick to anger
haply: perhaps
267 **truncheon:** baton, swagger-stick
268 **out of that:** as a result of that
269–270 **whose qualification ... again:** who will not be truly
appeased again
272 **prefer:** advance, promote
273 **impediment:** hindrance, obstacle
277 **warrant:** promise
278 **his necessaries:** Othello's belongings
281 **apt ... credit:** likely and easily believable
282 **howbeit:** even though
283 **constant:** faithful
285 **most dear:** loving (and costly)
286 **Not ... lust:** not only for lust
peradventure: perhaps
287 **stand accountant:** am accountable
288 **diet:** feed
289 **For that:** because
290 **leaped ... seat:** had sex with my wife
291 **inwards:** guts
293 **am evened:** have got even
297 **this ... Venice:** Roderigo
trace: check, hold back

> • *Why do you think Roderigo goes along with Iago's
> instructions?*

anger Cassio, either by speaking too loud, or tainting
his discipline, or from what other course you please,
which the time shall more favourably minister.

RODERIGO   Well.

IAGO   Sir, he's rash and very sudden in choler, and haply
with his truncheon may strike at you: provoke him
that he may; for even out of that will I cause these of
Cyprus to mutiny; whose qualification shall come
into no true taste again but by the displanting of   270
Cassio. So shall you have a shorter journey to your
desires by the means I shall then have to prefer them;
and the impediment most profitably removed,
without the which there were no expectation of our
prosperity.

RODERIGO   I will do this, if you can bring it to any opportunity.

IAGO   I warrant thee. Meet me by and by at the citadel, I
must fetch his necessaries ashore. Farewell.

RODERIGO   Adieu.   [*Exit* RODERIGO

IAGO   That Cassio loves her, I do well believe it;   280
That she loves him, 'tis apt and of great credit.
The Moor, howbeit that I endure him not,
Is of a constant, loving, noble nature,
And I dare think he'll prove to Desdemona
A most dear husband. Now I do love her too;
Not out of absolute lust, though peradventure
I stand accountant for as great a sin,
But partly led to diet my revenge
For that I do suspect the lusty Moor
Hath leaped into my seat. The thought whereof   290
Doth like a poisonous mineral gnaw my inwards;
And nothing can or shall content my soul
Till I am evened with him, wife for wife;
Or failing so, yet that I put the Moor
At least into a jealousy so strong
That judgment cannot cure. Which thing to do
If this poor trash of Venice, whom I trace

Iago says he will use Roderigo to destroy Cassio's reputation with Othello. Iago believes Cassio, too, has been with Emilia. He wants to make Othello love him as a loyal servant even while he is driving him mad.

298 **stand ... on:** is up to my challenge
299 **have ... hip:** catch Cassio off balance (as in wrestling)
300 **Abuse him:** tell lies about him
     rank garb: disgusting manner
301 **For ... too:** for I fear Cassio too has had sex with my wife
303 **egregiously:** blatantly
304 **practising upon:** plotting against
305 **Even to madness:** even to the extent of driving him mad
     here: in my mind

> • *How do you respond to Iago's claims about Emilia's affairs?*

The Herald announces that it is certain that the Turkish fleet has been destroyed and that Othello wants everyone to celebrate the triumph in whatever way they choose, as this is also his wedding feast.

2   **certain tidings:** definite information
3   **importing ... perdition:** concerning the complete destruction
4   **triumph:** celebrating the triumph
6   **addiction:** preferred method of celebrating
8   **nuptial:** marriage
8–9 **So much ... proclaimed:** this is everything he wanted announced
9   **All ... open:** all duties are suspended

> • *Why do you think Shakespeare included this speech?*

Othello orders Cassio to take charge of the guard to ensure the celebrations do not get out of hand.

1   **look you to the guard:** take charge of the guards
2   **honourable stop:** restraint that is respected
3   **Not to:** so as not to
     outsport discretion: let the party get out of hand

For his quick hunting, stand the putting on,
I'll have our Michael Cassio on the hip,
Abuse him to the Moor in the rank garb –   300
For I fear Cassio with my night-cap too –
Make the Moor thank me, love me, and reward me
For making him egregiously an ass,
And practising upon his peace and quiet,
Even to madness. 'Tis here, but yet confused.
Knavery's plain face is never seen till used.   [*Exit*

Scene

Enter OTHELLO'S HERALD, *with a proclamation; people*

HERALD   It is Othello's pleasure, our noble and valiant
general, that upon certain tidings now arrived
importing the mere perdition of the Turkish fleet, every
man put himself into triumph; some to dance, some to
make bonfires, each man to what sport and revels his
addiction leads him. For, besides these beneficial news,
it is the celebration of his nuptial. So much was his
pleasure should be proclaimed. All offices are open,
and there is full liberty of feasting from this present
hour of five till the bell have told eleven. Heaven bless   10
the isle of Cyprus, and our noble general Othello!
                                        [*Exeunt*

Scene 3

Enter OTHELLO, DESDEMONA, CASSIO, *and* ATTENDANTS

OTHELLO   Good Michael, look you to the guard tonight.
Let's teach ourselves that honourable stop,
Not to outsport discretion.

Cassio replies that Iago knows what to do and is very reliable – however he will oversee everything. Othello then takes Desdemona away to bed – he feels they've earned the delayed pleasure of their wedding night. Cassio calls Iago to guard duty, but Iago points out there is another hour's revelry and says Othello cannot be blamed for going to bed early with so desirable a woman. In response to Iago's references to Desdemona's sexiness, Cassio comments on her exceptional beauty and character. Iago tries to persuade Cassio to have a drink with him and some Cypriots, but Cassio declines.

4 **hath direction:** has been instructed
5 **But notwithstanding:** nevertheless
5–6 **with my … to it:** I will take personal responsibility for it
6 **honest:** dependable
7 **with your earliest:** as early as you can
9 **The purchase … ensue:** the deal has been made, the benefits are to follow. Othello is using a business metaphor to refer to the fact that although they are married they have not yet had sex.
10 **profit:** pleasure
13 **Not this hour:** not at this hour
14 **cast us:** rejected our company
   made wanton the night: had a night of lovemaking
16 **sport for Jove:** sexy enough for Jupiter (chief of the Greek gods, renowned for seducing maidens)
19 **warrant:** guarantee
   full of game: always keen for sex
21–22 **sounds a parley to provocation:** arouses sexual interest (sounds a parley is a military term describing the trumpet call to a meeting)
23 **inviting:** attractive
24 **alarum:** incitement, rousing call (alarum is another military term to describe a call to arms)
26 **happiness … sheets:** may they have a good night's lovemaking
27 **stoup:** flagon
27–28 **a brace … gallants:** a pair of local lads
28 **fain … measure:** be happy to drink
32 **courtesy:** social etiquette

> • *How do Cassio and Othello talk about Iago's character and abilities?*

CASSIO	Iago hath direction what to do;
	But notwithstanding, with my personal eye
	Will I look to't.
OTHELLO	Iago is most honest.
	Michael, good night. Tomorrow with your earliest
	Let me have speech with you. [*To* DESDEMONA] Come
	my dear love,
	The purchase made, the fruits are to ensue:
	That profit's yet to come 'tween me and you.
	Good night.

10

[*Exeunt* OTHELLO, DESDEMONA, *and* ATTENDANTS

Enter IAGO

CASSIO	Welcome Iago; we must to the watch.
IAGO	Not this hour lieutenant; 'tis not yet ten o'th'clock.
	Our general cast us thus early for the love of his
	Desdemona: who let us not therefore blame. He hath
	not yet made wanton the night with her; and she is
	sport for Jove.
CASSIO	She's a most exquisite lady.
IAGO	And, I'll warrant her, full of game.
CASSIO	Indeed she's a most fresh and delicate creature.

20

IAGO	What an eye she has! Methinks it sounds a parley to
	provocation.
CASSIO	An inviting eye, and yet methinks right modest.
IAGO	And when she speaks, is it not an alarum to love?
CASSIO	She is indeed perfection.
IAGO	Well, happiness to their sheets. Come lieutenant, I
	have a stoup of wine; and here without are a brace of
	Cyprus gallants that would fain have a measure to the
	health of black Othello.
CASSIO	Not tonight, good Iago. I have very poor and
	unhappy brains for drinking. I could well wish
	courtesy would invent some other custom of
	entertainment.

30

Cassio says he has a poor head for drink: he has had one
drink and already feels tipsy, but he reluctantly agrees to let
in Iago's drinking companions. Iago tells the audience that
they are quarrelsome types, especially if they've had a few
drinks, and that one more drink will get Cassio going. He is
confident of making Cassio provoke a quarrel which will
disturb the peace.

34 **but:** only
37 **craftily qualified:** carefully watered down
   innovation: influence
38 **here:** in his head
   infirmity: weakness
39 **task:** challenge
45 **fasten … him:** get him to have one more drink
47 **full of … offence:** quarrelsome and offensive
50 **caroused:** drunk toasts
51 **potations pottle-deep:** bottles full of drink
   he's to watch: he's on guard
52 **else:** others
   noble swelling spirits: lads with high opinions of themselves
53 **hold … distance:** easily provoked if they think their honour
   has been questioned
54 **The very elements:** absolutely typical of the spirit
55 **flustered:** got light-headed
57 **action:** quarrelsome behaviour
59 **consequence … dream:** the outcome confirms my
   prognostication
61 **'Fore God:** by God
   a rouse: a drink

- *How 'honest' does Iago seem to be here?*
- *What is the effect of Cassio, the senior officer, doing as Iago asks him (43–44), especially as it 'dislikes' him?*

IAGO	O, they are our friends. But one cup; I'll drink for you.
CASSIO	I have drunk but one cup tonight, and that was craftily qualified too; and behold what innovation it makes here. I am unfortunate in the infirmity and dare not task my weakness with any more.
IAGO	What, man! 'Tis a night of revels; the gallants desire it. 40
CASSIO	Where are they?
IAGO	Here, at the door. I pray you call them in.
CASSIO	I'll do't, but it dislikes me. [*Exit* CASSIO
IAGO	If I can fasten but one cup upon him, With that which he hath drunk tonight already, He'll be as full of quarrel and offence As my young mistress' dog. Now my sick fool Roderigo, Whom love hath turned almost the wrong side out, To Desdemona hath tonight caroused 50 Potations pottle-deep; and he's to watch. Three else of Cyprus, noble swelling spirits, That hold their honours in a wary distance, The very elements of this warlike isle, Have I tonight flustered with flowing cups And they watch too. Now 'mongst this flock of drunkards, Am I to put our Cassio in some action That may offend the isle. But here they come;

Enter CASSIO, MONTANO, *and* GENTLEMEN; *servants following with wine*

	If consequence do but approve my dream, My boat sails freely both with wind and stream. 60
CASSIO	'Fore God, they have given me a rouse already.
MONTANO	Good faith, a little one; not past a pint, as I am a soldier.

Iago sings a drinking song and Cassio, now well and truly
drunk, says he likes it. Iago says it is an English song, the
English being great drinkers. Cassio proposes Othello's
health and Iago drinks to England and drunkenness, singing
another song which Cassio thinks even better. Iago offers to
repeat it but Cassio says he disapproves of such things.

65	**canakin:** a small drinking can
68	**span:** a short time
73	**potting:** drinking
	Your Dane: Danes generally
74	**swag-bellied:** with a sagging belly
76	**exquisite:** expert
77	**facility:** ease
78	**he sweats ... Almain:** to drink a German under the table doesn't even make him sweat
82	**I'll ... justice:** I'll keep pace with you
85	**crown:** coin (five shillings or 25p in today's currency)
86	**sixpence ... dear:** too expensive by sixpence (2p)
87	**lown:** crook
88	**wight:** person
89	**low degree:** low status
91	**auld:** old
93	**exquisite:** beautiful
96–97	**that does those things:** sings drunken songs

> • *Why might this section of the play appeal especially to an
> English audience? What tone does it add to the play?*

IAGO	Some wine ho!
	[*Sings*] And let me the canakin clink, clink;
	And let me the canakin clink;
	A soldier's a man;
	O man's life's but a span
	Why then let a soldier drink.
	Some wine boys! 70
CASSIO	'Fore God an excellent song.
IAGO	I learned it in England, where indeed they are most potent in potting. Your Dane, your German, and your swag-bellied Hollander – drink ho! – are nothing to your English.
CASSIO	Is your Englishman so exquisite in his drinking?
IAGO	Why he drinks you with facility your Dane dead drunk; he sweats not to overthrow your Almain; he gives your Hollander a vomit, ere the next pottle can be filled. 80
CASSIO	To the health of our general!
MONTANO	I am for it, lieutenant; and I'll do you justice.
IAGO	O sweet England!
	King Stephen was and-a worthy peer,
	His breeches cost him but a crown
	He held them sixpence all too dear,
	With that he called the tailor lown.
	He was a wight of high renown,
	And thou art but of low degree.
	'Tis pride that pulls the country down, 90
	Then take thine auld cloak about thee.
	Some wine ho!
CASSIO	'Fore God this is a more exquisite song than the other.
IAGO	Will you hear't again?
CASSIO	No; for I hold him to be unworthy of his place that does those things. Well, God's above all; and there be souls must be saved, and there be souls must not be saved.

Iago humours Cassio. Cassio, without wishing to push his
claims, hopes to be saved from hell – asserts that he will be
saved ahead of Iago, being his superior officer. Insisting that
he is not drunk, he leaves drunkenly. Montano sets the guard
and Iago makes some sarcastic remarks about Cassio's fitness;
he fears that Othello's trust in him is misplaced, and tells
Montano that Cassio always drinks himself to sleep. This
worries Montano, who suggests that Othello should be told.

104 **by your leave:** if you don't mind me saying so
104–105 **the lieutenant … ancient:** Cassio believes that the
    souls of officers of higher rank (e.g. lieutenant) will be
    saved ahead of those of lower rank (e.g. ancient). A
    drunken utterance.
114 **platform:** artillery position
    set the watch: set up guard duty (Montano takes charge
    because Cassio has left, drunk)
115 **this fellow:** i.e. Cassio
117 **give direction:** give orders
118 **just equinox:** precise counter-balance
119 **The one … other:** equinox meant literally twenty-four
    hours divided equally into day and night. So Cassio's virtue
    and vice are equal.
121 **odd time:** chance moment
123 **evermore:** always
124 **watch … set:** stay awake while the clock goes round twice
125 **If drink … cradle:** if drink does not soothe him to sleep

> • *In what way is Iago influencing Montano's view of
> Cassio?*

IAGO	It's true, good lieutenant.	100

IAGO   It's true, good lieutenant.   100

CASSIO   For mine own part – no offence to the general,
nor any man of quality – I hope to be saved.

IAGO   And so do I too lieutenant.

CASSIO   Ay but, by your leave, not before me; the lieutenant is
to be saved before the ancient. Let's have no more of
this; let's to our affairs. God forgive us our sins.
Gentlemen, let's look to our business. Do not think,
gentlemen, I am drunk: this is my ancient, this is my
right hand, and this is my left. I am not drunk now: I
can stand well enough and I speak well enough.   110

GENTLEMEN   Excellent well.

CASSIO   Why very well then; you must not think then that I am
drunk.   [Exit

MONTANO   To the platform, masters; come, let's set the watch.

IAGO   You see this fellow that is gone before,
He is a soldier fit to stand by Caesar
And give direction. And do but see his vice;
'Tis to his virtue a just equinox,
The one as long as the other. 'Tis pity of him.
I fear the trust Othello puts him in,   120
On some odd time of his infirmity
Will shake this island.

MONTANO   But is he often thus?

IAGO   'Tis evermore the prologue to his sleep:
He'll watch the horologe a double set,
If drink rock not his cradle.

MONTANO   It were well
The general were put in mind of it:
Perhaps he sees it not; or his good nature
Prizes the virtue that appears in Cassio
And looks not on his evils. Is not this true?

Enter RODERIGO

IAGO   [*Aside*] How now, Roderigo!   130

Iago, aside, sends Roderigo after Cassio to start a fight.
Montano says again that Othello should be told about
Cassio's weakness, but Iago refuses, saying he wants to help
Cassio overcome this. A fight is heard and Cassio enters,
pursuing Roderigo and accusing him of questioning his
competence. Montano tries to calm Cassio, but Cassio turns
on him. Iago, aside, tells Roderigo to raise the alarm, and
calls for peace. He warns Cassio that he's heading for
humiliation.

133 **hazard:** take a risk with
    place: position, office
    second: deputy
134 **ingraft:** fundamental, innate
142 **twiggen-bottle:** bottle covered in wickerwork (Cassio is
    describing the fragile state to which his attacker will be
    reduced)
144 **prate:** blather
146 **mazzard:** head (the word basically meant a drinking bowl)
149–150 **cry a mutiny:** raise the alarm that there is a street
    brawl
151 **God's will:** let God's will be done (a call for peace)
153 **Here's a goodly watch indeed:** this is a fine example of
    guard duty
154 **Diablo:** the devil
156 **ashamed:** dishonoured

• *How does Iago manipulate events here?*

I pray you after the lieutenant go.

[*Exit* RODERIGO

MONTANO And 'tis great pity that the noble Moor
Should hazard such a place as his own second
With one of an ingraft infirmity.
It were an honest action to say
So to the Moor.

IAGO   Not I, for this fair island.
I do love Cassio well and would do much
To cure him of this evil.

[*Cry within* 'Help, Help!']

                    But hark what noise?

Enter CASSIO *pursuing* RODERIGO

CASSIO Zounds, you rogue, you rascal!

MONTANO What's the matter, lieutenant?   140

CASSIO A knave teach me my duty? I'll beat the knave into a
twiggen-bottle.

RODERIGO Beat me?

CASSIO Dost thou prate, rogue?   [*Strikes* RODERIGO

MONTANO Nay, good lieutenant; I pray you sir, hold your hand.

CASSIO Let me go sir, or I'll knock you o'er the mazzard.

MONTANO Come, come, you're drunk.

CASSIO Drunk!   [*They fight*

IAGO [*Aside to* RODERIGO] Away I say; go out and cry a
mutiny.   [*Exit* RODERIGO   150

Nay, good lieutenant. God's will, gentlemen!
Help ho! – Lieutenant – sir – Montano – sir –
Help masters! Here's a goodly watch indeed.

                    [*Bell rings*

Who's that which rings the bell? Diablo, ho!
The town will rise. God's will, lieutenant, hold;
You will be ashamed for ever!

Othello enters and threatens death to anyone who continues
fighting. Montano is wounded and threatens Cassio with
death. Othello asks Iago what happened. Iago says he doesn't
know how the brawl started and wishes he'd not been
involved. Cassio declines to speak. Othello says he is shocked
to remember that Montano has a reputation for peaceful
responsibility.

158 **I am hurt to the death**: Montano thinks he is mortally
wounded
He dies: I'll kill him
Hold … lives: stop fighting or you will die
163 **turned Turks**: become uncivilised barbarians
166 **carve … rage**: vent his anger by using his sword
167 **Holds … light**: is risking his life
upon his motion: the moment he moves
169 **propriety**: decent and respectable state
171 **On thy … thee**: I order you to speak according to your
loyalty to me
173 **In quarter, and in terms**: in relationship and good
manners
174 **devesting**: undressing
175 **As … men**: as if the movement of some planet had driven
them mad
176 **tilting**: charging
178 **peevish odds**: bad-tempered dispute
179–180 **would … part of it**: I would rather have lost my legs
in battle than have been part of this fracas
181 **you … forgot**: you have forgotten your position and duty
182 **wont**: accustomed
183 **gravity**: seriousness
185 **The … noted**: you are well known for
186 **censure**: judgement
187 **unlace**: undo

> • *How effectively does Othello gain control here? By what
> means?*

Enter OTHELLO *and* ATTENDANTS

OTHELLO	What is the matter here?
MONTANO	Zounds, I bleed still. I am hurt to the death. He dies.
OTHELLO	Hold for your lives!
IAGO	Hold ho! Lieutenant sir – Montano – gentlemen! – Have you forgot all sense of place and duty? 160 Hold! The general speaks to you. Hold, hold, for shame.
OTHELLO	Why, how now, ho! From whence ariseth this? Are we turned Turks, and to ourselves do that Which heaven hath forbid the Ottomites? For Christian shame, put by this barbarous brawl. He that stirs next to carve for his own rage Holds his soul light; he dies upon his motion. Silence that dreadful bell; it frights the isle From her propriety. What is the matter, masters? Honest Iago, that looks dead with grieving, 170 Speak, who began this? On thy love I charge thee.
IAGO	I do not know. Friends all but now, even now, In quarter, and in terms like bride and groom Devesting them for bed, and then but now, As if some planet had unwitted men, Swords out, and tilting one at others' breasts In opposition bloody. I cannot speak Any beginning to this peevish odds; And would in action glorious I had lost Those legs that brought me to a part of it. 180
OTHELLO	How comes it Michael, you are thus forgot?
CASSIO	I pray you pardon me: I cannot speak.
OTHELLO	Worthy Montano, you were wont to be civil; The gravity and stillness of your youth The world hath noted; and your name is great In mouths of wisest censure. What's the matter That you unlace your reputation thus,

Montano says that he is seriously wounded and Iago can explain for him. Othello says he's in danger of losing his temper – he must know who started the brawl, and whoever it was will be dismissed. He again asks Iago who started it. Iago says he would never wish to harm Cassio, and is sure that the truth will not harm him. He describes how Cassio pursued a person crying for help.

188 **spend:** barter, exchange
opinion: reputation
190 **hurt to danger:** wounded so seriously that my life is threatened
192 **offends me:** causes me pain
193 **aught:** anything
195 **self-charity:** taking care of oneself
198 **blood:** passionate anger
199 **collied:** darkened
200 **Assays:** tries
203 **rout:** brawl
204 **approved:** found guilty
205 **had twinned with me:** were my twin
206 **Shall lose me:** will lose my trust and favour
207 **Yet wild:** still volatile
208 **manage:** carry out
209 **on … safety:** in the very place which is supposed to guarantee the security of the island
211 **partially affined:** favouring one side
leagued in office: sharing a duty
213 **Touch … near:** Don't press me on such a painful matter
217 **nothing wrong him:** do him no harm

> • *Why does Othello say he is in danger of losing his temper?*
> • *How does Montano's speech (211–213) play right into Iago's hands?*

And spend your rich opinion for the name
Of a night-brawler? Give me answer to it.

MONTANO Worthy Othello, I am hurt to danger.   190
Your officer Iago can inform you,
While I spare speech, which something now offends
  me,
Of all that I do know; nor know I aught
By me that's said or done amiss this night,
Unless self-charity be sometimes a vice,
And to defend ourselves it be a sin
When violence assails us.

OTHELLO   Now by heaven,
My blood begins my safer guides to rule,
And passion, having my best judgment collied,
Assays to lead the way. Zounds, if I stir,   200
Or do but lift this arm, the best of you
Shall sink in my rebuke. Give me to know
How this foul rout began, who set it on;
And he that is approved in this offence,
Though he had twinned with me, both at a birth,
Shall lose me. What, in a town of war
Yet wild, the people's hearts brimful of fear,
To manage private and domestic quarrel,
In night, and on the court and guard of safety
'Tis monstrous. Iago, who began't?   210

MONTANO If partially affined or leagued in office,
Thou dost deliver more or less than truth,
Thou art no soldier.

IAGO   Touch me not so near.
I had rather have this tongue cut from my mouth
Than it should do offence to Michael Cassio.
Yet I persuade myself, to speak the truth
Shall nothing wrong him. This it is, general.
Montano and myself being in speech,
There comes a fellow crying out for help,
And Cassio following him with determined sword   220
To execute upon him. Sir, this gentleman

Iago followed the person but couldn't keep up and came
back to find Cassio and Montano fighting. He has no more
to say except that Cassio must have been enraged by some
insult from the man who fled. Othello believes Iago has been
soft on Cassio and dismisses Cassio from his position as
lieutenant. Desdemona enters, Othello tells her all is well,
offers Montano a surgeon, tells Iago to restore order in the
town, and retires to bed.

222 **Steps in to:** confronts
     entreats his pause: asks him to stop
224 **Lest … clamour:** in case, because of his shouting
226 **I … rather:** I thought it better to return
228 **high in oath:** cursing loudly
234 **men are men:** men will be macho
235 **little wrong:** minor injustice
238 **strange indignity:** mysterious insult
239 **pass:** overlook
240 **mince:** play down
243 **raised up:** woken up
247 **Myself … surgeon:** I will pay for a surgeon for you
249 **distracted:** disturbed
251 **balmy slumbers:** sweet and peaceful sleep

> • *What is the dramatic impact of Desdemona's entrance
> and almost immediate exit?*

Steps in to Cassio, and entreats his pause.
Myself the crying fellow did pursue,
Lest by his clamour – as it so fell out –
The town might fall in fright. He, swift of foot,
Outran my purpose; and I returned the rather
For that I heard the clink and fall of swords,
And Cassio high in oath; which till tonight
I ne'er might say before. When I came back –
For this was brief – I found them close together,   230
At blow and thrust, even as again they were
When you yourself did part them.
More of this matter can not I report.
But men are men; the best sometimes forget.
Though Cassio did some little wrong to him,
As men in rage strike those that wish them best,
Yet surely Cassio I believe received
From him that fled some strange indignity,
Which patience could not pass.

OTHELLO   I know, Iago,
Thy honesty and love doth mince this matter,   240
Making it light to Cassio. Cassio, I love thee;
But nevermore be officer of mine.

Enter DESDEMONA, *attended*

Look if my gentle love be not raised up.
I'll make thee an example.

DESDEMONA   What is the matter, dear?

OTHELLO   All's well now, sweeting;
Come away to bed. Sir, for your hurts,
Myself will be your surgeon. Lead him off.

[MONTANO *is led off*

Iago, look with care about the town,
And silence those whom this vile brawl distracted.
Come, Desdemona, 'tis the soldiers' life   250
To have their balmy slumbers waked with strife.

[*Exeunt all but* IAGO *and* CASSIO

Cassio remains, mortified with shame. Iago tells him that reputation is often won or lost undeservedly, and adds that men lose their reputation only if they believe they have done so. Iago assures Cassio that he should appeal to Othello because his dismissal merely fitted the momentary needs. Cassio feels so guilty that he cannot do so, and curses the spirit of wine. When Iago asks him whom he was pursuing, he says he knows nothing.

252 **hurt:** wounded
257 **bestial:** merely animal
260 **sense:** feeling
261 **idle:** empty, trivial
262 **imposition:** obligation put upon a person
265 **to ... again:** to win back the general's good opinion
265–266 **You ... mood:** You are dismissed now only because of his temper
266 **in policy:** for the political needs of the moment
267 **in malice:** real ill-will
 offenceless: innocent
268 **imperious:** dominating
 Sue: appeal
272 **speak parrot:** talk meaninglessly
273 **discourse fustian:** debate like a fool
277 **What:** who
282 **nothing wherefore:** nothing about the reason
284 **pleasance:** pleasure
 revel: revelry
285 **applause:** self-approval

> • *What is the impact of Iago's analogy in lines 267–268?*

IAGO	What, are you hurt, lieutenant?
CASSIO	Ay, past all surgery.
IAGO	Marry God forbid!
CASSIO	Reputation, reputation, reputation! O I have lost my reputation. I have lost the immortal part of myself, and what remains is bestial. My reputation, Iago, my reputation!
IAGO	As I am an honest man, I thought you had received some bodily wound; there is more sense in that than in reputation. Reputation is an idle, and most false imposition; oft got without merit, and lost without deserving. You have lost no reputation at all, unless you repute yourself such a loser. What man, there are ways to recover the general again. You are but now cast in his mood – a punishment more in policy than in malice – even so as one would beat his offenceless dog to affright an imperious lion. Sue to him again, and he's yours.
CASSIO	I will rather sue to be despised than to deceive so good a commander with so slight, so drunken, and so indiscreet an officer. Drunk! And speak parrot! And squabble! Swagger! Swear! And discourse fustian with one's own shadow! O thou invisible spirit of wine, if thou hast no name to be known by, let us call thee devil.
IAGO	What was he that you followed with your sword? What had he done to you?
CASSIO	I know not.
IAGO	Is't possible?
CASSIO	I remember a mass of things, but nothing distinctly; a quarrel, but nothing wherefore. O God, that men should put an enemy in their mouths to steal away their brains; that we should with joy, pleasance, revel and applause transform ourselves into beasts.

260

270

280

Iago asks Cassio why he seems clear-headed now, and Cassio explains that drunkenness has been replaced by anger – he despises himself. Iago says Cassio must fix the situation he is in. He reminds Cassio that he is his friend and suggests that that because Desdemona is so influential and generous, Cassio should appeal to her. This will be sure to mend things.

289 **wrath:** anger
      unperfectness: failing, imperfection
290 **frankly:** freely, honestly and unreservedly
291 **moraller:** examiner of morality
293 **befallen:** turned out
296 **Hydra:** many-headed snake killed by Hercules (Greek myth)
296–297 **such an answer:** i.e. that I am a drunkard
297–298 **now ... by and by ... presently:** at one moment ... the next ... immediately
299 **inordinate:** over the limit
      unblessed: evil
300 **ingredience:** evil
301 **familiar:** friendly (also familiars were animals used by witches for black magic)
304 **approved:** confirmed
305 **at a time:** once in a while
306–307 **Our general's ... general:** Our general's wife now commands him
307 **for that:** because
309 **mark:** attention
      denotement: observation
      parts: good qualities
310 **importune:** beg earnestly for
312 **free:** generous
      apt: ready
315 **splinter:** heal by applying a splint
      my fortunes: all I have
316 **lay:** bet
319 **protest:** offer it
320 **think it freely:** absolutely believe it
      betimes: early

> • *What are the implications in Iago's speech (301–303)*
> *when he calls wine 'a good familiar creature' and*
> *reminds Cassio of his love for him?*

IAGO	Why, but you are now well enough. How came you thus recovered?
CASSIO	It hath pleased the devil drunkenness to give place to the devil wrath; one unperfectness shows me another, to make me frankly despise myself.

290

IAGO	Come, you are too severe a moraller. As the time, the place, and the condition of this country stands, I could heartily wish this had not so befallen; but since it is as it is, mend it for your own good.
CASSIO	I will ask him for my place again; he shall tell me I a drunkard. Had I as many mouths as Hydra, such an answer would stop them all. To be now a sensible man, by and by a fool, and presently a beast! O strange! Every inordinate cup is unblessed and the ingredience is a devil.

300

IAGO	Come come, good wine is a good familiar creature, if it be well used; exclaim no more against it. And good lieutenant, I think you think I love you.
CASSIO	I have well approved it sir. I drunk!
IAGO	You or any man living may be drunk at a time, man. I'll tell you what you shall do. Our general's wife is now the general. I may say so in this respect, for that he hath devoted and given up himself to the contemplation, mark, and denotement of her parts and graces. Confess yourself freely to her; importune her help to put you in your place again. She is of so free, so kind, so apt, so blessed a disposition, she holds it a vice in her goodness not to do more than she is requested. This broken joint between you and her husband, entreat her to splinter; and my fortunes against any lay worth naming, this crack of your love shall grow stronger than it was before.

310

CASSIO	You advise me well.
IAGO	I protest, in the sincerity of love and honest kindness.
CASSIO	I think it freely; and betimes in the morning I will

320

Cassio agrees to act on this advice and leaves. Iago challenges the audience to say he is a villain when his advice to Cassio is sound: Desdemona is kind enough to plead for Cassio and Othello would do anything for Desdemona. Iago will use this to his advantage by telling Othello that Desdemona lusts after Cassio. Roderigo enters, defeated.

321 **undertake for me:** take up my cause
322 **desperate of:** despairing about
327 **free:** open
328 **Probal to thinking:** can be checked by thinking it through
    course: route
330 **inclining:** amenable, sympathetic
    subdue: win over
331 **suit:** appeal, cause
    framed as fruitful: as naturally generous
332 **the free elements:** the creative forces of nature
333 **were't:** even if it were
334 **All … sin:** all the signs and symbols that represent the fact that human sin has been redeemed by Christ's death – in short, his faith
335 **enfettered:** bound
336 **list:** wishes
337 **appetite:** desire
337–338 **play … function:** be all-powerful over his frail reason
339 **counsel:** advise
    parallel course: plan that runs in line with Desdemona's inclinations
340 **Divinity of hell:** the Devil
341 **put on:** inspire
342 **suggest:** tempt
344 **Plies:** appeals to
346 **pestilence:** poisonous idea
347 **repeals:** wants him reinstated
349 **credit:** trust
350 **pitch:** sticky black substance (virtue is traditionally white)
352 **enmesh:** entangle
353 **chase:** hunt
354 **fills up the cry:** makes up the numbers in the pack (of hounds)

> • *With what attitude do you imagine Iago will address the audience in his opening question (326–329)?*

	beseech the virtuous Desdemona to undertake for me. I am desperate of my fortunes if they check me here.
IAGO	You are in the right. Good night lieutenant, I must to the watch.
CASSIO	Good night, honest Iago. [*Exit*
IAGO	And what's he then that says I play the villain,

When this advice is free I give and honest,
Probal to thinking, and indeed the course
To win the Moor again? For 'tis most easy
Th'inclining Desdemona to subdue   330
In any honest suit; she's framed as fruitful
As the free elements. And then for her
To win the Moor – were't to renounce his baptism,
All seals and symbols of redeemed sin –
His soul is so enfettered to her love,
That she may make, unmake, do what she list,
Even as her appetite shall play the god
With his weak function. How am I then a villain
To counsel Cassio to this parallel course,
Directly to his good? Divinity of hell,   340
When devils will the blackest sins put on,
They do suggest at first with heavenly shows,
As I do now. For whiles this honest fool
Plies Desdemona to repair his fortunes,
And she for him pleads strongly to the Moor,
I'll pour this pestilence into his ear,
That she repeals him for her body's lust;
And by how much she strives to do him good,
She shall undo her credit with the Moor.
So will I turn her virtue into pitch,   350
And out of her own goodness make the net
That shall enmesh them all.

Enter RODERIGO

                                        How now, Roderigo?

| RODERIGO | I do follow here in the chase, not like a hound that hunts but one that fills up the cry. My money is almost |

Roderigo has failed: he has spent all his money, taken a
beating and plans to return to Venice, a wiser man. Iago tells
Roderigo that clever plans take time. Cassio is out of the way
– this is a start. Iago advises Roderigo to go to bed, then
tells the audience he will set Emilia up to plead to
Desdemona for Cassio. He himself will get Othello to
observe Cassio pleading to Desdemona. He has found his
plan.

356 **cudgelled:** beaten
    issue: outcome
357 **so much:** this much and no more
358 **a little more wit:** a little wiser
361 **by degrees:** in stages
362 **wit:** native wit, cleverness
363 **dilatory:** slow-moving
365 **cashiered Cassio:** caused Cassio to be dismissed
366 **other things:** things in general
    fair: beautiful
367 **be ripe:** ripen and rot
368 **Content ... awhile:** be patient for the moment
    By th'mass: good heavens
370 **billeted:** lodged
373 **move for:** speak up for
376 **jump:** at exactly the right moment
377 **Soliciting:** pleading for favours from
378 **Dull ... delay:** Don't let the plan fail through apathy and
    delay

> • *How readily does Roderigo accept Iago's advice?*
> • *How do you imagine Iago delivering the last part of this*
>   *speech after Roderigo's exit?*

spent; I have been tonight exceedingly well
cudgelled; and I think the issue will be, I shall have
so much experience for my pains; and so, with no
money at all, and a little more wit, return again to
Venice.

IAGO　　　　How poor are they that have not patience.　　　　360
What wound did ever heal but by degrees?
Thou know'st we work by wit, and not by witchcraft;
And wit depends on dilatory time.
Does't not go well? Cassio hath beaten thee,
And thou by that small hurt, hast cashiered Cassio.
Though other things grow fair against the sun,
Yet fruits that blossom first will first be ripe.
Content thyself awhile. By th'mass, 'tis morning;
Pleasure and action make the hours seem short.
Retire thee, go where thou art billeted.　　　　370
Away I say, thou shalt know more hereafter.
Nay get thee gone.　　　　　　　　　　⌊*Exit* RODERIGO
　　　　　　　　　　　　　　Two things are to be done;
My wife must move for Cassio to her mistress;
I'll set her on;
Myself the while to draw the Moor apart,
And bring him jump when he may Cassio find
Soliciting his wife. Ay, that's the way;
Dull not device by coldness and delay.

　　　　　　　　　　　　　　　　　　　[*Exit*

CTIVITIES

Keeping track

Scene 1

1 In what order do the main characters arrive on Cyprus? Between which two characters is there the longest delay? What happens during this time?
2 How does Cassio behave to Desdemona? How does Iago interpret this? How does he use it?
3 In what mood is Othello when he arrives? How does Iago see his reunion with Desdemona?
4 What do we learn at the end of the scene about Iago's plans?

Scene 3

1 What are Othello's orders to Cassio and why? What are Othello's intentions for the night?
2 What is the first stage of Iago's plan? How does he put it into action?
3 How does Iago 'orchestrate' the drunken brawl for his own ends and then ensure that it is Cassio who is dismissed?
4 How does Iago manipulate Cassio for his own ends? What are his future plans?

Discussion

Scene 1

1 Iago reveals much of his intentions to the audience at the end of the scene. Explore his words and actions from the time of his arrival in Cyprus and discuss how his intentions are discernible in his behaviour. Consider especially how an actor might play him between his entrance (line 82) and line 164. How do you think his interaction with his wife should be played?
2 Similarly, look at Cassio's words and actions from his arrival to his exit. Iago says much to us about Cassio, but how do you think Cassio should be acted? Is he as Iago suggests – smooth and lustful – or do you see him in another way? Consider in particular what he says about Desdemona, and how he relates to her.
3 Discuss Othello's role in this scene.
4 Discuss the symbolic possibilities of moving the action of the play from Venice to Cyprus. Consider: the Venetians surviving the storm; the Turks being destroyed by the storm; the passing of the storm and the removal of the real need for Othello to be in Cyprus; the reunion of Othello and Desdemona; the activities of Iago.

Scene 3

1 Othello and Cassio plan to ensure the stability of Cyprus by good discipline in not letting the celebration get out of hand. Discuss how Iago, by his cleverness, by good fortune and through the other characters' actions, succeeds in completely undermining their plans.

2 Discuss Othello's actions as a commander. How well does he investigate and then judge?

3 Desdemona makes a fleeting appearance in this scene, yet she is much in the minds of Othello, Iago and Cassio. Explore the scene and discuss the contrasts in their views of her.

4 Do you think everyone but Iago is a fool? How many people call Iago 'honest'? Why do they believe him?

5 The pleasures and problems of drinking and its effects are themes in this scene. Discuss its significance for the various characters – and Iago's plot.

Close study

Scene 1

1 (a) Look at the language Shakespeare uses to describe the storm in lines 1–51. What are the implications of the following words used to describe its actions and effects: 'high-wrought' (2); 'ruffianed' (7); 'chidden' (12); 'quench' (15); 'molestation' (16); 'enchafed' (17); 'banged' (21)?
   (b) Are there any indications in this passage to show why the Venetian ships were able to survive the storm while the Turkish fleet was not?

2 In lines 61–87 Cassio describes and greets Desdemona. Look at the language he uses. How do you respond to it? What does it tell us about Cassio? What effect might it have on our response to Desdemona?

3 From line 100 to line 157, Iago speaks, in many ways, like the clown in a comedy. He is challenged by Desdemona and Emilia to be witty and to find ways of praising women. Look at how he does it. Is he merely helping to pass the time while they wait to see if Othello arrives safely, or, as with others of Shakespeare's clowns, do his words have other significance? What insights do we get into his attitude to his wife and women in general? What is the impact of his final line (157)? How do you respond to Desdemona's and Cassio's comments on Iago's 'folly' (158–163)?

4 Look at what Cassio says about his manners (97–99). Now consider how he should behave to Desdemona as Iago speaks his lines 162–174. What do these two speeches tell us about Cassio and Iago? How is Iago's imagination working? Is Cassio giving him anything definite to work on?

5 The reunion of Othello and Desdemona (177–194) is brief. From the evidence in the text, how do you imagine this greeting should be played? How do their emotional responses to this moment differ and contrast? How is this seen in their manner of expression? How does Iago's aside (195–197) alter the mood for the audience, and what perspective does it offer?

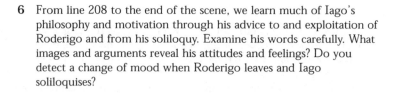

6 From line 208 to the end of the scene, we learn much of Iago's philosophy and motivation through his advice to and exploitation of Roderigo and from his soliloquy. Examine his words carefully. What images and arguments reveal his attitudes and feelings? Do you detect a change of mood when Roderigo leaves and Iago soliloquises?

Scene 3

1 In lines 14–25, Cassio and Iago exchange their views of Desdemona. What are the implications of their views? What do they tell us about the two characters and how they relate?

2 In his soliloquy (45–58), Iago speaks of 'this flock of drunkards' (56). Who are they and what is his attitude to them, revealed in the way he speaks about them? What is his mood in the final rhyming couplet (59–60)?

3 In lines 61–113, Cassio gets increasingly drunk. Shakespeare gives him lines which both show his loss of control and reveal some of his inner preoccupations. What do you learn about him?

4 In lines 114–135, how would you direct the actors to play Roderigo's entrance and exit, and Iago's aside 130–131 to him? What impact would you intend this moment to have on the audience?

5 Compare Othello's attempt to control the brawl (157–171) with his efforts in Act 1 Scene 2 (59–61).

6 (a) Consider the following passages of Othello's speeches: 162–164, 165, 183–189, 206–210. What has disturbed him most about the brawl and those involved in it?
(b) How do you respond to Iago's image describing the friendships that prevailed before the brawl (172–174), and to the image he uses to describe the change in mood (175)? In what ways are they appropriate?
(c) In 197–210 Othello begins by saying that he is in danger of losing his temper. Look at the style, rhythm and diction of this whole speech. Is he almost out of control? Do you think he might be putting on a performance?

7 In lines 211–213, Montano challenges Iago to tell the unbiased truth. In the speech which follows (213–239) Iago gives an account of the action of the brawl with some comments of his own. As a result, Othello dismisses Cassio (242). What is there in Iago's speech which might have persuaded Othello to take this course?

8 Lines 252–325.
(a) Up to line 304, Cassio constantly expresses self-condemnation and disgust. What does he criticise himself for? What are his values?

(b) What arguments and attitudes does Iago offer him to boost his morale in the same passage?

(c) From 305–325, Iago persuades Cassio to a course of action. How does he do it? What ideas about Othello and Desdemona does he use? Why is Cassio persuaded, considering his own view of Desdemona and Othello?

9 Lines 326–352.

(a) Iago challenges the audience to say that he plays the villain (326). What are the implications of this question and the fact that it is directed to the audience? What kind of character is he? How does the speech that follows enlighten us? Is he a villain? Is he the devil?

(b) What view of Desdemona does Iago express? What is the effect of the final images in lines 350–352?

10 Lines 352–378. Roderigo enters, every bit as hurt and defeated as Cassio was earlier. Iago bends him to his will. How does he do this? Are there any similarities in his methods here with those he used on Cassio? What do these consecutive scenes with Cassio and Roderigo tell us about Iago? In what mood does Iago end the scene?

Imagery

In this act there are three aspects of the poetic language and imagery which you might find it interesting to focus on.

1 Look at Scene 1 up to line 207, the point at which Othello has arrived safely on Cyprus, greeted Desdemona and disembarked all his equipment. Pay attention to the ways in which characters describe the sea and the storm, and the sense of peace, safety and optimism which follows it. What impact do their descriptions have on you? You might wish to contrast the language and imagery used by the characters in lines 1–17 to describe the storm as they see it with Othello's words at 178–194 and 197–207.

2 The language and imagery used by characters to speak about other characters reveals much about themselves (as well as those they describe). In Scenes 1 and 3, note the language used by:
   • Cassio, Iago and Roderigo to describe Desdemona (e.g. Act 2 Scene 1, 61–65; Act 2 Scene 1, 217–230; Act 2 Scene 1, 244–245)
   • Iago to describe Othello, Cassio, Roderigo, women in general and himself. (e.g. Act 2 Scene 1, 216–306)
   • Othello to describe Iago and Cassio. (e.g. Act 2 Scene 3, 1–7)

3 Look at the ways in which characters speak of order and discipline on the one hand and disorder and indiscipline on the other. As part of this, contrast Cassio's and Iago's language about wine and drinking. How do these contrasts affect your sense of the developing drama?

Key scene

Scene 3 line 13 – end.

At the end of Scene 1, Iago tells the audience what his aims and motives are, and how he plans to proceed. He says his plan is 'here, but yet confused'. Study Scene 3 to see how he succeeds in discrediting Cassio through words and actions. Does he seem still to be 'confused'? Is he an opportunist, or does he seem to be following a preconceived plan? Try to describe for yourself what his methods are. This will help you when you watch him trying to bring his plans to a conclusion through Acts 3, 4 and 5.

Writing

1 Focusing on Scene 1, argue if there is any evidence for Iago's idea that there is potential for an affair between Desdemona and Cassio. You might consider:
   • Cassio's descriptions of Desdemona before she arrives
   • Cassio's greeting of Emilia and his explanation of it
   • Cassio's attentions to Desdemona
   • Iago's observations about Cassio and Desdemona together.
2 Explain your view of Cassio and his role in the drama on the evidence of Act 2.
   You might consider:
   • his concern for Othello and care for Desdemona
   • his concern for discipline
   • his awareness of his own weakness with drink
   • his shame
   • the way in which Iago plans to use him
   • your responses to his behaviour.
3 Look back at Act 1 Scene 2 (55–91) when Othello prevents a street fight with Brabantio's men. Now write a comparison of his effectiveness in handling that situation with the one involving Cassio, Roderigo and Montano in Act 2 Scene 3. Pay particular attention to his language, especially:
   • the words he uses to assert his authority
   • how he speaks of himself
   • the responses of the other characters
   • the effectiveness of his commands.

In an attempt to regain Othello's favour, Cassio employs
some musicians to play for Othello and Desdemona the
morning after their wedding night. The Clown enters, tells
the musicians that their music is no good, makes a dirty joke
about their instruments' tails being like flaccid penises, and
pays them to stop playing and go. Cassio asks the Clown to
stop playing games and fetch Emilia to speak with him.

1   **content your pains:** pay for your work
      *Stage direction: Enter Clown – 'clown' has a double
      significance: fool, jester (and therefore witty); or country
      person, rustic*
2–3   **bid … general:** wish the general a good morning (after his
      wedding night)
4   **speak i'th'nose:** make a nasal sound (the Neapolitan accent
      was supposed to sound nasal)
6   **wind instruments:** like bagpipes
7   **marry:** certainly, for sure (literally 'by St Mary')
8   **tail:** penis; also, a pun on tale, a story
10   **a wind instrument:** musical pipe (with a pun meaning
      anus)
16–17 **to 't again:** play some more
      as they say: it is generally known
23   **keep … quillets:** stop quibbling over words
25   **stirring:** awake

> • *What is the mood of this passage by contrast with the end
>   of Act 2?*

ACT THREE

Scene

Enter CASSIO *and some* MUSICIANS

CASSIO   Masters, play here; I will content your pains;
Something that's brief; and bid 'Good morrow,
  general'.
Enter CLOWN   [*Music*

CLOWN   Why masters, have your instruments been in Naples,
that they speak i'th'nose thus?

1ST MUSICIAN How sir, how?

CLOWN   Are these, I pray you, wind instruments?

1ST MUSICIAN Ay, marry are they, sir

CLOWN   O, thereby hangs a tail.

1ST MUSICIAN Whereby hangs a tale sir?

CLOWN   Marry sir, by many a wind instrument that I know.   10
But masters, here's money for you; and the general so
likes your music that he desires you for love's sake to
make no more noise with it.

1ST MUSICIAN Well sir, we will not.

CLOWN   If you have any music that may not be heard, to't
again. But, as they say, to hear music the general does
not greatly care.

1ST MUSICIAN We have none such, sir.

CLOWN   Then put up your pipes in your bag, for I'll away.
Go, vanish into air, away.   [*Exeunt* MUSICIANS   20

CASSIO   Dost thou hear, mine honest friend?

CLOWN   No, I hear not your honest friend; I hear you.

CASSIO   Prithee keep up thy quillets. There's a poor piece of
gold for thee; if the gentlewoman that attends the
general's wife be stirring, tell her there's one Cassio

The Clown agrees, with more word play. Iago appears.
Cassio tells him what he has done, and Iago agrees to help by
getting Othello out of the way. Cassio thanks him and Iago
goes. Emilia enters and tells Cassio that Othello and
Desdemona are discussing his dismissal and that Desdemona
is speaking up for him. Emilia continues by telling Cassio
that Othello wants to reinstate him, and is only waiting for
the right time. Cassio nevertheless presses for an opportunity
to speak to Desdemona alone.

28 **stirring:** having sex
   stir: move (but echoing the sexual innuendo above)
28–29   **seem to notify:** tell (but expressed in an over-polite way
   to mock Cassio)
33 **made bold:** taken the liberty
34 **suit:** request
36 **Procure ... access:** admit me to her presence (but Cassio's
   words, which have a note of formality, also carry the
   unintended connotation of obtaining a prostitute)
41 **A Florentine:** i.e. even one of my own countrymen could not
   be more kind than Iago (a Venetian)
43 **your displeasure:** your loss of favour (with Othello)
45 **stoutly:** strongly
46 **of great fame:** highly respected
47 **great affinity:** importantly connected
   in wholesome wisdom: it was only sensible
48–49 **might ... you:** had no alternative but to dismiss you
49 **needs ... likings:** needs no one to beg for you other than his
   own preference
50 **by the front:** directly
51 **bring you in again:** restore you to your post
52 **fit:** it is appropriate
53 **advantage:** opportunity
   discourse: conversation

> • *How might an audience react to Iago's and Emilia's
> support of Cassio?*

	entreats her a little favour of speech. Wilt thou do
	this?
CLOWN	She is stirring sir. If she will stir hither, I shall seem
	to notify unto her.
CASSIO	Do, good my friend.

Enter IAGO

[*Exit* CLOWN

               In happy time, Iago.   30

IAGO   You have not been abed then?

CASSIO   Why no; the day had broke before we parted.
I have made bold, Iago,
To send in to your wife; my suit to her
Is that she will to virtuous Desdemona
Procure me some access.

IAGO   I'll send her to you presently;
And I'll devise a mean to draw the Moor
Out of the way, that your converse and business
May be more free.

CASSIO   I humbly thank you for't. [*Exit* IAGO] I never knew   40
A Florentine more kind and honest.

[*Enter* EMILIA

EMILIA   Good morrow, good lieutenant. I am sorry
For your displeasure; but all will sure be well.
The general and his wife are talking of it,
And she speaks for you stoutly. The Moor replies
That he you hurt is of great fame in Cyprus,
And great affinity, and that in wholesome wisdom
He might not but refuse you. But he protests he loves
    you,
And needs no other suitor but his likings
To take the safest occasion by the front   50
To bring you in again.

CASSIO   Yet I beseech you,
If you think fit, or that it may be done,
Give me advantage of some brief discourse
With Desdemon alone.

Emilia lets Cassio in and says she will put him where he can speak freely.

56 **bosom:** innermost thoughts and feelings
   much bound: very obliged

Othello gives Iago letters for the pilot to take to the ship which will carry them to Venice. He will go off and inspect the fortifications.

2 **do my duties:** pay my respects
3 **works:** fortifications
4 **Repair:** return

Desdemona promises Cassio that she will strive to bring him and Othello together again, and Emilia says Iago is equally concerned. Cassio pledges his allegiance to Desdemona whatever happens.

2 **All my abilities:** all that I can
3 **warrant:** promise
5 **honest:** Desdemona joins Othello and Cassio in the habit of calling Iago 'honest'
7 **Bounteous:** generous

EMILIA   Pray you come in;
I will bestow you where you shall have time
To speak your bosom freely.

CASSIO   I am much bound to you.
                                            [*Exeunt*

Scene ❷ ──────────

Enter OTHELLO, IAGO, *and* GENTLEMEN

OTHELLO   These letters give, Iago, to the pilot,
And by him do my duties to the senate.
That done, I will be walking on the works;
Repair there to me.

IAGO   Well, my good lord, I'll do't.

OTHELLO   This fortification, gentlemen, shall we see't?

GENTLEMEN   We'll wait upon your lordship.   [*Exeunt*

Scene ❸ ──────────

Enter DESDEMONA, CASSIO, *and* EMILIA

DESDEMONA   Be thou assured, good Cassio, I will do
All my abilities in thy behalf.

EMILIA   Good madam, do. I warrant it grieves my husband
As if the cause were his.

DESDEMONA   O that's an honest fellow. Do not doubt, Cassio,
But I will have my lord and you again
As friendly as you were.

CASSIO   Bounteous madam,
Whatever shall become of Michael Cassio,
He's never anything but your true servant.

Desdemona explains that Othello's distance from Cassio is diplomatic and temporary. Cassio fears that it may become permanent. Desdemona assures him of her full support; she says she would rather die than give up on Cassio and encourages him to be optimistic. When Othello and Iago enter, Cassio, despite Desdemona's invitation to stay, leaves feeling guilty. Iago makes his exit seem suspicious to Othello.

12 **in strangeness:** like a stranger
13 **politic:** diplomatic, politically necessary
15 **nice:** thin
16 **breed itself:** develop, extend
    out of circumstance: beyond its actual causes and needs
17 **supplied:** taken over by someone else
19 **doubt:** fear, suspect
20 **warrant:** guarantee
    Assure thee: be assured
21 **a friendship:** an act of friendship
22 **article:** detail
23 **I'll … tame:** I'll keep him awake to tame him (as animals were)
    talk … patience: talk to him about you until he can bear it no longer
24 **board:** meal table
    shrift: confessional
27 **solicitor:** person who puts your case
33 **Unfit … purposes:** not in the right frame of mind to do myself any good
34 **do your discretion:** do as you see fit

> * *Why does Cassio fear Othello's policy may be permanent (lines 14–17)?*
> * *How would you stage the arrival of Iago and Othello at the very moment Cassio is with Desdemona?*

DESDEMONA	I know't, I thank you. You do love my lord. 10
	You have known him long, and be you well assured
	He shall in strangeness stand no farther off
	Than in a politic distance.
CASSIO	Ay, but lady,
	That policy may either last so long,
	Or feed upon such nice and waterish diet,
	Or breed itself so out of circumstance,
	That I being absent and my place supplied,
	My general will forget my love and service.
DESDEMONA	Do not doubt that. Before Emilia here,
	I give thee warrant of thy place. Assure thee, 20
	If I do vow a friendship, I'll perform it
	To the last article. My lord shall never rest.
	I'll watch him tame and talk him out of patience;
	His bed shall seem a school, his board a shrift;
	I'll intermingle everything he does
	With Cassio's suit. Therefore be merry, Cassio,
	For thy solicitor shall rather die
	Than give thy cause away.
	Enter OTHELLO *and* IAGO
EMILIA	Madam, here comes my lord.
CASSIO	Madam, I'll take my leave. 30
DESDEMONA	Why stay, and hear me speak.
CASSIO	Madam, not now. I am very ill at ease,
	Unfit for mine own purposes.
DESDEMONA	Well, do your discretion. [*Exit* CASSIO
IAGO	Ha! I like not that.
OTHELLO	What dost thou say?
IAGO	Nothing, my lord; or if – I know not what.
OTHELLO	Was not that Cassio parted from my wife?
IAGO	Cassio, my lord? No, sure, I cannot think it,
	That he would sneak away so guilty-like,
	Seeing you coming.

Desdemona says Cassio has been to see her, and she pleads with Othello to make peace. She thinks Cassio is loyal; she asks Othello to call him back. Desdemona tells Othello that Cassio is so depressed that she sympathises. She repeats her request to call him back. Othello declines, so she points out that, but for the circumstances, Cassio's fault deserved only a private reprimand. She wonders if she would deny him a request so feebly.

42 **suitor:** one who pleads (but also a man seeking a woman's attention)
43 **languishes in:** is in a state of collapse because of
47 **present reconciliation take:** accept his immediate attempt to make peace
52 **sooth:** truly
humbled: ashamed
55 **Desdemon:** Shakespeare omits the final 'a' of Desdemona for the sake of the rhythm: thus, the final syllable '-mon' should be stressed
63 **penitent:** repentant
64 **trespass:** fault
in our common reason: by normal standards
65–66 **Save … best:** except that the general rule is that even the best must be made example of in wartime
66–67 **not almost … check:** is almost a small enough fault to merit merely a private reprimand

OTHELLO	I do believe 'twas he. 40
DESDEMONA	How now, my lord? I have been talking with a suitor here, A man that languishes in your displeasure.
OTHELLO	Who is't you mean?
DESDEMONA	Why your lieutenant Cassio. Good my lord, If I have any grace or power to move you, His present reconciliation take. For if he be not one that truly loves you, That errs in ignorance, and not in cunning, I have no judgment in an honest face. 50 I prithee call him back.
OTHELLO	Went he hence now?
DESDEMONA	Ay, sooth; so humbled That he hath left part of his grief with me To suffer with him. Good love, call him back.
OTHELLO	Not now, sweet Desdemon, some other time.
DESDEMONA	But shall't be shortly?
OTHELLO	The sooner, sweet, for you.
DESDEMONA	Shall't be tonight at supper?
OTHELLO	No, not tonight.
DESDEMONA	Tomorrow dinner then?
OTHELLO	I shall not dine at home. I meet the captains at the citadel.
DESDEMONA	Why then tomorrow night, or Tuesday morn, 60 On Tuesday noon, or night, on Wednesday morn; I prithee name the time, but let it not Exceed three days. In faith he's penitent And yet his trespass, in our common reason – Save that they say the wars must make example Out of their best – is not almost a fault T'incur a private check. When shall he come? Tell me Othello. I wonder in my soul, What you would ask me that I should deny,

She reminds him of Cassio's support in his wooing of her.
Othello agrees to see Cassio – but at a time of his own
choosing. Desdemona insists that she is not requesting a
special favour but merely advising Othello something for his
own good. He repeats that he will deny her nothing, but asks
to be left alone. She goes, confirming that he should follow
his own wishes and she will obey. Othello expresses his
absolute love for her and the fatal effects of losing her. Iago
begins to question Othello as to whether Cassio knew
Desdemona while they were wooing. Othello confirms this.

70	**mammering:** hesitating
72	**dispraisingly:** critically
74	**bring him in:** reinstate him
76	**boon:** special favour
79	**sue:** beg
	a peculiar profit: something for your own good
80	**suit:** request
81	**to touch … indeed:** genuinely to exploit your love for me
82	**poise … weight:** serious and problematic importance
83	**fearful:** uncertain
84	**Whereon:** on the strength of this
88	**fancies:** desires
90	**Excellent wretch:** a term of affection, but its quality as an oxymoron (see Glossary page 305) gives it a disturbing impact
90–91	**perdition … thee:** may my soul be damned if I don't love you
92	**Chaos is come again:** the world will end (as it began) in chaos
97	

> • *Why does Othello give in to Desdemona's requests?*
> • *Why do you think Othello asks Desdemona to leave him to himself (84–85) when Iago is still present?*

But for a … thought: only to satisfy my idle curiosity

Or stand so mammering on? What! Michael Cassio,   70
That came a-wooing with you, and so many a time –
When I have spoke of you dispraisingly –
Hath ta'en your part; to have so much to do
To bring him in? By'r Lady, I could do much –

OTHELLO   Prithee, no more. Let him come when he will;
I will deny thee nothing.

DESEMONA   Why, this is not a boon;
'Tis as I should entreat you wear your gloves,
Or feed on nourishing dishes, or keep you warm,
Or sue to you to do a peculiar profit
To your own person. Nay, when I have a suit   80
Wherein I mean to touch your love indeed,
It shall be full of poise and difficult weight,
And fearful to be granted.

OTHELLO   I will deny thee nothing.
Whereon, I do beseech thee, grant me this,
To leave me but a little to myself.

DESDEMONA   Shall I deny you? No. Farewell, my lord.

OTHELLO   Farewell, my Desdemona, I'll come to thee straight.

DESDEMONA   Emilia, come. Be as your fancies teach you;
Whate'er you be, I am obedient.

                      [*Exeunt* DESDEMONA *and* EMILIA

OTHELLO   Excellent wretch! Perdition catch my soul   90
But I do love thee; and when I love thee not,
Chaos is come again.

IAGO   My noble lord –

OTHELLO   What dost thou say, Iago?

IAGO   Did Michael Cassio, when you wooed my lady,
Know of your love?

OTHELLO   He did, from first to last. Why dost thou ask?

IAGO   But for a satisfaction of my thought;
No further harm.

OTHELLO   Why of thy thought, Iago?

Iago continues to ask questions about Cassio, without revealing his thoughts or motives, until Othello snaps and insists he must be hiding some monstrous thought because of his questions about Cassio's behaviour with Desdemona. He wants to know what it is. Iago confirms his loyalty to Othello, and Othello points out that his mysterious behaviour is therefore all the more worrying. Iago says he could swear to Cassio's honesty.

100 **went between us:** acted as a go-between
107 **some monster:** something monstrous
111 **of my counsel:** had my confidence
113 **contract ... together:** frown and furrow your brow
115 **conceit:** idea
119 **weigh'st:** evaluate
120 **stops:** hesitations, pauses
    affright: disturb
122 **tricks of custom:** typical or habitual tricks or ruses
123–124 **close dilations ... rule:** secret revelations, coming from the heart, which even the strongest desires cannot control

- *What is the irony of Othello's words (121–124)?*

IAGO	I did not think he had been acquainted with her.	
OTHELLO	O yes, and went between us very oft.	100
IAGO	Indeed?	
OTHELLO	Indeed? Ay, indeed. Discern'st thou aught in that? Is he not honest?	
IAGO	Honest, my lord?	
OTHELLO	Honest? Ay, honest.	
IAGO	My lord, for aught I know.	
OTHELLO	What dost thou think?	
IAGO	Think, my lord?	
OTHELLO	Think, my lord? Alas, thou echoest me, As if there were some monster in thy thought Too hideous to be shown. Thou dost mean something. I heard thee say even now, thou lik'st not that, When Cassio left my wife. What didst not like? And when I told thee he was of my counsel In my whole course of wooing, thou cried'st 'Indeed?' And didst contract and purse thy brow together, As if thou then hadst shut up in thy brain Some horrible conceit. If thou dost love me, Show me thy thought.	110
IAGO	My lord, you know I love you.	
OTHELLO	I think thou dost. And for I know thou'rt full of love and honesty, And weigh'st thy words before thou giv'st them breath, Therefore these stops of thine affright me more. For such things in a false disloyal knave Are tricks of custom; but in a man that's just They're close dilations, working from the heart, That passion cannot rule.	120
IAGO	For Michael Cassio, I dare be sworn I think that he is honest.	
OTHELLO	I think so too.	

Iago says that men should be what they seem. Othello agrees, and Iago repeats his faith in Cassio. This makes Othello suspicious. Iago replies that he has a right to keep his speculative thoughts to himself. Othello points out that it is wronging a friend to keep secret a possible wrong. Iago says that he could be wrong – he has a tendency to find faults where there are none. He adds that it would not be good if he revealed his unsubstantiated thoughts. Othello wants clarification.

127 **would ... none:** I wish they would seem not to be what they are

132 **As ... ruminate:** as you think things over

135 **to that ... free to:** to that which not even slaves are bound to do

137 **As where's ... whereinto:** for example, what place is there into which

139 **uncleanly apprehensions:** corrupt ideas

140 **leets:** days when courts are in session
law-days: days when courts are in session
in session: like judges

141 **meditations lawful:** decent thoughts

143 **but think:** even suspect

143–144 **mak'st ... thoughts:** keep your suspicions a secret from him

145 **perchance ... guess:** perhaps I am wrong in my understanding

146 **it is ... plague:** it is an innate flaw in my character

147 **jealousy:** suspicion

148 **Shapes:** creates, imagines
wisdom: good sense

149 **imperfectly conceits:** mistakenly imagines

150 **build ... trouble:** create a problem

151 **scattering ... observance:** confused and uncertain ideas

152 **quiet:** peace of mind

156 **immediate jewel:** most valuable treasure

> • *Why does Othello think Iago is not telling him everything?*

IAGO	Men should be what they seem;
	Or those that be not, would they might seem none.
OTHELLO	Certain, men should be what they seem.
IAGO	Why then, I think Cassio's an honest man.
OTHELLO	Nay, yet there's more in this. 130
	I prithee speak to me as to thy thinkings,
	As thou dost ruminate, and give thy worst of thoughts
	The worst of words.
IAGO	Good my lord, pardon me.
	Though I am bound to every act of duty,
	I am not bound to that all slaves are free to.
	Utter my thoughts? Why, say they are vile and false?
	As where's that palace whereinto foul things
	Sometimes intrude not? Who has a breast so pure,
	But some uncleanly apprehensions
	Keep leets and law-days, and in session sit 140
	With meditations lawful?
OTHELLO	Thou dost conspire against thy friend, Iago,
	If thou but think'st him wronged, and mak'st his ear
	A stranger to thy thoughts.
IAGO	I do beseech you,
	Though I perchance am vicious in my guess –
	As I confess it is my nature's plague
	To spy into abuses, and oft my jealousy
	Shapes faults that are not – that your wisdom,
	From one that so imperfectly conceits,
	Would take no notice, nor build yourself a trouble 150
	Out of his scattering and unsure observance.
	It were not for your quiet nor your good,
	Nor for my manhood, honesty, wisdom,
	To let you know my thoughts.
OTHELLO	What dost thou mean?
IAGO	Good name in man and woman, dear my lord,
	Is the immediate jewel of their souls.
	Who steals my purse, steals trash; 'tis something,
	nothing;

Iago philosophises that reputation is the most important thing. Othello presses further, but Iago refuses to say more. When Othello grunts in frustration, Iago warns him against jealousy. Othello is distraught. He cannot understand why Iago has mentioned jealousy. He says that if he were ever jealous he would deal with it immediately. The mere fact that his wife is very attractive will not make him jealous. He needs evidence.

159 **filches:** steals
160–161 **not enriches ... indeed:** does not enrich him, and
    bankrupts me
162 **if ... hand:** even if you had control of my heart
163 **custody:** control
165–166 **mock ... on:** makes the person who is jealous more
    and more ridiculous
166 **cuckold:** man whose wife is unfaithful
167 **Who ... wronger:** who is certain that his wife is unfaithful
    but doesn't love her
168 **what ... o'er:** what a hellish time the man spends
169 **dotes:** is infatuated
172 **fineless:** infinite
173 **ever:** always
175 **Why ... this:** Why are you talking to me about jealousy?
176 **make ... jealousy:** spend my life being jealous
177 **still:** always
    changes of the moon: every change of the moon
178–179 **to be once ... resolved:** as soon as I suspect
    something
    I will deal with it immediately
179 **Exchange me for:** change me into
180 **turn ... soul:** focus my mind
181 **exsufflicate ... surmises:** overblown and rotten imaginings
182 **Matching thy inference:** in keeping with what you imply
    'Tis not ... jealous: It does not make me jealous
186 **from ... merits:** based on the fact that I scarcely deserve
    her
187 **revolt:** unfaithfulness
188 **had eyes:** could see what I was like
189 **see:** witness

> • *Why does Iago speak about 'good name' (155–161) in his
> scheme to unhinge Othello, when he has spoken so
> dismissively of 'reputation' to Cassio?*

'Twas mine, 'tis his, and has been slave to thousands;
But he that filches from me my good name
Robs me of that which not enriches him,   160
And makes me poor indeed.

OTHELLO   By heaven, I'll know thy thoughts.

IAGO   You cannot, if my heart were in your hand,
            Nor shall not, whilst 'tis in my custody.

OTHELLO   Ha!

IAGO   O beware my lord of jealousy;
            It is the green-eyed monster which doth mock
            The meat it feeds on. That cuckold lives in bliss
            Who certain of his fate loves not his wronger,
            But O, what damned minutes tells he o'er
            Who dotes, yet doubts, suspects, yet fondly loves.

OTHELLO   O misery!   170

IAGO   Poor and content is rich, and rich enough;
            But riches fineless is as poor as winter
            To him that ever fears he shall be poor.
            Good God, the souls of all my tribe defend
            From jealousy!

OTHELLO   Why, why is this?
            Think'st thou I'd make a life of jealousy,
            To follow still the changes of the moon
            With fresh suspicions? No, to be once in doubt
            Is once to be resolved. Exchange me for a goat,
            When I shall turn the business of my soul   180
            To such exsufflicate and blown surmises,
            Matching thy inference. 'Tis not to make me jealous
            To say my wife is fair, feeds well, loves company,
            Is free of speech, sings, plays, and dances well;
            Where virtue is, these are more virtuous.
            Nor from mine own weak merits will I draw
            The smallest fear or doubt of her revolt,
            For she had eyes, and chose me. No Iago,
            I'll see before I doubt; when I doubt, prove;
            And on the proof, there is no more but this –   190

Iago says he now feels free to warn Othello to watch his
wife. He does not want Othello's open spirit to be exploited.
He adds that Desdemona deceived her father by marrying
Othello, and points out that Desdemona was only pretending
to be afraid of Othello in order to deceive her father. Othello
agrees. Iago says this is proof of her powers of deception.
Othello says he is indebted to Iago and denies that he is
worried. Iago warns Othello not to elaborate on his
thoughts.

194 **franker:** more open
as I am bound: as is my duty
195 **Receive:** hear
197 **Wear:** keep
secure: confidently unconcerned
199 **self-bounty:** natural generosity
200 **our ... disposition:** the attitudes of Venetian women
202 **their best conscience:** the best they can offer in terms of
moral conscience
206 **shake:** shudder with fright
207 **Why ... then:** well, there you are (i.e. it shows she's
deceitful)
208 **seeming:** deceptive appearance, act
209 **seel:** sew up, blind (an image from hawking, where the
bird's eyes were blindfolded during training)
close as oak: as tight as oak-grain
212 **bound:** in debt
214 **Not a jot:** not the tiniest amount
217–219 **I am ... suspicion:** I beg you not to stretch what I say
to wider and more shocking conclusions, nor to go further
than being suspicious

> • *What does Iago only now (192–194) say he feels free to*
> *speak out of love and duty?*

Away at once with love or jealousy.

IAGO   I am glad of this; for now I shall have reason
To show the love and duty that I bear you
With franker spirit. Therefore, as I am bound,
Receive it from me. I speak not yet of proof.
Look to your wife; observe her well with Cassio;
Wear your eyes thus, not jealous nor secure.
I would not have your free and noble nature,
Out of self-bounty, be abused. Look to't.
I know our country disposition well;   200
In Venice they do let God see the pranks
They dare not show their husbands; their best
    conscience
Is not to leave't undone, but keep't unknown.

OTHELLO   Dost thou say so?

IAGO   She did deceive her father, marrying you;
And when she seemed to shake, and fear your looks,
She loved them most.

OTHELLO   And so she did.

IAGO   Why, go to then;
She that so young could give out such a seeming,
To seel her father's eyes up close as oak –
He thought 'twas witchcraft – but I am much to
    blame;   210
I humbly do beseech you of your pardon
For too much loving you.

OTHELLO   I am bound to thee for ever.

IAGO   I see this hath a little dashed your spirits.

OTHELLO   Not a jot, not a jot.

IAGO   I' faith I fear it has.
I hope you will consider what is spoke
Comes from my love. But I do see y'are moved.
I am to pray you not to strain my speech
To grosser issues, nor to larger reach
Than to suspicion.

Iago affirms that Cassio is his friend. Othello says he is only a little disturbed, and is sure of Desdemona's honesty. He wonders how people can betray their true natures. Iago seizes on this, and points out that Desdemona's rejection of marriage to Venetian men was abnormal. He fears she may compare Othello unfavourably. Othello orders Iago to go, but asks him to report and for Emilia to watch Desdemona. Othello wonders why he married. He trusts Iago. Iago returns and insists Othello should not dwell on this matter. He advises him not to reinstate Cassio yet, but to keep a close watch on how Desdemona pleads for him.

221 **vile success:** disgraceful consequences
222 **my ... at:** I did not intend
224 **I ... but:** I am certain
226 **nature ... itself:** a personality straying from its true character
228 **Not ... matches:** to reject many proposals of marriage
229 **clime:** country
complexion, and degree: nature and status
231 **rank:** corrupt
232 **disproportion:** corruption
233 **in position:** positively
234 **Distinctly:** specifically
235 **will:** desires
recoiling: returning
236 **May ... forms:** may eventually compare you with the appearance of men of her country to your disadvantage
237 **happily:** perhaps
244 **scan:** examine
249 **strain his entertainment:** press too hard for his reinstatement

- *At 213, 214 and 223, Iago observes that Othello is disturbed. Look at Othello's responses. What is the effect of Iago's observations?*
- *Why does Iago return so soon (243)?*

OTHELLO   I will not.

IAGO   Should you do so my lord,   220
          My speech should fall into such vile success
          Which my thoughts aimed not. Cassio's my worthy
               friend –
          My lord, I see y'are moved.

OTHELLO   No, not much moved.
          I do not think but Desdemona's honest.

IAGO   Long live she so. And long live you to think so.

OTHELLO   And yet, how nature erring from itself –

IAGO   Ay, there's the point: as, to be bold with you,
          Not to affect many proposed matches
          Of her own clime, complexion, and degree,
          Whereto we see in all things nature tends.   230
          Foh! One may smell in such a will most rank,
          Foul disproportion, thoughts unnatural
          But pardon me, I do not in position
          Distinctly speak of her, though I may fear
          Her will, recoiling to her better judgment,
          May fall to match you with her country forms,
          And happily repent.

OTHELLO   Farewell, farewell.
          If more thou dost perceive, let me know more.
          Set on thy wife to observe. Leave me, Iago.

IAGO   [*Going*] My lord, I take my leave.   240

OTHELLO   Why did I marry? This honest creature doubtless
          Sees and knows more, much more, than he unfolds.

IAGO   [*Returns*] My lord, I would I might entreat your
               honour
          To scan this thing no further. Leave it to time.
          Although 'tis fit that Cassio have his place,
          For sure he fills it up with great ability,
          Yet if you please to hold him off awhile,
          You shall by that perceive him and his means.
          Note if your lady strain his entertainment

Othello says he will not lose his self-control. Iago leaves and Othello decides he will be rid of Desdemona if he proves her false. He is sure she has deserted him because he is black and old. He curses marriage for infatuating men with creatures whose desires they cannot control. Desdemona enters, and Othello is unable to believe that she is guilty. Desdemona calls him to dinner with his guests and notices his faint answer.

250 **importunity:** appeals
252 **Let ... fears:** assume that my thoughts have gone too far
253 **As ... am:** as I have good cause to fear I have
254 **hold her free:** consider her innocent
255 **government:** self-control
257 **qualities:** types of people
       with a learned spirit: from a thorough experience
258 **haggard:** untamed hawk
259 **jesses:** leather straps attached to a hawk's legs in training
260 **whistle her off:** let her fly off
       let her ... wind: let her fly free where the wind takes her
261 **prey at fortune:** survive as best she can
       Haply: perhaps
262 **soft parts:** easy manner
263 **chamberers:** ladies' men
263–264 **declined ... years:** descending into the depths of age
269 **vapour:** stinking air
272 **Prerogatived ... base:** they have less chance than the lowest in society of avoiding being cuckolded
273 **destiny unshunnable:** inevitable fate
274–275 **Even ... quicken:** As soon as we are born we are predestined to it. (The sign of the cuckold was a pair of horns.)
276 **heaven mocks itself:** heaven itself is a mockery
278 **generous:** nobly born
280 **I am to blame:** It is my fault I am late for dinner (but also with the implication that he has made a mistake in marrying Desdemona)

> • *How do you think Othello should respond to Desdemona's entrance (275)?*

	With any strong or vehement importunity;	250
	Much will be seen in that. In the meantime,	
	Let me be thought too busy in my fears,	
	As worthy cause I have to fear I am,	
	And hold her free, I do beseech your honour.	

OTHELLO   Fear not my government.

IAGO   I once more take my leave.   [*Exit*

OTHELLO   This fellow's of exceeding honesty,
           And knows all qualities with a learned spirit
           Of human dealings. If I do prove her haggard,
           Though that her jesses were my dear heart-strings,
           I'd whistle her off, and let her down the wind   260
           To prey at fortune. Haply, for I am black
           And have not those soft parts of conversation
           That chamberers have; or, for I am declined
           Into the vale of years – yet that's not much –
           She's gone. I am abused, and my relief
           Must be to loathe her. O curse of marriage!
           That we can call these delicate creatures ours,
           And not their appetites. I had rather be a toad,
           And live upon the vapour of a dungeon,
           Than keep a corner in the thing I love   270
           For others' uses. Yet 'tis the plague of great ones,
           Prerogatived are they less than the base;
           'Tis destiny unshunnable, like death.
           Even then this forked plague is fated to us
           When we do quicken. Look, where she comes.

           Enter DESDEMONA *and* EMILIA

           If she be false, o then heaven mocks itself.
           I'll not believe't.

DESDEMONA   How now, my dear Othello?
           Your dinner, and the generous islanders
           By you invited, do attend your presence.

OTHELLO   I am to blame.

DESDEMONA   Why do you speak so faintly?   280
           Are you not well?

Othello complains of a headache. Desdemona offers to bind his head. Othello pushes the offered handkerchief away. Desdemona drops it and Othello tells her to leave it. Othello and Desdemona leave and Emilia picks it up and says she will give it to Iago since he has often said he wanted it. She says she will have it copied. Iago enters and, after he has casually accused her of promiscuity, she tells him about the handkerchief.

282 **pain upon my forehead:** a headache, but also with the implication of a cuckold's horns
283 **watching:** staying awake
285 **napkin:** handkerchief
289 **remembrance:** keepsake
290 **wayward:** unpredictable
292 **conjured:** made her swear
293 **reserves it evermore:** always keeps it
294 **work ta'en out:** embroidery copied (As the handkerchief is very dear to Desdemona, and as Iago is very keen to have it for unknown reasons, a copy is the only solution.)
297 **I ... fantasy:** I am only doing it to humour his whim
299 **chide:** tell off
300 **thing:** Iago deliberately twists Emilia's meaning – 'thing' was a crude way of referring to the female sexual organ
     common: shared by all

• *What is Emilia's attitude to her husband here?*

OTHELLO	I have a pain upon my forehead here.
DESDEMONA	Faith, that's with watching; 'twill away again. Let me but bind it hard, within this hour It will be well.
OTHELLO	Your napkin is too little.

[He puts the handkerchief from him, and she drops it

	Let it alone. Come, I'll go in with you.
DESDEMONA	I am very sorry that you are not well.

[Exeunt OTHELLO *and* DESDEMONA

EMILIA	I am glad I have found this napkin. This was her first remembrance from the Moor. My wayward husband hath a hundred times 290 Wooed me to steal it. But she so loves the token, For he conjured her she should ever keep it, That she reserves it evermore about her To kiss and talk to. I'll have the work ta'en out, And give't Iago. What he will do with it, Heaven knows, not I; I nothing but to please his fantasy.

Enter IAGO

IAGO	How now, what do you here alone?
EMILIA	Do not you chide; I have a thing for you.
IAGO	A thing for me? It is a common thing – 300
EMILIA	Ha?
IAGO	To have a foolish wife.
EMILIA	O, is that all? What will you give me now For that same handkerchief?
IAGO	What handkerchief?
EMILIA	What handkerchief? Why, that the Moor first gave to Desdemona, That which so often you did bid me steal.
IAGO	Hast stol'n it from her?

Despite Emilia's protests, Iago takes the handkerchief. Emilia goes and Iago says he will leave it in Cassio's lodgings and let him find it. Such a trivial thing could provoke Othello's jealousy further. Othello enters, and Iago senses that nothing will bring him peace. Othello is thinking of Desdemona's deception, and Iago says he should stop. Othello dismisses him.

309 **negligence:** accident
310 **to th'advantage:** by good fortune
312 **earnest:** keen
315 **of import:** important
318 **Be not ... on't:** pretend you know nothing about it
320 **Trifles ... air:** trivial and insignificant things
321 **confirmations:** evidence
322 **holy writ:** The Bible, believed to be infallibly true
324 **conceits:** ideas
325 **to distaste:** to be unpalatable
326 **with a little:** after a little while
327 **mines of sulphur:** hell (the mines of sulphur burned inextinguishably and were traditionally believed to be located between Italy and Sicily, in the Aeolian Isles)
328 **poppy, mandragora:** narcotic drugs (from opium and mandrake)
329 **drowsy syrups:** sleep-inducing potions
330 **medicine:** influence
331 **owedst:** owned, had
333 **set ... rack:** set me up for torture (the rack was an instrument of torture which stretched the body to breaking point)
335 **but:** only
336 **sense:** knowledge

- **What does Othello's thought at 334–335 echo?**

EMILIA	No faith; she let it drop by negligence,
	And to th'advantage, I being here, took't up. 310
	Look, here it is.
IAGO	A good wench; give it me.
EMILIA	What will you do with't, that you have been so
	earnest
	To have me filch it?
IAGO	[*Snatching it*] Why, what is that to you?
EMILIA	If it be not for some purpose of import,
	Give't me again. Poor lady, she'll run mad
	When she shall lack it.
IAGO	Be not acknown on't. I have use for it.
	Go, leave me. [*Exit* EMILIA
	I will in Cassio's lodging lose this napkin,
	And let him find it. Trifles light as air 320
	Are to the jealous confirmations strong
	As proofs of holy writ. This may do something.
	The Moor already changes with my poison.
	Dangerous conceits are in their natures poisons,
	Which at the first are scarce found to distaste,
	But, with a little, act upon the blood,
	Burn like the mines of sulphur. I did say so.
	Enter OTHELLO
	Look where he comes. Not poppy, nor mandragora,
	Nor all the drowsy syrups of the world
	Shall ever medicine thee to that sweet sleep 330
	Which thou owedst yesterday.
OTHELLO	Ha, ha – false to me?
IAGO	Why, how now, general? No more of that.
OTHELLO	Avaunt, be gone! Thou hast set me on the rack.
	I swear 'tis better to be much abused,
	Than but to know't a little.
IAGO	How now my lord?
OTHELLO	What sense had I of her stol'n hours of lust?

Othello says he was happy when he knew nothing of
Desdemona's unfaithfulness. He would have been happy if
the whole army had had her as long as he did not know.
Now he has no peace and feels everything that made his life
worthwhile has gone. He insists Iago prove Desdemona is a
whore. He wishes to see certain proof. Iago tries to protest.
Othello turns on Iago in rage and says that, if Iago is
deceiving him, he may as well sink deeper into evil deeds
because nothing he does in future could ever be worse.

340 **wanting:** missing
341 **let … know't:** as long as he doesn't know it
343 **general:** whole
344 **Pioners and all:** even the lowliest trench-diggers
345 **So:** as long as
347 **plumed troops:** soldiers with feathered helmets
348 **make ambition virtue:** lead to good ambitions (*or* give
      ambitious men the opportunity to distinguish themselves)
349 **trump:** trumpet, bugle
350 **fife:** military pipe
351 **all quality:** all the fine qualities that war brings out
352 **circumstance:** ceremonial
353 **mortal engines:** heavy artillery
      rude throats: rough voices (i.e. of cannons being fired)
354 **Th'immortal … counterfeit:** imitate the terrifying crash of
      immortal Jove's thunderbolts
355 **occupation:** purpose in life
358 **ocular:** visible, before my eyes
363 **probation:** proof
367 **remorse:** sorrow for having done wrong

> • *Why does Othello call Iago 'Villain' (357)? How is he*
> *making Iago's task clearer in this speech?*

I saw't not, thought it not, it harmed not me.
I slept the next night well, fed well, was free and
   merry;
I found not Cassio's kisses on her lips.
He that is robbed, not wanting what is stol'n,   340
Let him not know't, and he's not robbed at all.

IAGO   I am sorry to hear this.

OTHELLO   I had been happy, if the general camp,
Pioners and all, had tasted her sweet body,
So I had nothing known. O now, for ever
Farewell the tranquil mind; farewell content;
Farewell the plumèd troops, and the big wars
That make ambition virtue. O, farewell.
Farewell the neighing steed, and the shrill trump,
The spirit-stirring drum, th'ear-piercing fife,   350
The royal banner, and all quality,
Pride, pomp and circumstance of glorious war,
And o you mortal engines, whose rude throats
Th'immortal Jove's dread clamours counterfeit,
Farewell. Othello's occupation's gone.

IAGO   Is't possible my lord?

OTHELLO   Villain, be sure thou prove my love a whore,
Be sure of it. Give me the ocular proof,
Or by the worth of mine eternal soul,
Thou hadst been better have been born a dog   360
Than answer my wakèd wrath.

IAGO   Is't come to this?

OTHELLO   Make me to see't: or at the least, so prove it,
That the probation bear no hinge nor loop
To hang a doubt on; or woe upon thy life.

IAGO   My noble lord –

OTHELLO   If thou dost slander her and torture me,
Never pray more; abandon all remorse;
On horror's head horrors accumulate;
Do deeds to make heaven weep, all earth amazed:
For nothing canst thou to damnation add   370

Iago reacts with well-simulated shock that Othello should
think such a thought and says he will learn never to be
honest or love again. Othello relents, but cannot be sure
what he thinks of Desdemona or Iago. He insists on proof,
saying that in his present situation he is suicidal. Iago
dismisses the idea that Othello should actually spy on
Desdemona and Cassio having sex. He says it would be very
hard to arrange.

372 **sense:** sensitivity
373 **God ... you:** God be with you
     take mine office: dismiss me from my post
     O wretched fool: Iago is speaking of himself
377 **profit:** lesson
378 **sith:** since
380 **wise:** wordly-wise
381 **that ... for:** what it tries to achieve
385 **Dian's visage:** the face of the virgin goddess Diana
386–388 **If there be ... it:** if there are nooses, knives, poison,
     fire or drowning streams by which to commit suicide, I will
     not put up with this torment
388 **satisfied:** given proof
393 **supervisor:** eye-witness
     grossly gape on: crudely spy on
394 **topped:** with a man on top of her (as in sexual intercourse).
     Iago is being crude
396 **prospect:** situation
397 **bolster:** share a pillow
398 **More:** other
401 **prime, hot:** sexually rampant

> • *What are Iago's tactics in his two speeches beginning at*
>   *371 and 380*

Greater than that.

IAGO   O grace! O heaven defend me!
Are you a man? Have you a soul or sense?
God bu'y you; take mine office. O wretched fool,
That liv'st to make thine honesty a vice.
O monstrous world! Take note, take note, o world!
To be direct and honest is not safe.
I thank you for this profit, and from hence
I'll love no friend, sith love breeds such offence.

OTHELLO   Nay, stay – thou shouldst be honest.

IAGO   I should be wise; for honesty's a fool,   380
And loses that it works for.

OTHELLO   By the world,
I think my wife be honest, and think she is not.
I think that thou art just, and think thou art not.
I'll have some proof. Her name that was as fresh
As Dian's visage, is now begrimed and black
As mine own face. If there be cords, or knives,
Poison, or fire, or suffocating streams,
I'll not endure it. Would I were satisfied.

IAGO   I see, sir, you are eaten up with passion.
I do repent me that I put it to you.   390
You would be satisfied?

OTHELLO   Would? Nay, and I will.

IAGO   And may. But how? How satisfied my lord?
Would you, the supervisor, grossly gape on,
Behold her topped?

OTHELLO   Death and damnation! O!

IAGO   It were a tedious difficulty, I think,
To bring them to that prospect. Damn them then,
If ever mortal eyes do see them bolster
More than their own. What then? How then?
What shall I say? Where's satisfaction?
It is impossible you should see this,   400
Were they as prime as goats, as hot as monkeys,

Iago asks if Othello will accept circumstantial evidence.
Othello wants a strong reason for Iago's suspicions. Iago
describes how he heard Cassio speak in his sleep to
Desdemona about keeping their love a secret and even acted
out love-making. Though Iago reminds Othello he's merely
been recounting Cassio's dream, Othello is certain it is about
a real sexual encounter. Iago agrees it is likely, but says they
have seen nothing. He asks about Desdemona's handkerchief.

402 **salt:** sexually rampant
   in pride: on heat
   gross: crude
404 **imputation ... circumstances:** allegations and clear
   circumstantial evidence
407 **living:** essential
408 **office:** responsibility
410 **Pricked:** driven
412 **raging:** aching
414 **loose of soul:** unrestrained, undisciplined
419 **gripe:** grip
   wring: clasp
426 **foregone conclusion:** an event that has already happened
427 **shrewd doubt:** fair suspicion
428 **thicken:** confirm
429 **thinly:** less certainly
430 **yet:** as yet
433 **Spotted with strawberries:** with strawberries embroidered
   on it

> • *Why does Iago say he does 'not like the office' (408)?*

As salt as wolves in pride, and fools as gross
As ignorance made drunk. But yet, I say,
If imputation and strong circumstances,
Which lead directly to the door of truth,
Will give you satisfaction, you might have't.

OTHELLO   Give me a living reason she's disloyal.

IAGO   I do not like the office.
But sith I am entered in this cause so far,
Pricked to't by foolish honesty and love,   410
I will go on. I lay with Cassio lately,
And being troubled with a raging tooth,
I could not sleep.
There are a kind of men so loose of soul
That in their sleeps will mutter their affairs;
One of this kind is Cassio.
In sleep I heard him say, 'Sweet Desdemona,
Let us be wary, let us hide our loves',
And then, sir, would he gripe and wring my hand,
Cry 'O, sweet creature,' then kiss me hard,   420
As if he plucked up kisses by the roots,
That grew upon my lips; then laid his leg
Over my thigh, and sighed and kissed, and then
Cried 'Cursed fate that gave thee to the Moor!'

OTHELLO   O monstrous! Monstrous!

IAGO   Nay, this was but his dream.

OTHELLO   But this denoted a foregone conclusion.

IAGO   'Tis a shrewd doubt, though it be but a dream:
And this may help to thicken other proofs
That do demonstrate thinly.

OTHELLO   I'll tear her all to pieces.

IAGO   Nay, but be wise; yet we see nothing done.   430
She may be honest yet. Tell me but this,
Have you not sometimes seen a handkerchief,
Spotted with strawberries, in your wife's hand?

OTHELLO   I gave her such a one; 'twas my first gift.

Iago tells Othello that he has seen Cassio wiping his beard with the handkerchief. Othello is reduced to thoughts of murder. Othello declares that his vengeful thoughts are irresistible and swears to carry them out. Iago commits himself to Othello's service in this.

440 **slave:** might refer to Desdemona or to Cassio

443 **fond:** foolish

446 **hearted throne:** throne that rules in my heart

447 **fraught:** burden

448 **For … tongues:** he feels as though his chest is crammed with poisonous snakes (aspic=asp)

451 **Pontic sea:** Black Sea

452 **compulsive:** unrelenting

453 **Ne'er … ebb:** never ebbs

454 **Propontic:** Sea of Marmara, at the south-west corner of the Black Sea whose currents flow through it and out through the narrow straits known as …
Hellespont: Dardanelles

451–458 This whole image is about a vast amount of water being forced through a narrow space

457 **capable and wide:** fittingly huge

458 **marble:** hard and shining

459 **In … of:** with the proper respect for

460 **I here … words:** I make a solemn promise

462 **elements:** earth, air, fire and water – the whole of creation
clip: surround, embrace

464 **execution:** exercise, use

- *What does Othello's repeated cry of 'blood' indicate?*
- *Do you think Othello is referring to Desdemona or Cassio as 'slave' in line 440? What are your reasons?*

IAGO	I know that: but such a handkerchief – I am sure it was your wife's – did I today See Cassio wipe his beard with.

OTHELLO	If it be that –

IAGO	If it be that, or any that was hers, It speaks against her with the other proofs.

OTHELLO	O, that the slave had forty thousand lives. 440 One is too poor, too weak for my revenge. Now do I see 'tis true. Look here, Iago, All my fond love thus do I blow to heaven. 'Tis gone. Arise, black vengeance, from the hollow hell. Yield up, o love, thy crown and hearted throne To tyrannous hate. Swell, bosom, with thy fraught, For 'tis of aspics' tongues.

IAGO	Yet be content

OTHELLO	O, blood, blood, blood!

IAGO	Patience, I say; your mind perhaps may change. 450

OTHELLO	Never Iago. Like to the Pontic sea, Whose icy current and compulsive course Ne'er feels retiring ebb, but keeps due on To the Propontic and the Hellespont; Even so my bloody thoughts with violent pace Shall ne'er look back, ne'er ebb to humble love, Till that a capable and wide revenge Swallow them up. Now, by yond marble heaven, In the due reverence of a sacred vow I here engage my words. [*Kneels*

IAGO	Do not rise yet. [*Kneels* 460 Witness you ever-burning lights above, You elements that clip us round about, Witness that here Iago doth give up The execution of his wit, hands, heart, To wronged Othello's service. Let him command,

Othello promises him rewards if Iago kills Cassio, and Iago says it is as good as done. Othello says he will find a means to kill Desdemona himself, and appoints Iago his lieutenant. Iago swears loyalty for ever.

466 **remorse:** sympathy, compassion
467 **What ... ever:** however murderous the task
468 **vain:** empty
    acceptance bounteous: promise of generous reward
469 **upon ... to't:** immediately put your commitment to the test
473 **lewd minx:** lecherous creature
475 **furnish me:** provide myself
476 **fair devil:** i.e. Desdemona
    lieutenant: i.e. Othello's new deputy, replacing Cassio

> • *Why does Iago ask Othello to spare Desdemona's life (472)?*

Desdemona asks the Clown to go and find Cassio.

1 **sirrah:** a way of addressing someone who was socially inferior
2 **lies:** tell lies
5 **'tis stabbing:** means certain death
7 **To ... lie:** if I were to tell you where he is staying I would be lying
9 **devise:** invent, make up
12 **edified:** informed (mock-polite)

And to obey shall be in me remorse,
What bloody business ever.

                                        [*They rise*

OTHELLO   I greet thy love,
Not with vain thanks, but with acceptance bounteous,
And will upon the instant put thee to't.
Within these three days let me hear thee say   470
That Cassio's not alive.

IAGO   My friend is dead;
'Tis done at your request. But let her live.

OTHELLO   Damn her, lewd minx! O, damn her, damn her!
Come, go with me apart, I will withdraw
To furnish me with some swift means of death
For the fair devil. Now art thou my lieutenant.

IAGO   I am your own for ever.   [*Exeunt*

Scene

Enter DESDEMONA, EMILIA, *and* CLOWN

DESDEMONA   Do you know, sirrah, where Lieutenant Cassio lies?

CLOWN   I dare not say he lies anywhere.

DESDEMONA   Why, man?

CLOWN   He's a soldier, and for one to say a soldier lies, 'tis
stabbing.

DESDEMONA   Go to. Where lodges he?

CLOWN   To tell you where he lodges is to tell you where I lie.

DESDEMONA   Can anything be made of this?

CLOWN   I know not where he lodges, and for me to devise a
lodging, and say he lies here, or he lies there, were to   10
lie in mine own throat.

DESDEMONA   Can you inquire him out, and be edified by report?

The Clown agrees to look for Cassio, but only after making some puns which question Cassio's honour. Desdemona asks Emilia where her handkerchief is, and Emilia says she doesn't know. Desdemona says she would rather have lost her money, and that the loss of the handkerchief would make Othello jealous if he were a jealous person. As Othello enters, Desdemona says she will not leave him until Cassio is reinstated. Othello comments in an aside on how hard it is to act lovingly to Desdemona. He comments on her hand's youthfulness and fertility, but his words reveal his suspicions.

13 **catechize the world:** interrogate everyone (Catechism is the use of question and answer in Christian teaching.)
16 **moved:** pleaded with
18 **compass:** range
    wit: intelligence
20 **Where should I lose:** where might I have lost
23 **crusadoes:** Portuguese gold coins with the sign of the cross on them
    but: if it were not for the fact that
28 **humours:** moods
31 **O ... dissemble:** how hard it is to pretend (not to be angry or jealous)
33 **moist:** a moist palm indicated both youth and lust
35 **argues fruitfulness:** is a sign of fertility (but also lust)
    liberal: generous (but also promiscuous)
36 **Hot:** passionate
37 **sequester:** separation
    liberty: freedom (but also promiscuity)
38 **castigation:** disciplinary punishment
41 **frank:** open, revealing

> • *Why does Emilia deny knowledge of Desdemona's handkerchief?*
> • *What is the impact of Desdemona's comments in 23–26 and 27–28?*

CLOWN	I will catechize the world for him; that is, make questions, and by them answer.
DESDEMONA	Seek him, bid him come hither; tell him I have moved my lord on his behalf, and hope all will be well.
CLOWN	To do this is within the compass of man's wit, and therefore I will attempt the doing of it.

[*Exit*

DESDEMONA	Where should I lose that handkerchief, Emilia?	20
EMILIA	I know not, madam.	
DESDEMONA	Believe me, I had rather have lost my purse Full of crusadoes. And, but my noble Moor Is true of mind, and made of no such baseness As jealous creatures are, it were enough To put him to ill-thinking.	
EMILIA	Is he not jealous?	
DESDEMONA	Who? He? I think the sun where he was born Drew all such humours from him.	
EMILIA	Look where he comes.	

Enter OTHELLO

DESDEMONA	I will not leave him now till Cassio Be called to him. How is't with you, my lord?	30
OTHELLO	Well, my good lady. [*Aside*] O, hardness to dissemble! How do you, Desdemona?	
DESDEMONA	Well, my good lord.	
OTHELLO	Give me your hand. This hand is moist, my lady.	
DESDEMONA	It yet has felt no age, nor known no sorrow.	
OTHELLO	This argues fruitfulness, and liberal heart. Hot, hot and moist. This hand of yours requires A sequester from liberty, fasting, and prayer, Much castigation, exercise devout; For here's a young and sweating devil here That commonly rebels. 'Tis a good hand, A frank one.	40

Desdemona reminds Othello of his promise. She tells Othello she has sent for Cassio. Othello complains of a cold and asks to borrow Desdemona's handkerchief, insisting on the one he gave her. She says she does not have it, which he sees as a fault. He says it has magic properties which will bring destruction if it is lost and describes the handkerchief's mystical qualities.

43-44 The hearts … not hearts: in the past, people gave their hands in marriage as a sign of giving their hearts; now, when people give their hands, you cannot trust that they are giving their hearts (i.e. Othello has lost faith in the marriage vows Desdemona made to him)

46 chuck: darling, love (literally, little chicken)

48 salt and sorry rheum: stinging, miserable and runny cold – also a concealed reference to tears

54 charmer: magician, prophet

56 amiable: lovable

63 darling: dearest possession

64 perdition: destruction, damnation

66 web: weaving

67 sybil: female prophet

67-68 that … compasses: who had lived two hundred years

69 fury: trance, frenzy

> • *What is the effect of the broken lines 49–51?*

DESDEMONA   You may indeed say so;
                 For 'twas that hand that gave away my heart.

OTHELLO   A liberal hand. The hearts of old gave hands;
                 But our new heraldry is hands, not hearts.

DESDEMONA   I cannot speak of this. Come now, your promise.

OTHELLO   What promise, chuck?

DESDEMONA   I have sent to bid Cassio come speak with you.

OTHELLO   I have a salt and sorry rheum offends me.
                 Lend me thy handkerchief.

DESDEMONA   Here my lord.

OTHELLO   That which I gave you.

DESDEMONA   I have it not about me.   50

OTHELLO   Not?

DESDEMONA   No faith, my lord.

OTHELLO   That is a fault. That handkerchief
                 Did an Egyptian to my mother give,
                 She was a charmer, and could almost read
                 The thoughts of people. She told her, while she kept
                    it,
                 'Twould make her amiable, and subdue my father
                 Entirely to her love; but if she lost it
                 Or made a gift of it, my father's eye
                 Should hold her loathed, and his spirits should hunt
                 After new fancies. She, dying, gave it me,   60
                 And bid me, when my fate would have me wive
                 To give it her. I did so; and take heed on't,
                 Make it a darling like your precious eye.
                 To lose, or give't away were such perdition
                 As nothing else could match.

DESDEMONA   Is't possible?

OTHELLO   'Tis true. There's magic in the web of it.
                 A sibyl, that had numbered in the world
                 The sun to course two hundred compasses,
                 In her prophetic fury sewed the work.

Othello insists on Desdemona producing the handkerchief.
Desdemona continues to press Othello about Cassio and says
his worry about the handkerchief is a ploy to divert her.
In the end, Othello storms out.

70 **hallowed:** holy, sacred
71 **mummy:** a substance made from mummified human flesh
72 **Conserved of:** prepared from
73 **veritable:** true, able to be verified
    look to't well: take good care of it
76 **startlingly and rash:** stutteringly and wildly
77 **out o' th' way:** lost
79 **an if:** if
84 **misgives:** is disturbed
86 **sufficient:** capable
87 **talk me:** talk to me
88 **all his time:** all his life in the army
92 **to blame:** at fault, not fair

> • *Why does Desdemona's pursuit of Cassio's case inflame*
> *Othello? Is she entirely innocent in avoiding the subject*
> *of the handkerchief?*

	The worms were hallowed that did breed the silk, 70
	And it was dyed in mummy, which the skilful
	Conserved of maidens' hearts.

DESDEMONA   Indeed? Is't true?

OTHELLO   Most veritable, therefore look to't well.

DESDEMONA   Then would to God that I had never seen it.

OTHELLO   Ha! Wherefore?

DESDEMONA   Why do you speak so startlingly and rash?

OTHELLO   Is't lost? Is't gone? Speak: is't out o'th'way?

DESDEMONA   Heaven bless us!

OTHELLO   Say you?

DESDEMONA   It is not lost.
            But what an if it were?

OTHELLO   How?

DESDEMONA   I say it is not lost.

OTHELLO   Fetch't, let me see't.   80

DESDEMONA   Why, so I can but I will not now.
            This is a trick to put me from my suit.
            Pray you let Cassio be received again.

OTHELLO   Fetch me the handkerchief. My mind misgives.

DESDEMONA   Come, come;
            You'll never meet a more sufficient man.

OTHELLO   The handkerchief.

DESDEMONA   I pray, talk me of Cassio.

OTHELLO   The handkerchief.

DESDEMONA   A man that all his time
            Hath founded his good fortunes on your love,
            Shared dangers with you –   90

OTHELLO   The handkerchief.

DESDEMONA   I'faith you are to blame.

OTHELLO   Zounds!   [*Exit*

Emilia asks again if Othello is not jealous, and Desdemona
says that she has never seen him like this before. She is
distressed at the importance of the handkerchief. Iago and
Cassio enter, discussing Cassio's reinstatement. Cassio
explains to Desdemona the hopelessness of his situation.
Desdemona regrets that Othello is not in the right mood for
her appeals, but concludes by saying she will do all she can
for Cassio.

96   'Tis ... man: it takes us (women) more than a year or two
     to find out what a man is really like
98   hungerly: hungrily
101 no other way: i.e. to win Othello's favour back
     she: Desdemona
102 importune: beg insistently
106 Exist: be valued
     be a member of: have a share of
107 office: dutifulness
109 mortal: fatal
111 purposed ... futurity: intended worthy behaviour in the
     future
112 ransom me: win me back, buy me back
113 But ... benefit: at least to know this is the case would be a
     benefit for me
114 forced content: artificial satisfaction
115–116 shut ... alms: give myself up to some other way of life
     and seek fortune's charity
117 advocation: appeal
     in tune: in harmony (i.e. with Othello)
119 favour: appearance
     humour: temperament
120 sanctified: holy
122 blank: centre of the target
124–125 more I will ... dare: I will do more for you than I
     would dare do for myself

- *In what way is Cassio's and Iago's arrival so timely?*
- *How has Desdemona's attitude to Othello changed here?*

EMILIA   Is not this man jealous?

DESDEMONA   I ne'er saw this before.
Sure, there's some wonder in this handkerchief;
I am most unhappy in the loss of it.

EMILIA   'Tis not a year or two shows us a man.
They are all but stomachs, and we all but food;
They eat us hungerly, and when they are full,
They belch us.

Enter IAGO *and* CASSIO

Look you, Cassio and my husband.   100

IAGO   There is no other way; 'tis she must do't.
And lo, the happiness! Go, and importune her.

DESDEMONA   How now, good Cassio, what's the news with you?

CASSIO   Madam, my former suit. I do beseech you
That by your virtuous means I may again
Exist, and be a member of his love
Whom I, with all the office of my heart,
Entirely honour. I would not be delayed.
If my offence be of such mortal kind
That nor my service past, nor present sorrows,   110
Nor purposed merit in futurity,
Can ransom me into his love again
But to know so must be my benefit.
So shall I clothe me in a forced content,
And shut myself up in some other course
To fortune's alms.

DESDEMONA   Alas thrice-gentle Cassio!
My advocation is not now in tune;
My lord is not my lord; nor should I know him,
Were he in favour as in humour altered.
So help me every spirit sanctified,   120
As I have spoken for you all my best,
And stood within the blank of his displeasure
For my free speech. You must awhile be patient.
What I can do I will; and more I will
Than for myself I dare. Let that suffice you.

Iago says that if Othello is angry it must be serious and so he will go and find him. Desdemona assumes it is a state matter and regrets that she argued with him. Desdemona says she never gave him a reason to be jealous and Emilia points out that jealous people don't need a reason. Desdemona prays that Othello won't be jealous.

128–131 I have seen … angry: I have seen cannons blast his lines of troops into smithereens, and, with power like the devil's, blow away the man beside him (then, it is implied, he has remained calm); if he is angry now, it must be very serious

130 from … arm: beside him

131 Puffed: blown away

132 Something of moment: it must be something of great importance

133 matter: substance, something definite

135 unhatched practice: secret conspiracy

136 made demonstrable: disclosed

137 puddled: clouded

138 wrangle with: argue about

139 object: concern

140 endues: leads

141 members: limbs

143 observancy: attention

144 bridal: wedding day
Beshrew me much: a gentle oath against herself

145 unhandsome … am: unskilful fighter that I am

146 Arraigning: accusing
unkindness: uncharacteristic behaviour

147 suborned the witness: made myself give false evidence against him

148 indicted: accused

150 conception: fanciful idea
toy: whim

> • *Do you think that Desdemona really believes Othello is troubled by affairs of state?*

IAGO   Is my lord angry?

EMILIA   He went hence but now
And certainly in strange unquietness.

IAGO   Can he be angry? I have seen the cannon
When it hath blown his ranks into the air,
And, like the devil, from his very arm   130
Puffed his own brother – and is he angry?
Something of moment then. I will go meet him.
There's matter in't indeed, if he be angry.

DESDEMONA   I prithee do so.   [*Exit* IAGO
                Something sure of state,
Either from Venice, or some unhatched practice
Made demonstrable here in Cyprus to him,
Hath puddled his clear spirit; and in such cases
Men's natures wrangle with inferior things,
Though great ones are their object. 'Tis even so;
For let our finger ache, and it endues   140
Our other healthful members even to a sense
Of pain. Nay, we must think men are not gods,
Nor of them look for such observancy
As fits the bridal. Beshrew me much, Emilia,
I was, unhandsome warrior as I am,
Arraigning his unkindness with my soul;
But now I find I had suborned the witness,
And he's indicted falsely.

EMILIA   Pray heaven it be state matters, as you think,
And no conception nor no jealous toy   150
Concerning you.

DESDEMONA   Alas the day! I never gave him cause.

EMILIA   But jealous souls will not be answered so;
They are not ever jealous for the cause,
But jealous for they're jealous. It is a monster
Begot upon itself, born on itself.

DESDEMONA   Heaven keep that monster from Othello's mind.

EMILIA   Lady, amen.

Desdemona decides to continue Cassio's suit. Desdemona
and Emilia go and Bianca enters. Cassio greets her and she
berates him for avoiding her. He explains that he has been
worried, and promises to devote time to her and asks her to
copy the handkerchief. Bianca assumes he has got it from a
new lover. Cassio dismisses her suspicions and swears he is
being truthful. He tells her he found it and likes it and wants
it copied before it's reclaimed.

160 **fit:** amenable, ready to listen
161 **effect it:** bring it about
    uttermost: utmost ability
163 **Save you:** God save you (a simple greeting)
    make you from home: are you doing away from home
167 **What ... away:** Why have you stayed away for a week?
168–169 **And lovers' ... times:** And with time of absence being
    harder to bear and seeming longer for parted lovers than
    real time?
171 **with ... pressed:** been tortured under the weight of
    depressing thoughts
172 **continuate:** uninterrupted
173 **Strike ... score:** pay off this debt (score means a bill to be
    paid as well as the number 20)
174 **Take ... out:** copy this embroidery for me
175 **token:** lover's gift
176 **To ... cause:** I see now there is a real reason for your
    hurtful absence
177 **Go to:** control yourself
181 **in good troth:** I promise you
183 **demanded:** asked for

- *Why does Bianca complain so forcefully (166–170)?*
- *What is the irony of Bianca's reaction (174–177) to the handkerchief?*

DESDEMONA	I will go seek him. Cassio, walk hereabout.
	If I do find him fit, I'll move your suit, 160
	And seek to effect it to my uttermost.
CASSIO	I humbly thank your ladyship.

                    [*Exeunt* DESDEMONA *and* EMILIA

Enter BIANCA

BIANCA	Save you, friend Cassio.
CASSIO	What make you from home?
	How is it with you, my most fair Bianca?
	I'faith, sweet love, I was coming to your house.
BIANCA	And I was going to your lodging, Cassio.
	What, keep a week away? Seven days and nights?
	Eight score eight hours? And lovers' absent hours
	More tedious than the dial eight score times?
	O weary reckoning!
CASSIO	Pardon me Bianca, 170
	I have this while with leaden thoughts been pressed,
	But I shall in a more continuate time
	Strike off this score of absence. Sweet Bianca,

              [*Gives her* DESDEMONA'S *handkerchief*

	Take me this work out.
BIANCA	O Cassio, whence came this?
	This is some token from a newer friend.
	To the felt absence now I feel a cause.
	Is't come to this? Well, well.
CASSIO	Go to, woman
	Throw your vile guesses in the devil's teeth,
	From whence you have them. You are jealous now
	That this is from some mistress, some remembrance. 180
	No, in good troth, Bianca.
BIANCA	Why, whose is it?
CASSIO	I know not neither. I found it in my chamber.
	I like the work well. Ere it be demanded –
	As like enough it will – would have it copied.

Cassio asks Bianca to leave him because he is waiting to see Othello and it won't help his cause if he's seen with a woman. Bianca reluctantly agrees to go – she has to put up with this treatment.

186 **Wherefore?:** Why?
187 **attend on:** wait for
188 **no addition:** no advantage
189 **womaned:** in the company of a woman
191 **bring ... way:** take me with you
195 **be circumstanced:** live with this treatment

> • *How is Shakespeare developing the importance of the handkerchief in the plot? Consider, for instance, the fact that Cassio likes the handkerchief enough to have it copied.*

	Take it and do't, and leave me for this time.
BIANCA	Leave you? Wherefore?
CASSIO	I do attend here on the general, And think it no addition, nor my wish, To have him see me womaned.
BIANCA	Why, I pray you?
CASSIO	Not that I love you not.
BIANCA	But that you do not love me. 190 I pray you bring me on the way a little, And say if I shall see you soon at night.
CASSIO	'Tis but a little way that I can bring you, For I attend here. But I'll see you soon.
BIANCA	'Tis very good: I must be circumstanced. [*Exeunt*

ACTIVITIES

Keeping track

Scene 1

1 Why does the Clown send Cassio's musicians away?
2 What are Othello's plans for Cassio?

Scene 2

Given the arrangements made by Emilia at the end of Scene 1, what is the purpose of this scene?

Scene 3

1 What does Desdemona say she will do on Cassio's behalf?
2 How does Iago make use of Cassio's exit when he and Othello arrive?
3 How do Othello and Desdemona part?
4 What means does Iago use to arouse Othello's jealousy?
5 How does Desdemona's handkerchief come into and become a vital component of the plot?
6 It is clear that Othello is obsessed with one thing which Iago eventually provides in two ways. What does Othello want, and what does Iago give him?
7 What is Othello's response? How does it affect Iago?

Scene 4

1 Desdemona describes Othello as 'true of mind' (24). How does Othello belie this description as soon as he enters? What does he imply about her when he greets her? How does he test whether Desdemona has the handkerchief he gave her? How does she react to his insistence that she should fetch the handkerchief?
2 What explanations for Othello's anger does Desdemona offer? What alternative does Emilia consider?
3 Why does Cassio give Desdemona's handkerchief to Bianca? How does she react to this? Why does he not wish to be seen with Bianca at this point?

Discussion

Scene 1

Cassio presses to talk to Desdemona even after he hears that she is already speaking up for him, and that Othello wants to reinstate him and is only waiting for the right time. On this evidence and that of the play so far, are there any grounds for the suspicions Iago will later put in Othello's mind?

Scene 3

1 Discuss your responses to the characters at this stage. Do you have any sympathy for Othello by the end of the scene? Do you see him as fool, villain, or in some more complex way? Do you enjoy Iago's cleverness, view him as a straight villain or find that he resists one simple label? Is Desdemona an innocent, a fool, too good to be true or a more interesting character altogether? How do you respond to Cassio's pressure for Desdemona to speak for him? Is he a coward or guilty for departing when Othello arrives?

2 This is the pivotal scene of the play. Before it began Othello was blissfully in love with Desdemona. By the end of it, he is devising a means by which to kill her. Discuss how and why this transformation has come about. Use your answers to 2, 4, 5, 6 and, perhaps, 7 in 'Keeping track' as a basis for your discussion.

3 In this scene, Shakespeare is bringing his play to a point from which there is no turning back. Discuss his use of characters, their actions and words, and the dropping of the handkerchief as essential elements in the making of this critical scene.

Scene 4

1 The first part of this scene involving the Clown (1–19) is frequently cut from modern productions. Discuss why you think Shakespeare may have written this episode and what the play might gain or lose by its omission.

2 Consider the end of the scene from Bianca's entrance (163) to the end. The fact that Cassio has given Desdemona's handkerchief to Bianca could be recounted at a suitable point later in the play. Discuss what Shakespeare adds to his play and its themes by writing this episode.

Close study

Scene 1

Lines 4–30.

1 What is the significance of the Clown instantly dismissing the musicians Cassio hired to sweeten Othello? Is there any significance in the Clown's sexual joke about wind instruments/tails/tales?

2 What might the significance be of Othello not caring to hear music?

3 What do the repetition of 'honest' (21–22) and the Clown's reply that he does not hear 'your honest friend' imply?

4 What is the implication of the Clown's innuendo in line 28?

Scene 3

1 Lines 1–28.
- What is the tone of Cassio's words to Desdemona?
- In lines 20–28, Desdemona commits herself to pressing Cassio's case. What do you think of the way she does this?

2 Lines 29–92.
- Iago begins this section with three brief speeches and says no more. Why is this?
- How does Desdemona represent Cassio or Othello in this passage? How does she present the value of her advice? How do you interpret Desdemona's feelings for Cassio and her readiness to help him?
- Othello says to Desdemona 'I will deny thee nothing'. What is the tone and dramatic significance of this line?
- How do you interpret Othello's words at the end of this section – in terms of his feelings and state of mind?

3 Lines 93–191.
- In this passage, Iago further undermines Othello's confidence in Cassio and Desdemona. Look closely at his methods and Othello's responses. What uncertainties in Othello does he play on? Some key lines in this passage you might consider are: 94–95; 97–98; 104; 106–108; 115–120; 124–133; 152–193.
- Consider the impact of the expressions in 164–169; 171–175; 179–182.
- In what ways are lines 192–199 a turning point?

4 Lines 191–268.
- What ideas about Desdemona does Iago directly or indirectly put in Othello's mind?
- In line 212, Othello declares his everlasting commitment to Iago: 'I am bound to thee for ever'. Compare this ominous commitment to the one Iago makes in the last words of this same scene. What do these ominous commitments suggest about the relationship between Othello and Iago?
- What is the effect on Othello when he first dismisses Iago (237–242)? To what purpose does Iago return (248–255)? What is the effect (256–277)? What is the impact of Othello's language in lines 258–277?

5 Lines 328–477.
  • What is the impact of the image Othello uses in line 333?
  • What do you understand about Othello from lines 336–355? What is his idea of emotional security? How does he value himself and his life?
  • How do Othello's words in lines 357–364 indicate his obsession with evidence?
  • How do you understand the images Othello uses in lines 368–369 and 384–386?
  • How does Iago deliver his first piece of 'evidence' (392–424)? Consider especially the impact of 393–394; 400–403; 411–424.
  • In lines 425–438, how does Iago pretend to be concerned about justice? What is the effect on Othello?
  • From line 442, Othello makes a commitment. What is it? How does his language in lines 442–448, 449, and 451–460 express this?
  • From line 460 to the end of the scene Othello and Iago kneel together then rise. What does this symbolise? How does their language reinforce this symbolism?

Scene 4

1 Lines 1–19. Explore the play on the word 'lie' in this passage. What is its significance beyond the Clown's role as a man of wit and entertainment? Look ahead to Act 4 Scene 1 lines 29–36. How is the significance of this passage in Act 3 brought into sharper focus by what follows in Act 4?
2 Lines 33–45. Explore this passage in which Othello takes Desdemona's hand. What is the full significance of the language he uses? What thoughts and feelings does it reveal in him? How might an audience respond? How does Desdemona?
3 Lines 49–72. What is the effect of Othello's 'story behind the handkerchief'? What does it reveal about Othello that he should want to tell it at this point? Look especially at the significance of his language in lines 54–55, 57–60 and 64–65. Consider also the significance of Othello's account of the making of the handkerchief?
4 In lines 72–92 (exit Othello), how does Shakespeare indicate Othello's state of mind?
5 In what way is Emilia's role developing in the play through this scene? Consider her responses to the situation and how they differ from Desdemona's.
6 Consider Desdemona's lines in 116–161. In what way is her response to Othello altering? How does she express her thoughts and feelings? How do you interpret her character here? Is 'innocent' the right word?

Imagery

There are two strands of poetic language which you may find particularly interesting and revealing to study:

1 The idea of the 'monstrous' – that which is horrifying and unnatural, a 'monster' – is not new in this play, and you could well research it in the earlier acts. Here, in Act 3, it is used by Iago to describe jealousy – 'green-eyed monster' – and by Othello to describe what he believes is Desdemona's infidelity. Pay attention to this strand of language and other references to jealousy and infidelity and think about their impact.

2 Othello says in lines 91–92 of Scene 3 that if he does not love Desdemona 'Chaos is come again'. As the scene develops, and in Scene 4, we see increasing signs of 'chaos' in Othello's expression, both in imagery and style of speech, as he descends into obsessive jealousy. Study this development in Othello's language. What does it reveal to you? What impact does it have?

Key scene

Scene 3: From the beginning to line 255 (Iago's exit)

At the end of Act 2 Scene 3, we watch Iago work hard to persuade first Cassio, then Roderigo, to do what he wants. We also know that, after the disturbance of the street brawl, Othello and Desdemona have returned to their long-delayed wedding night. In Act 3 Scene 1, Cassio is assured by Emilia that Desdemona and Othello are discussing him and that Othello still 'loves' Cassio and will find an opportunity to reinstate him; he sacked him only for political reasons. Yet, by the end of Scene 3, Othello has ordered Iago to organise Cassio's death and has sworn to devise a means of killing Desdemona himself. A mad jealousy has emerged in him.

It is in this key passage that the tragic change is brought about. The words and actions of Cassio, Desdemona, and Emilia – all of them behaving quite 'innocently' – fatally conspire to make Othello, whose mind is prompted by Iago, believe that Desdemona is unfaithful to him with Cassio. Here are two examples. Desdemona (10–13) tells Cassio that Othello is only keeping 'a politic distance' from him, and that all will be well. Cassio, despite this, not wanting Othello to forget him, insists that Desdemona speak for him and she, out of the goodness of her heart, undertakes to do so with all her energy. Then, at line 34,

Cassio exits, not wanting Othello to see him out of an understandable sense of shame. Othello is provoked by Iago to see this as a guilty departure, and hears Desdemona's protests on Cassio's behalf as a sign of her attraction to him.

This passage is at the centre of the play. Key questions about the tragedy are brought sharply into focus:

1 Was the final tragedy inevitable because of this fatal combination of characters?
2 Is Iago responsible for Othello's descent into jealousy or is he merely exploiting the opportunities Othello and the others supply him?
3 Is Othello an innocent victim of Iago's malice, an unstably jealous man or simply inexperienced in love?

You should study the passage with these questions in mind and develop your own views. The way you see Othello here will affect your final view of the tragedy as a whole. You would do well to continue these studies through to the end of Scene 3 (and beyond). Pay particular attention to the 'accident' of the dropped handkerchief.

Writing

1 Study the role of Emilia in this act. Write an interpretation of her character, motives and actions, and explain how important you think her role is. You might consider:
   • her role as a messenger
   • her various comments about jealousy and her observations of Othello
   • her behaviour and feelings in relation to the handkerchief
   • her relationship with Desdemona.
2 Explain how you think Act 3 affects the audience's feelings about Othello. You might consider:
   • whether you see him as victim of Iago or not
   • his change from love to loathing
   • your response to his language
   • his plans for Desdemona and Cassio.
3 'For all that Iago is acting out of hatred, there is much for the audience to enjoy in the cleverness of his manipulations of Othello.' How do you respond to this idea? In your answer you should think about the way Iago has previously taken the audience into his confidence: we know what he is going to do. Perhaps, in some sense, we are on his side?

Othello and Iago enter in the middle of a conversation about what is acceptable behaviour in a woman and what constitutes flirting or infidelity. Iago reminds Othello of the handkerchief and Othello says he had almost forgotten it – but cannot do so.

1 **Will you think so?:** Do you really believe this?
2 **unauthorized:** illegal, not allowed (i.e. adulterous)
6–8 **It is hypocrisy ... tempt heaven:** pretending to do evil but actually doing good (i.e. the reverse of 'hypocrisy' as we normally use it, pretending to do good, but actually doing evil)
9 **So they ... venial slip:** if they don't give in to temptation, it is only a trivial sin
13 **bestow't:** give it to
14 **honour:** chastity
16 **essence:** underlying, invisible reality
17 **They have it very oft that have it not:** those who seem to have honour often do not
20 **O it ... memory:** the memory of it overwhelms my mind
21–22 **As doth ... to all:** Othello compares the memory of the handkerchief to the raven, said in mythology to perch on houses where there was disease and death, thereby warning others to stay away

• *Why does Iago introduce the handkerchief when he does?*

ACT FOUR

Scene 1

Enter OTHELLO *and* IAGO

IAGO Will you think so?

OTHELLO   Think so, Iago?

IAGO   What!
To kiss in private?

OTHELLO   An unauthorized kiss.

IAGO Or to be naked with her friend in bed,
An hour or more, not meaning any harm?

OTHELLO Naked in bed, Iago, and not mean harm?
It is hypocrisy against the devil.
They that mean virtuously, and yet do so,
The devil their virtue tempts, and they tempt heaven.

IAGO So they do nothing, 'tis a venial slip.

But if I give my wife a handkerchief –   10

OTHELLO What then?

IAGO Why then 'tis hers, my lord; and being hers,
She may, I think, bestow't on any man.

OTHELLO She is protectress of her honour too;
May she give that?

IAGO Her honour is an essence that's not seen;
They have it very oft that have it not.
But for the handkerchief –

OTHELLO By heaven, I would most gladly have forgot it!
Thou said'st – O it comes o'er my memory   20
As doth the raven o'er the infected house,
Boding to all – he had my handkerchief.

IAGO Ay, what of that?

Iago continues to torment Othello, first implying and then
stating that he has heard Cassio boast about having had sex
with Desdemona. Othello is deeply disturbed by the
supposed evidence of confession and the handkerchief and
collapses. While Othello lies in a trance, Iago gloats over this
evidence that his plan is working. Cassio enters.

25–29 as knaves ... must blab: there are some men out there
who, once they've had a woman (either by their own
persistent attempts at seduction or by her weakness of will in
resisting) can't stop talking about it

31 No more ... unswear: he'll deny having said it

36 belie her: tell lies about her
Zounds: an oath (by God's wounds)

37 that's fulsome: vile, obscene

38 confess ... hanged: proverbial expression meaning 'you're
lying'

40–41 Nature ... instruction: No one would take on such a
dark passion without having some provocation

42 Pish!: very strong, anguished outcry

46–48 Thus credulous ... reproach: in this way too-trusting
people are tricked, trapped, and many sexually virtuous
women are wrongfully accused

> • *Why does Othello fall in a trance?*
> • *Iago refers to his 'medicine' (46). What do you think of*
>   *this choice of word for his treatment of Othello?*

OTHELLO	That's not so good now.
IAGO	What If I had said I had seen him do you wrong? Or heard him say – as knaves be such abroad, Who having by their own importunate suit Or voluntary dotage of some mistress Convinced or supplied them, cannot choose But they must blab –
OTHELLO	Hath he said anything?
IAGO	He hath, my lord; but be you well assured, 30 No more than he'll unswear.
OTHELLO	What hath he said?
IAGO	Faith, that he did – I know not what he did.
OTHELLO	What? What?
IAGO	Lie –
OTHELLO	With her?
IAGO	With her? On her. What you will.
OTHELLO	Lie with her? Lie on her? We say lie on her when they belie her. Lie with her – Zounds, that's fulsome. Handkerchief – confessions – handkerchief! To confess and be hanged for his labour – first to be hanged, and then to confess. I tremble at it. Nature would not invest herself in 40 such shadowing passion without some instruction. It is not words that shake me thus. Pish! Noses, ears, and lips. Is't possible? Confess – handkerchief! O devil!

[Falls in a trance

IAGO	Work on, My medicine, work! Thus credulous fools are caught, And many worthy and chaste dames, even thus, All guiltless, meet reproach. What ho, my lord! My lord, I say! Othello!

Enter CASSIO

Iago asks Cassio to withdraw because Othello's fits can be
violent. He tells Cassio he wants to speak with him on an
important matter after Othello has recovered. Cassio agrees.
Othello revives, and Iago's question about his head prompts
him to think Iago sees him with the horns of a cuckold. Iago
comments that there are many cuckolds in the world.

51 **an epilepsy:** a fit
53 **forbear:** hold back
54 **lethargy:** stupor, coma
    have … course: run its course undisturbed
59 **on great occasion:** about a very important matter
61 **Dost … me?:** Othello is asking whether Iago is mocking him
    about the cuckold's horns he supposes are on his head
    by heaven: an oath used to emphasise sincerity
62 **Would:** I wish, if only
    fortune: situation, fate
63 **horned man:** cuckold
64–65 **There's many … a civil monster:** in that case there are
    many beasts and monsters in every city
67–68 **Think … with you:** remember that every married man is
    in your situation
68–70 **There's millions … peculiar:** millions of people every
    night are unfaithful and think they're alone in an uncommon
    experience
71 **fiend's arch-mock:** devil's best trick
72 **lip:** kiss
    wanton: adulterous woman
    secure couch: a bed (i.e. sexual relationship) supposedly free
    from suspicion
73 **suppose her chaste:** believe her to be virtuous
73–74 **No … she shall be:** I'd rather know and, knowing I'm a
    cuckold, know that she's a whore
76 **Confine … list:** restrict yourself to being a patient listener

> • *Look at Iago's lines 71–73. Do you think he may be*
> *speaking from experience?*

How now Cassio?

CASSIO	What's the matter? 50
IAGO	My lord is fall'n into an epilepsy.
	This is his second fit: he had one yesterday.
CASSIO	Rub him about the temples.
IAGO	No, forbear.

The lethargy must have his quiet course,
If not, he foams at mouth, and by and by
Breaks out to savage madness. Look, he stirs.
Do you withdraw yourself a little while,
He will recover straight. When he is gone,
I would on great occasion speak with you.

[*Exit* CASSIO

How is it, general? Have you not hurt your head? 60

OTHELLO Dost thou mock me?

IAGO   I mock you? No, by heaven.
Would you would bear your fortune like a man.

OTHELLO A horned man's a monster and a beast.

IAGO There's many a beast then in a populous city,
And many a civil monster.

OTHELLO Did he confess it?

IAGO   Good sir, be a man.
Think every bearded fellow that's but yoked
May draw with you. There's millions now alive
That nightly lie in those unproper beds
Which they dare swear peculiar. Your case is better. 70
O 'tis the spite of hell, the fiend's arch-mock,
To lip a wanton in a secure couch,
And to suppose her chaste! No, let me know,
And knowing what I am, I know what she shall be.

OTHELLO O, thou art wise, 'tis certain.

IAGO   Stand you awhile apart,
Confine yourself but in a patient list.
Whilst you were here o'erwhelmed with your grief –

Iago tells Othello that while he was unconscious Cassio arrived
and is soon to return. He tells Othello to hide himself so that
he can observe Iago ask Cassio about his affair with
Desdemona. Othello agrees and withdraws. Iago tells the
audience that he is going to ask Cassio about Bianca, a
prostitute who adores Cassio. Iago knows that Cassio cannot
help laughing when he hears of Bianca – and he knows that the
watching Othello will believe Cassio is talking about
Desdemona. Cassio enters.

79   **shifted:** moved
80   **laid good ... ecstasy:** gave good explanations for your trance
81   **Bade ... return:** told him to return soon
82   **encave:** hide
83   **mark ... scorns:** note the sneers, the mocking comments and
       obvious scorn
85   **anew:** again
87   **cope:** copulate with
88   **Marry:** an oath (by the Virgin Mary)
89   **all in all spleen:** consumed with rage
91   **cunning in my patience:** waiting with all my wits about me
92–93 **That's not ... in all:** there's nothing wrong with that, but
       keep yourself under control
93   **withdraw:** stand aside
94   **question Cassio of Bianca:** ask Cassio about Bianca
95–96 **housewife ... clothes:** a woman who earns food and
       clothing by selling her body
97   **dotes on:** adores, is besotted with
97–98 **as 'tis ... by one:** it is the curse of the prostitute to be
       wanted by many men but to want only one
99   **refrain:** stop
102 **unbookish:** ignorant, uneducated
      construe: interpret
103 **light:** frivolous
104 **Quite in the wrong:** in the wrong way
105–106 **The worser ... kills me:** I feel worse because you address
      me by the title whose lack is causing my trouble
107 **Ply ... sure on't:** work on Desdemona and you will be certain
      of having your position back
108 **if ... power:** if this request were given to Bianca to make

> • *Why do you think Iago describes Othello's jealousy as*
> *'unbookish'?*

A passion most unsuiting such a man –
Cassio came hither. I shifted him away,
And laid good 'scuses upon your ecstasy;   80
Bade him anon return and here speak with me,
The which he promised. Do but encave yourself,
And mark the fleers, the gibes, and notable scorns
That dwell in every region of his face.
For I will make him tell the tale anew,
Where, how, how oft, how long ago, and when
He hath, and is again to cope your wife.
I say, but mark his gestures. Marry, patience,
Or I shall say y'are all in all in spleen
And nothing of a man.

OTHELLO   Dost thou hear, Iago?   90
I will be found most cunning in my patience.
But – dost thou hear? – most bloody.

IAGO   That's not amiss,
But yet keep time in all. Will you withdraw?

                                        [OTHELLO *retires*

Now will I question Cassio of Bianca,
A housewife that by selling her desires
Buys herself bread and clothes; it is a creature
That dotes on Cassio – as 'tis the strumpet's plague
To beguile many and be beguiled by one.
He when he hears of her cannot refrain
From the excess of laughter.

Enter CASSIO

                                        Here he comes.   100
As he shall smile, Othello shall go mad;
And his unbookish jealousy must construe
Poor Cassio's smiles, gestures, and light behaviours,
Quite in the wrong. How do you now, lieutenant?

CASSIO   The worser that you give me the addition
Whose want even kills me.

IAGO   Ply Desdemona well and you are sure on't.
Now if this suit lay in Bianca's power,

Othello hears Cassio laughing at the idea that Bianca loves
him, but believes he is laughing about his affair with
Desdemona. Iago says that Bianca has been saying that
Cassio will marry her. Cassio laughs at this, and says he has
no intention of doing so: the idea of marrying is entirely
Bianca's. Iago beckons Othello to listen closely as Cassio
describes how 'she' accosted him.

109 **speed:** prosper, succeed
     caitiff: thing, wretch (affectionate, in this instance)
113 **denies ... it out:** makes a feeble show of denying it, and
     laughs it off
114 **Do you hear:** have you heard
     importunes: begs persistently
115 **tell it o'er:** say it again
     Go to ... well said: go on with it, keep going, it's good
116 **gives it out:** tells everyone
119 **Do you triumph:** are you gloating
     Roman: Roman generals rode in triumph through Rome
     after great victories
120 **customer:** one who has customers (i.e. a prostitute)
120–121 **Prithee ... unwholesome:** please credit me with the
     intelligence not to do something so demeaning
123 **so, so, so:** a huntsman's cry to encourage his hounds
124 **Faith:** in faith, truly
     the cry goes: the story is, so people say
125 **say true:** be serious
126 **I am ... else:** call me a liar if it's not true
127 **scored:** wounded (i.e. made a point)
128 **giving out:** story
128–130 **She is ... promise:** she is convinced I will marry her
     because she wants it, not because I have promised to
132 **haunts:** follows, shadows
134 **bauble:** trinket, cheap adornment (meaning Bianca)
135 **by this hand:** an oath meaning 'truly'
     falls me ... neck: falls on my neck like this
136–137 **gesture imports it:** his actions express it
138 **lolls:** drapes herself
     hales: tugs

> • *Which words of Cassio's especially show his attitude to
> Bianca?*

	How quickly should you speed.	
CASSIO	Alas poor caitiff!	
OTHELLO	Look how he laughs already.	110
IAGO	I never knew a woman love man so.	
CASSIO	Alas, poor rogue! I think i'faith she loves me.	
OTHELLO	Now he denies it faintly, and laughs it out.	
IAGO	Do you hear, Cassio?	
OTHELLO	Now he importunes him To tell it o'er. Go to, well said, well said.	
IAGO	She gives it out that you shall marry her. Do you intend it?	
CASSIO	Ha, ha, ha!	
OTHELLO	Do you triumph, Roman? Do you triumph?	
CASSIO	I marry her? What? A customer! Prithee bear some charity to my wit; do not think it so unwholesome. Ha, ha, ha!	120
OTHELLO	So, so, so, so: they laugh that win.	
IAGO	Faith the cry goes that you shall marry her.	
CASSIO	Prithee say true.	
IAGO	I am a very villain else.	
OTHELLO	Have you scored me? Well.	
CASSIO	This is the monkey's own giving out. She is persuaded I will marry her out of her own love and flattery, not out of my promise.	130
OTHELLO	Iago beckons me; now he begins the story.	
CASSIO	She was here even now; she haunts me in every place. I was the other day talking on the sea-bank with certain Venetians, and thither comes the bauble and, by this hand, falls me thus about my neck –	
OTHELLO	Crying 'o dear Cassio!' as it were. His gesture imports it.	
CASSIO	So hangs, and lolls, and weeps upon me; so hales, and pulls me. Ha, ha, ha!	

Othello infers that Desdemona took Cassio to bed and vows
vengeance. Bianca enters and Othello now suspects Cassio of
promiscuity. Bianca believes that Cassio has received the
handkerchief from another lover and refuses to copy the
embroidery. She exits saying that if he doesn't come to
supper tonight he'll have to wait until she's next ready.
Cassio, prompted by Iago, goes after Bianca to calm her
down. Othello emerges wanting to murder Cassio.

140 **plucked:** pulled
141–142 **I see ... it to:** I see you, but not yet the manner of my
         revenge
144 **Before me!:** expression of surprise
145 **such another:** no other than, the very same
      fitchew: literally a polecat, renowned for being smelly
147 **the devil ... dam:** the devil and his mother (a curse)
149–150 **take ... work:** copy the pattern
150 **A likely piece of work:** a likely story (i.e. a lie)
152 **some minx's token:** a present from some other lover
153 **hobby-horse:** the woman you rode (i.e. had sex with)
156 **that should be:** that must be
157–158 **An you'll ... prepared for:** if you come to supper
         tonight, that's all right by me. If you don't, you'll come
         when I'm ready (implying never)
160 **rail:** make a noise about it
      else: otherwise
161 **sup:** eat
162 **I intend so:** I mean to
163 **chance:** happen
      very fain: very much like to
165 **Prithee ... will you:** Please go on, what do you want to
      say?
166 **Go to, say no more:** Not now. Go.
168 **vice:** sin

• *What is the significance of Bianca's use of the word
'minx' (152)? What is ironic about this usage?*

OTHELLO	Now he tells how she plucked him to my chamber. 140
	O, I see that nose of yours, but not that dog I shall
	throw it to!
CASSIO	Well, I must leave her company.
	Enter BIANCA
IAGO	Before me! Look where she comes.
CASSIO	'Tis such another fitchew. Marry, a perfumed one.
	What do you mean by this haunting of me?
BIANCA	Let the devil and his dam haunt you. What did you
	mean by that same handkerchief you gave me even
	now? I was a fine fool to take it. I must take out the
	work? A likely piece of work, that you should find it 150
	in your chamber, and know not who left it there.
	This is some minx's token, and I must take out the
	work? There, give it your hobby-horse; wheresoever
	you had it, I'll take out no work on't
CASSIO	How now, my sweet Bianca! How now, how now?
OTHELLO	By heaven, that should be my handkerchief.
BIANCA	An you'll come to supper tonight, you may. An you
	will not, come when you are next prepared for.
	[*Exit*
IAGO	After her, after her!
CASSIO	Faith I must, she'll rail in the street else. 160
IAGO	Will you sup there?
CASSIO	Faith I intend so.
IAGO	Well, I may chance to see you; for I would very fain
	speak with you.
CASSIO	Prithee come, will you?
IAGO	Go to; say no more.
	[*Exit* CASSIO
OTHELLO	[*Comes forward*] How shall I murder him, Iago?
IAGO	Did you perceive how he laughed at his vice?

Iago confirms that the handkerchief is the one Othello gave to Desdemona. Othello moves between thoughts of revenge and feelings of love for Desdemona. He hardens his heart finally and threatens to chop Desdemona into small pieces.

175 **I would … a-killing:** I'd like to kill him so slowly it would take nine years

182 **command him tasks:** get him to do whatever she asks

183 **that's … way:** that's not the line of thought you must take

185–186 **she will … a bear:** she could tame a wild bear with her singing

187 **plenteous:** abundant
invention: imagination

188 **She's … this:** these qualities make her hypocrisy the greater

190 **condition:** character, temperament

191 **too gentle:** too soft, too yielding

194–196 **If you … nobody:** If you are so indulgent about her sin, give her licence to go on sinning – if it doesn't affect you, it won't affect anyone

197 **messes:** little bits (as of food)

> • *Look at Iago's one-line responses to Othello. How does he move Othello from wanting to kill Cassio (175) to planning to kill Desdemona (201)?*

OTHELLO	O Iago!	
IAGO	And did you see the handkerchief?	170
OTHELLO	Was that mine?	
IAGO	Yours, by this hand. And to see how he prizes the foolish woman your wife; she gave it him, and he hath giv'n it his whore.	
OTHELLO	I would have him nine years a-killing. A fine woman, a fair woman, a sweet woman!	
IAGO	Nay, you must forget that.	
OTHELLO	Ay, let her rot and perish, and be damned tonight, for she shall not live. No, my heart is turned to stone; I strike it, and it hurts my hand. O the world hath not a sweeter creature; she might lie by an emperor's side and command him tasks.	180
IAGO	Nay, that's not your way.	
OTHELLO	Hang her, I do but say what she is: so delicate with her needle, an admirable musician. O, she will sing the savageness out of a bear. – Of so high and plenteous wit and invention.	
IAGO	She's the worse for all this.	
OTHELLO	O a thousand thousand times – and then of so gentle a condition.	190
IAGO	Ay, too gentle.	
OTHELLO	Nay, that's certain – but yet the pity of it, Iago. O Iago, the pity of it, Iago!	
IAGO	If you are so fond over her iniquity, give her patent to offend; for if it touch not you, it comes near nobody.	
OTHELLO	I will chop her into messes. Cuckold me!	
IAGO	O 'tis foul in her.	
OTHELLO	With mine officer.	
IAGO	That's fouler.	200
OTHELLO	Get me some poison Iago; this night. I'll not	

Othello concludes that he will poison Desdemona this very
night: he will no longer allow her seductive beauty to distract
him. Iago encourages Othello to strangle Desdemona in her
bed rather than poison her. This idea appeals to Othello
because it seems just that she should die where she has
sinned. Iago asks to be allowed to deal with Cassio and
Othello agrees. Lodovico arrives from Venice with a letter
from the Duke which Othello reads as Desdemona tells
Lodovico of the rift between him and Cassio. Othello seems
distracted by the letter.

202 **expostulate with her:** talk with her
203 **unprovide my mind:** make me lose my determination,
     distract me
205 **contaminated:** defiled
206 **justice:** fitness, aptness
207 **undertaker:** the one who undertakes to deal (with him)
209 **Excellent:** very, extremely
     What ... same: Whose trumpet is that?
210 **warrant:** wager, bet
215 **the instrument of their pleasures:** the letter (Othello is
     showing respect to the will, 'pleasures', of the senate)
219 **How does:** how is
221–222 **there's fall'n ... breach:** there is a bad break in the
     relationship between Cassio and Othello
225 **This fail ... will:** You must not fail to carry out these
     orders as you see fit
226 **He did ... paper:** he didn't speak; he's busy with the letter
227 **'twixt:** between

> • *Why does Iago say to Othello: "Tis Lodovico ... See, your
> wife is with him' (211–212)?*

	expostulate with her, lest her body and beauty unprovide my mind again. This night, Iago.
IAGO	Do it not with poison, strangle her in her bed, even the bed she hath contaminated.
OTHELLO	Good, good; the justice of it pleases; very good.
IAGO	And for Cassio, let me be his undertaker. You shall hear more by midnight.
OTHELLO	Excellent good. [A trumpet within What trumpet is that same?
IAGO	I warrant something from Venice. 210

Enter LODOVICO, DESDEMONA *and* ATTENDANTS

'Tis Lodovico. This comes from the Duke.
See, your wife is with him.

LODOVICO	Save you, worthy general.
OTHELLO	With all my heart, sir.
LODOVICO	The Duke and senators of Venice greet you. [*Gives him a letter*
OTHELLO	I kiss the instrument of their pleasures. [*Opens the letter, and reads*
DESDEMONA	And what's the news, good cousin Lodovico?
IAGO	I am very glad to see you, signor: Welcome to Cyprus.
LODOVICO	I thank you. How does Lieutenant Cassio?
IAGO	Lives, sir. 220
DESDEMONA	Cousin, there's fall'n between him and my lord An unkind breach; but you shall make all well.
OTHELLO	Are you sure of that?
DESDEMONA	My lord?
OTHELLO	[*Reads*] This fail you not to do as you will –
LODOVICO	He did not call; he's busy in the paper. Is there division 'twixt my lord and Cassio?

Desdemona, in talking to Lodovico, fuels Othello's anger. Lodovico wonders whether the letter has angered him because it orders his return to Venice and Cassio to take command. Othello strikes Desdemona and tells her to get out of his sight. She leaves. Lodovico asks Othello to call her back. Othello does, implying that Lodovico wants her for himself. He tells Lodovico that Desdemona can pretend to do his bidding while going her own way.

229 **T'atone them:** to reconcile them, bring peace between them
230 **Fire and brimstone:** an oath (Hell was said to contain these. Brimstone was sulphur, usually burning.)
    wise: in the know
231 **moved:** upset
233 **Deputing ... government:** appointing Cassio to replace him as governor
234 **By my troth:** an oath
    on't: of it
238 **Though ... saw't:** even though I had sworn I had seen it
    'Tis very much: it's an awful thing
239 **Make her amends:** make up for it, apologise for it
240–241 **If ... crocodile:** if the earth were awash with women's tears, each tear she sheds would be like those of a crocodile (which was believed to shed false tears to attract its victims)
244 **beseech:** ask
245 **What would you with her:** What do you want to do with her?
247 **Ay ... turn:** yes, you asked me to bring her back ('turn' has an implication of sexual intercourse)
248 **turn:** change, deceive (also, 'lie on her back' as a prostitute)
    and yet go on: still seem the same

> • *What do you imagine is the tone and feeling of Desdemona's line 'I will not stay' (242)?*

DESDEMONA	A most unhappy one. I would do much T'atone them, for the love I bear to Cassio.
OTHELLO	Fire and brimstone!
DESDEMONA	My lord?
OTHELLO	Are you wise? 230
DESDEMONA	What, is he angry?
LODOVICO	Maybe the letter moved him. For as I think, they do command him home, Deputing Cassio in his government.
DESDEMONA	By my troth, I am glad on't.
OTHELLO	Indeed?
DESDEMONA	My lord?
OTHELLO	I am glad to see you mad.
DESDEMONA	Why, sweet Othello –
OTHELLO	[*Strikes her*] Devil!
DESDEMONA	I have not deserved this.
LODOVICO	My lord, this would not be believed in Venice, Though I should swear I saw't. 'Tis very much. Make her amends; she weeps.
OTHELLO	O devil, devil! If that the earth could teem with woman's tears, 240 Each drop she falls would prove a crocodile. Out of my sight!
DESDEMONA	I will not stay to offend you. [*Goes*
LODOVICO	Truly, an obedient lady. I do beseech your lordship call her back.
OTHELLO	Mistress!
DESDEMONA	My lord?
OTHELLO	What would you with her, sir?
LODOVICO	Who I, my lord?
OTHELLO	Ay, you did wish that I would make her turn. Sir, she can turn, and turn, and yet go on,

Othello bitterly repeats the Senate's orders, noting that Cassio will have his place. He dismisses Desdemona, and leaves. Lodovico asks Iago why Othello has changed. Iago implies that he knows, but is unable to say. Lodovico wonders whether Othello was disturbed by the letter. Iago says he mustn't offer an opinion, but hints that he has seen worse from Othello. He tells Lodovico to follow Othello and then he will see what state he is in.

251 **Proceed ... tears:** carry on crying
252 **well-painted passion:** cleverly acted emotion
254 **mandate:** order
255 **Hence, avaunt:** Go from here (in an insulting and dismissive tone)
257 **entreat:** ask, beg
258 **Goats and monkeys!** a cry of rage (both animals were thought to be sexually potent and promiscuous)
260 **all in all sufficient:** completely competent
260–261 **Is this ... shake:** is this the person who could never be disturbed by emotion
261–263 **Whose solid ... pierce:** whose sound moral strength could not be wounded or destroyed by any weapon chance might throw at him
264 **Are his wits safe?:** Is he sane?
265–266 **I may ... might be:** I cannot speak my fear of what he might be
266–267 **If what he ... he were:** if Othello isn't all that he should be, I wish he were
268 **not so well:** not good
268–269 **yet would ... worst:** I wish I were certain he will not do anything worse
269 **Is it his use?:** is it his habit, does he usually behave like this?
270 **work upon his blood:** enrage him
271 **new-create this fault:** produce this failing for the first time
274–275 **his own ... speech:** his own behaviour will reveal him in such a way that I won't need to tell you
275–276 **Do but ... he continues:** just follow him and watch what he does next
277 **deceived in:** mistaken about

> • *How does Lodovico react to Othello's words and behaviour?*

And turn again. And she can weep, sir, weep;
And she's obedient, as you say, obedient,   250
Very obedient. – Proceed you in your tears. –
Concerning this sir – O, well-painted passion –
I am commanded home. – Get you away;
I'll send for you anon. – Sir, I obey the mandate,
And will return to Venice. – Hence, avaunt.

                        [*Exit* DESDEMONA

Cassio shall have my place. And sir, tonight,
I do entreat that we may sup together.
You are welcome sir, to Cyprus. – Goats and monkeys!
                                [*Exit*

LODOVICO	Is this the noble Moor whom our full senate
	Call all in all sufficient? Is this the nature 260
	Whom passion could not shake? Whose solid virtue
	The shot of accident, nor dart of chance
	Could neither graze nor pierce?
IAGO	He is much changed.
LODOVICO	Are his wits safe? Is he not light of brain?
IAGO	He's that he is. I may not breathe my censure
	What he might be. If what he might he is not,
	I would to heaven he were.
LODOVICO	What, strike his wife!
IAGO	Faith, that was not so well; yet would I knew
	That stroke would prove the worst.
LODOVICO	Is it his use?
	Or did the letters work upon his blood, 270
	And new-create this fault?
IAGO	Alas, alas!
	It is not honesty in me to speak
	What I have seen and known. You shall observe him,
	And his own courses will denote him so
	That I may save my speech. Do but go after,
	And mark how he continues.
LODOVICO	I am sorry that I am deceived in him. [*Exeunt*

Othello and Emilia enter in conversation about Desdemona
and Cassio. Emilia can give Othello no proof of any secret
affair between Desdemona and Cassio, and vows on her own
life that Desdemona is honest. Emilia, having defended
Desdemona, is sent by Othello to fetch her. He thinks she
has done her best to protect Desdemona and that Desdemona
is clever at hiding her crimes. Desdemona and Emilia return.

2   **Nor ever:** never, not once
5   **Each ... them:** every part of every word they spoke
8   **nor nothing:** or anything else
11 **durst:** dare
    wager ... honest: bet she is faithful
12 **Lay ... stake:** I'll bet my life
13 **it doth ... bosom:** the thought deceives you
15 **Let heaven ... curse:** let heaven pay him back with the curse
    put on the serpent in the Garden of Eden (to crawl on its
    belly, eat dust and be crushed by man, Gen 3:14–15)
17 **There's ... happy:** no man can be happily confident of his
    wife's faithfulness
17–18 **the purest ... slander:** (if Desdemona is unfaithful) then
    the purest wives will be sinful enough to deserve the slanders
    spoken about them
19 **She ... enough:** she says what she was bound to say (i.e. to
    try to clear Desdemona)
    simple: stupid, simple-minded
    bawd: woman who runs a bawdy house (brothel)
20 **That ... as much:** who could not make up this much of an
    answer
    This: Desdemona
    subtle: cunning
21 **A closet ... secrets:** one who keeps her crimes hidden as if
    locked up in a cupboard

- *In what tone does Emilia address Othello? How might an
  audience respond to her words?*
- *In line 19, after Emilia leaves, Othello says 'She says
  enough'. What does he mean?*

Scene

Enter OTHELLO *and* EMILIA

OTHELLO   You have seen nothing then?

EMILIA   Nor ever heard, nor ever did suspect.

OTHELLO   Yes, you have seen Cassio and she together.

EMILIA   But then I saw no harm; and then I heard
           Each syllable that breath made up between them.

OTHELLO   What, did they never whisper?

EMILIA   Never, my lord.

OTHELLO   Nor send you out o'th'way?

EMILIA   Never.

OTHELLO   To fetch her fan, her gloves, her mask, nor nothing?

EMILIA   Never my lord.

OTHELLO   That's strange.   10

EMILIA   I durst, my lord, to wager she is honest,
           Lay down my soul at stake. If you think other,
           Remove your thought: it doth abuse your bosom.
           If any wretch have put this in your head,
           Let heaven requite it with the serpent's curse;
           For if she be not honest, chaste, and true,
           There's no man happy; the purest of their wives
           Is foul as slander.

OTHELLO   Bid her come hither. Go.

                                            [*Exit* EMILIA

           She says enough; yet she's a simple bawd
           That cannot say as much. This is a subtle whore,   20
           A closet lock and key of villainous secrets;
           And yet she'll kneel and pray, I have seen her do't.

           Enter DESDEMONA *and* EMILIA

DESDEMONA My lord, what is your will?

Othello dismisses Emilia as if she were a brothel keeper.
Desdemona asks Othello what he means. He asks her what
she is and she replies that she is his wife. He tells her to
swear to it. Desdemona swears she is innocent, at which
point Othello weeps. Desdemona thinks his rage is because
her father has called them back to Venice.

23 **chuck:** chick, darling
25 **horrible fancy:** strange delusion
26 **Some ... function:** do your job (i.e. as brothel keeper)
27 **procreants:** people who are procreating, having sex
28 **cry 'hem':** give a warning cough
29 **Your mystery:** craft, trade
   dispatch: go
30 **import:** mean, signify
31 **understand ... words:** I can tell there's anger in your words
34 **damn thyself:** condemn yourself to hell
35 **one of heaven:** a heavenly creature, an angel
36–37 **Therefore ... honest:** therefore be damned twice: for
   sinning and for swearing, now, that you're honest
38 **false:** dishonest
41 **heavy day:** day that weighs heavily on the heart, sad day
42 **motive:** cause, motivation
43 **haply:** perhaps
44 **instrument:** cause
47 **try me with affliction:** test me with troubles. (The passage
   which begins here and continues until 52 refers to the Book
   of Job in the Old Testament from verse 15 of chapter 10.
   God tormented Job and he suffered it all with patience.
   Othello is saying that he would show the same patience.)
49 **Steeped ... lips:** soaked me in poverty up to my lips

OTHELLO	Pray, chuck, come hither.
DESDEMONA	What is your pleasure?
OTHELLO	Let me see your eyes; Look in my face.
DESDEMONA	What horrible fancy's this?
OTHELLO	[*To* EMILIA] Some of your function, mistress. Leave procreants alone and shut the door; Cough, or cry 'hem', if anybody come. Your mystery, your mystery. Nay, dispatch!

[*Exit* EMILIA

DESDEMONA	Upon my knees, what doth your speech import? 30 I understand a fury in your words, But not the words.
OTHELLO	Why, what art thou?
DESDEMONA	Your wife, my lord; your true and loyal wife.
OTHELLO	Come swear it; damn thyself, Lest being like one of heaven, the devils themselves Should fear to seize thee. Therefore be double-damned; Swear thou art honest.
DESDEMONA	Heaven doth truly know it.
OTHELLO	Heaven truly knows that thou art false as hell.
DESDEMONA	To whom my lord? With whom? How am I false?
OTHELLO	Ah Desdemona! Away, away, away! 40
DESDEMONA	Alas the heavy day! Why do you weep? Am I the motive of these tears, my lord? If haply you my father do suspect An instrument of this your calling back, Lay not your blame on me. If you have lost him, I have lost him too.
OTHELLO	Had it pleased heaven To try me with affliction, had they rained All kind of sores and shames on my bare head, Steeped me in poverty to the very lips,

Othello answers that he could have borne any affliction except Desdemona's unfaithfulness. Desdemona hopes Othello thinks her honest. He replies bitterly, yet cannot resist her beauty. She wants to know what sin she has committed. Othello seizes on the implications of 'commit' (i.e. commit adultery) and expresses his disgust at her. Desdemona insists on her Christian belief in keeping her body pure for her husband.

50 **utmost:** highest
52–54 **to make … finger at:** to make me a permanent object for mockery that will seem to last as long as the slow movement of time (the idea is that the hand of a clock moves so slowly that it appears to point everlastingly at the 'fixed figure' on the clock's dial – an image for the long, drawn-out suffering of scorn that Othello feels)
56 **garnered:** gathered
58–59 **The fountain … dries up:** the spring that gives me life without which I die (Othello is explaining that his love for Desdemona is the source of his life.)
60 **cistern:** tank (See Proverbs 5:15–18, where wives are likened to fountains; fidelity to drinking out of your own cistern.)
61 **knot and gender:** entwine and breed
Turn thy complexion: go pale
62 **Patience:** Othello is appealing to, addressing, patience personified as …
thou … cherubin: you young, rosy-lipped angel
64 **esteems:** thinks, believes
65–66 **as summer … blowing:** as flies in summer breed while they feed on carcasses in an abattoir ('shambles')
69 **ignorant sin:** sin I was unaware of
70 **this fair … book:** i.e. Desdemona, her self and body
72 **public commoner:** common whore
73–75 **I should make … thy deeds:** my cheeks would burn if I were even to say what you have been doing
76 **Heaven … at it:** it stinks to high heaven
77 **bawdy wind:** i.e. the wind is like a whore because it caresses everyone
77–79 **the bawdy … hear it:** even the promiscuous wind hides deep in the earth rather than hear of your deeds
80 **strumpet:** whore, harlot
82 **preserve this vessel:** keep my body

> • *What is there in Othello's language that tells us that he feels that Desdemona's sin affects the whole world and not just himself?*

	Given to captivity me and my utmost hopes,
	I should have found in some place of my soul
	A drop of patience. But alas, to make me
	A fixed figure for the time of scorn
	To point his slow unmoving finger at!
	Yet could I bear that too; well, very well;
	But there where I have garnered up my heart,
	Where either I must live, or bear no life,
	The fountain from the which my current runs,
	Or else dries up; to be discarded thence,
	Or keep it as a cistern for foul toads
	To knot and gender in. Turn thy complexion there,
	Patience, thou young and rose-lipped cherubin –
	Ay, there look grim as hell.
DESDEMONA	I hope my noble lord esteems me honest.
OTHELLO	O ay, as summer flies are in the shambles,
	That quicken even with blowing. O thou weed,
	Who art so lovely fair, and smell'st so sweet
	That the sense aches at thee, would thou hadst never
	been born.
DESDEMONA	Alas, what ignorant sin have I committed?
OTHELLO	Was this fair paper, this most goodly book,
	Made to write 'whore' upon? What committed?
	Committed? O thou public commoner,
	I should make very forges of my cheeks,
	That would to cinders burn up modesty,
	Did I but speak thy deeds. What committed?
	Heaven stops the nose at it, and the moon winks;
	The bawdy wind, that kisses all it meets
	Is hushed within the hollow mine of earth
	And will not hear it. What committed?
	Impudent strumpet!
DESDEMONA	By heaven, you do me wrong.
OTHELLO	Are not you a strumpet?
DESDEMONA	No, as I am a Christian.
	If to preserve this vessel for my lord

Line numbers: 50, 60, 70, 80

Othello sarcastically says he must have mistaken Desdemona for the Venetian whore who married Othello. He orders Emilia to lock the door and keep all this secret, and leaves. Emilia asks what is going on in Othello's mind, but Desdemona is stunned. She asks Emilia to put her wedding sheets on her bed and to fetch Iago.

82–84 If to ... am none: if it's not being a strumpet to keep myself only for my husband and away from any adulterous contact, then I am not a strumpet

85 as ... saved: as I hope for salvation

87 I cry ... then: I beg your pardon (sarcastic)

90 office ... St Peter: the job of guarding Hell's gate (as opposed to guarding heaven's gates, which is St Peter's job)

92 done our course: finished our business

93 keep our counsel: keep our conversation secret

94 conceive: imagine, think

103 But ... water: except those that should be said in tears

104 wedding sheets: wives were sometimes buried in their wedding sheets

> • *Why does Desdemona ask Emilia to fetch Iago? What is the dramatic impact of this choice?*

	From any other foul unlawful touch
	Be not to be a strumpet, I am none.
OTHELLO	What, not a whore?
DESDEMONA	No, as I shall be saved.
OTHELLO	Is't possible?
DESDEMONA	O heaven forgive us!
OTHELLO	I cry you mercy then.

OTHELLO I took you for that cunning whore of Venice
That married with Othello. [*Raises his voice*] You,
    mistress,
That have the office opposite to Saint Peter,   90
And keep the gate of hell –
Enter EMILIA

                               You, you, ay, you.
We have done our course; there's money for your
    pains.
I pray you turn the key, and keep our counsel.
                                     [*Exit*

EMILIA	Alas, what does this gentleman conceive?
	How do you, madam? How do you, my good lady?
DESDEMONA	Faith, half asleep.
EMILIA	Good madam, what's the matter with my lord?
DESDEMONA	With who?
EMILIA	Why, with my lord, madam.
DESDEMONA	Who is thy lord?
EMILIA	He that is yours, sweet lady. 100

DESDEMONA I have none. Do not talk to me, Emilia:
I cannot weep, nor answers have I none,
But what should go by water. Prithee, tonight
Lay on my bed my wedding sheets; remember –
And call thy husband hither.

EMILIA   Here's a change indeed.
                                   [*Exit*

Alone, Desdemona reflects on Othello's treatment of her and wonders what she has done to deserve it. Emilia returns with Iago, who asks Desdemona how she is: Emilia answers that Othello has called Desdemona a whore. Iago seems to try to comfort Desdemona. Emilia bitterly wonders why Desdemona passed up the opportunity of marrying a noble Venetian. Iago wants to know how Othello could have got into this mood. Emilia says that some villain must have made up lies about Desdemona.

106   **'Tis meet:** it is appropriate
107   **been behaved:** behaved
107–108 **stick ... misuse:** attach the lowest opinion to my smallest fault
112   **chid:** chided, criticised, told off
113   **I am ... chiding:** I am unused to being criticised
114   **bewhored her:** called her a whore
115   **despite:** spite, hatred
      heavy terms: violent abuse
119   **A beggar ... drink:** a drunken beggar
120   **callet:** slut
122   **none such:** not any such thing
124   **forsook:** given up, forsaken
      noble matches: opportunities for making a 'good' marriage
127   **fortune:** fate, lot
      Beshrew him: Curse him
128   **trick:** delusion
129   **eternal villain:** villain to be damned for eternity
130   **busy:** meddling, interfering
      insinuating: lying, slandering
131   **cogging:** deceiving
      cozening: devious
      slave: term of abuse
      to get ... office: in order to be promoted to some job
132   **devised:** plotted

- *What is Desdemona's response to Othello's treatment of her?*
- *What is the dramatic significance of Emilia's speech (129–132)?*

DESDEMONA	'Tis meet I should be used so, very meet.
	How have I been behaved, that he might stick
	The smallest opinion on my least misuse?

Enter EMILIA *with* IAGO

IAGO	What is your pleasure madam? How is't with you?
DESDEMONA	I cannot tell. Those that do teach young babes 110
	Do it with gentle means and easy tasks.
	He might have chid me so, for in good faith
	I am a child to chiding.
IAGO	What's the matter, lady?
EMILIA	Alas Iago, my lord hath so bewhored her,
	Thrown such despite and heavy terms upon her,
	That true heart cannot bear.
DESDEMONA	Am I that name, Iago?
IAGO:	What name, fair lady?
DESDEMONA	Such as she said my lord did say I was.
EMILIA	He called her whore. A beggar in his drink
	Could not have laid such terms upon his callet. 120
IAGO	Why did he so?
DESDEMONA	I do not know; I am sure I am none such.
IAGO	Do not weep, do not weep. Alas the day!
EMILIA	Hath she forsook so many noble matches,
	Her father, and her country, all her friends,
	To be called whore? Would it not make one weep?
DESDEMONA	It is my wretched fortune.
IAGO	Beshrew him for't!
	How comes this trick upon him?
DESDEMONA	Nay, heaven doth know.
EMILIA	I will be hanged if some eternal villain,
	Some busy and insinuating rogue, 130
	Some cogging, cozening slave, to get some office,
	Have not devised this slander; I'll be hanged else.
IAGO	Fie, there is no such man; it is impossible.

Emilia continues to curse the man she believes must have abused Desdemona to Othello, and compares him to the person who told Iago she had been with Othello. Iago tries to tell her to calm down and be quiet. Desdemona asks Iago to help her win Othello back, swearing that she has never been unfaithful to him. Iago suggests that state problems are behind Othello's mood.

135 **A halter pardon:** May he hang (a halter is a noose)
137 **what form:** i.e. what does her supposed lover look like
139 **base notorious:** low-born and infamous
    scurvy: disease-ridden
140 **thou'dst unfold:** you would reveal
142 **lash:** whip
143 **Speak within door:** Lower your voice (so that you can't be heard outside)
144 **them:** i.e. the neighbours
    squire: young fool
145 **that turned ... without:** turned your intelligence inside out (seams are on the inside)
146 **suspect ... Moor:** suspect that I had an affair with Othello
147 **Go to:** Shut up, stop it
151 **trespass:** sin
152 **discourse ... deed:** process of thought or action
154 **Delighted them:** i.e. my senses enjoyed
156–157 **shake ... divorcement:** reject me to live abandoned and destitute
158 **Comfort forswear me:** may all comfort leave me
159 **defeat my life:** kill me, ruin my life
160 **taint:** tarnish, spoil
161 **abhor:** disgust, appal
162 **addition:** name, title
163 **world's mass of vanity:** all the riches the world has to offer
164 **humour:** mood, temper
165 **does him offence:** causes him problems
166 **does chide with:** takes it out on

> • *What is the effect of Iago's response to Emilia's words against the person who abused Desdemona to Othello?*

DESDEMONA   If any such there be, heaven pardon him.

EMILIA   A halter pardon him, and hell gnaw his bones!
             Why should he call her whore? Who keeps her
                company?
             What place, what time, what form, what likelihood?
             The Moor's abused by some most villainous knave,
             Some base notorious knave, some scurvy fellow.
             O heaven, that such companions thou'dst unfold,   140
             And put in every honest hand a whip
             To lash the rascals naked through the world,
             Even from the east to th'west!

IAGO   Speak within door.

EMILIA   O fie upon them! Some such squire he was
             That turned your wit the seamy side without,
             And made you to suspect me with the Moor.

IAGO   You are a fool. Go to.

DESDEMONA   O good Iago,
             What shall I do to win my lord again?
             Good friend, go to him; for, by this light of heaven,
             I know not how I lost him. Here I kneel: 150
             If e'er my will did trespass 'gainst his love,
             Either in discourse of thought or actual deed;
             Or that mine eyes, mine ears, or any sense,
             Delighted them in any other form;
             Or that I do not yet, and ever did,
             And ever will – though he do shake me off
             To beggarly divorcement – love him dearly,
             Comfort forswear me. Unkindness may do much,
             And his unkindness may defeat my life,
             But never taint my love. I cannot say 'whore';   160
             It does abhor me now I speak the word;
             To do the act that might the addition earn
             Not the world's mass of vanity could make me.

IAGO   I pray you be content: 'tis but his humour.
             The business of the state does him offence,
             And he does chide with you.

Iago sends Desdemona and Emilia in to supper, saying that all will be well. Roderigo enters, claiming that Iago has mistreated him. He says Iago does not keep his promises, and he wants to finish with him. He has wasted a lot of his money wooing Desdemona. Roderigo threatens to go to Desdemona.

167 **If 'twere no other:** if that's all it is
   warrant: guarantee
168 **instruments:** i.e. musical instrument(s) used as a signal for supper
169 **stay the meat:** wait for their food
173 **What ... contrary:** What has shown that I've dealt with you unjustly?
174 **daff'st me:** put me off
   device: method, ploy
175–176 **keep'st ... conveniency:** stop me proceeding
178–179 **nor am ... suffered:** and I am not prepared to forget what I have already foolishly put up with
182 **are ... together:** are not the same thing
183 **charge:** accuse
184 **naught:** nothing
184–185 **wasted ... means:** wasted all my money and property
186–187 **corrupted a votarist:** persuaded a nun to sin
188–189 **returned ... respect:** and sent me promises of requital
190 **go to:** that's all right
192 **scurvy:** poor, despicable
192–193 **begin ... in it:** starting to find I'm being made a fool of
196 **return me:** return to me

> • *What is Roderigo's complaint against Iago?*

DESDEMONA   If 'twere no other –

IAGO   It is so, I warrant.
Hark how these instruments summon to supper;
The messengers of Venice stay the meat.
Go in, and weep not; all things shall be well.   170

                    [*Exeunt* DESDEMONA *and* EMILIA

                    Enter RODERIGO

How now Roderigo?

RODERIGO   I do not find that thou dealest justly with me.

IAGO   What in the contrary?

RODERIGO   Every day thou daff'st me with some device, Iago,
and rather, as it seems to me now, keep'st from me
all conveniency, than suppliest me with the least
advantage of hope. I will indeed no longer endure it;
nor am I yet persuaded to put up in peace what
already I have foolishly suffered.

IAGO   Will you hear me Roderigo?   180

RODERIGO   Faith, I have heard too much, for your words and
performances are no kin together.

IAGO   You charge me most unjustly.

RODERIGO   With naught but truth. I have wasted myself out of
my means. The jewels you have had from me to
deliver to Desdemona would half have corrupted a
votarist. You have told me she hath received them,
and returned me expectations and comforts of
sudden respect and acquaintance, but I find none.

IAGO   Well go to; very well.   190

RODERIGO   Very well, go to! I cannot go to, man; nor 'tis not
very well. Nay, I think it is scurvy, and begin to find
myself fopped in it.

IAGO   Very well.

RODERIGO   I tell you 'tis not very well. I will make myself
known to Desdemona. If she will return me my

Roderigo says he will ask Desdemona for his gifts (which she never received, Iago having kept them) to be returned, and promise to give up his suit. If not, he says he will challenge Iago. Iago tries to calm him by approving his determination and claiming that he has acted fairly. He agrees that Roderigo has had no success, and promises that satisfaction is about to be given. Iago tells Roderigo that Cassio is to take Othello's place. Roderigo assumes (rightly) that Othello and Desdemona will return to Venice. Iago, however, announces that Othello will go to Mauritania, taking Desdemona with him – unless some accident, such as Cassio's death, prevents them. He dares Roderigo to be the one to kill Cassio, which will remove Cassio and keep Desdemona in Cyprus.

197–198 **repent ... solicitation:** stop trying to seduce Desdemona by devious means
198–199 **seek satisfaction:** challenge to a duel
201–202 **I ... doing:** I intend
203 **mettle:** strength, determination
204 **do build ... opinion:** think more highly of you than I did before
206 **just exception:** fair complaint
207 **directly:** farily, honestly
208 **It ... appeared:** It doesn't look like it
214 **enjoy:** have sex with
215–216 **take me ... my life:** betray me from this world and devise a way of killing me
217 **within ... compass:** sensible and practical
218 **especial:** special, extraordinary
222 **Mauritania:** a part of North Africa
223–224 **his abode ... here:** his stay here be prolonged
224–225 **wherein ... Cassio:** nothing could make him stay as much as Cassio's removal
227 **uncapable of:** incapable of taking
230 **do yourself ... right:** do yourself a favour and a deserved service

• *What ultimatum does Roderigo present Iago with here?*

jewels, I will give over my suit and repent my unlawful
solicitation. If not, assure yourself I will seek
satisfaction of you.

IAGO   You have said now.   200

RODERIGO   Ay, and said nothing but what I protest intendment
of doing.

IAGO   Why, now I see there's mettle in thee; and even from
this instant do build on thee a better opinion than ever
before. Give me thy hand, Roderigo. Thou hast taken
against me a most just exception; but yet I protest I
have dealt most directly in thy affair.

RODERIGO   It hath not appeared.

IAGO   I grant indeed it hath not appeared and your
suspicion is not without wit and judgment. But,   210
Roderigo, if thou hast that in thee indeed, which I
have greater reason to believe now than ever – I mean
purpose, courage, and valour – this night show it. If
thou the next night following enjoy not Desdemona,
take me from this world with treachery and devise
engines for my life.

RODERIGO   Well, what is it? Is it within reason and compass?

IAGO   Sir, there is especial commission come from Venice to
depute Cassio in Othello's place.

RODERIGO   Is that true? Why, then Othello and Desdemona   220
return again to Venice.

IAGO   O no; he goes into Mauritania and takes away with
him the fair Desdemona, unless his abode be lingered
here by some accident; wherein none can be so
determinate as the removing of Cassio.

RODERIGO   How do you mean removing of him?

IAGO   Why, by making him uncapable of Othello's place –
knocking out his brains.

RODERIGO   And that you would have me to do?

IAGO   Ay, if you dare do yourself a profit and a right. He   230

Iago explains how he and Roderigo can waylay Cassio this coming night. He says he will give Roderigo compelling reasons to kill Cassio.

231 **harlotry:** prostitute
232–233 **If you** ... **thence:** if you watch for him leaving there
233–234 **fashion** ... **out:** make happen
234–235 **take** ... **pleasure:** attack him when it suits you
235–236 **second your attempt:** back you up
236 **fall between us:** between us we'll cause his death
237 **go** ... **me:** join me in this plan
238 **such** ... **death:** such a need for his death
238–239 **think** ... **on him:** think it your duty to kill him

> • *How far do you think from the evidence here that Roderigo is convinced by Iago?*

Lodovico takes his leave of Desdemona after Othello insists on accompanying him for a walk. Othello tells Desdemona to go straight to bed, dismiss Emilia and await him. Emilia suggests to Desdemona that Othello looks gentler.

1 **beseech:** beg
2 **pardon me:** please let me come with you
'twill: it will
6 **on th'instant:** immediately
7 **forthwith:** without delay
7–8 **Look't be done:** make sure it is done, see to it
10 **incontinent:** immediately

sups tonight with a harlotry, and thither will I go to
him. He knows not yet of his honourable fortune. If
you will watch his going thence, which I will fashion
to fall out between twelve and one, you may take
him at your pleasure. I will be near to second your
attempt, and he shall fall between us. Come, stand
not amazed at it, but go along with me. I will show
you such a necessity in his death that you shall think
yourself bound to put it on him. It is now high
supper-time and the night grows to waste. About it.   240

RODERIGO   I will hear further reason for this.

IAGO   And you shall be satisfied.   [*Exeunt*

Scene

Enter OTHELLO, LODOVICO, DESDEMONA, EMILIA, *and*
ATTENDANTS

LODOVICO   I do beseech you sir, trouble yourself no further.

OTHELLO   O pardon me; 'twill do me good to walk.

LODOVICO   Madam, good night. I humbly thank your ladyship.

DESDEMONA   Your honour is most welcome.

OTHELLO   Will you walk sir?
O, Desdemona.

DESDEMONA   My lord?

OTHELLO   Get you to bed on th'instant; I will be returned
forthwith. Dismiss your attendant there. Look't be
done.

DESDEMONA   I will, my lord.

[*Exeunt* OTHELLO, LODOVICO, *and* ATTENDANTS

EMILIA   How goes it now? He looks gentler than he did.

DESDEMONA   He says he will return incontinent.   10

Desdemona tells Emilia what Othello's instructions are and asks her to put out her nightdress. Emilia wishes Desdemona had never met Othello, but Desdemona reaffirms her love. Desdemona asks to be shrouded in her wedding sheets if she dies before Emilia. She remembers Barbary, a maid of her mother's who was abandoned by her lover, and died singing about disappointment in love. Desdemona and Emilia discuss Lodovico in complimentary terms, and then Desdemona sings Barbary's song.

14 **nightly wearing:** night-clothes
16 **would:** wish
17 **so … I:** I don't wish that
    my … him: my love makes me see the best in him
19 **unpin me:** undo my clothes (part of a maid's job)
21 **All's one:** it's all one to me, it doesn't matter now
23 **Come … talk:** nonsense
24 **Barbary:** the maid's name, perhaps implying she was from the Barbary Coast in Africa, or that she was a barbarian
26 **forsake:** abandon, desert
    song of willow: song about willow (willow is traditionally associated with weeping)
27 **thing:** song, ballad
    expressed her fortune: captured her situation
29–30 **I have … hang my head:** I can barely stop myself from hanging my head
31 **dispatch:** go
33 **proper man:** gentleman
36 **nether lip:** lower lip

- *What does Emilia wish and why?*
- *Why does Desdemona bring Lodovico into the conversation? What do they think of him?*

He hath commanded me to go to bed,
And bade me to dismiss you.

EMILIA   Dismiss me?

DESDEMONA   It was his bidding; therefore, good Emilia,
Give me my nightly wearing, and adieu.
We must not now displease him.

EMILIA   I would you had never seen him.

DESDEMONA   So would not I; my love doth so approve him;
That even his stubbornness, his checks, his frowns –
Prithee, unpin me – have grace and favour in them.

EMILIA   I have laid those sheets you bade me on the bed.   20

DESDEMONA   All's one. Good faith, how foolish are our minds!
If I do die before thee, prithee shroud me
In one of those same sheets.

EMILIA   Come, come, you talk.

DESDEMONA   My mother had a maid called Barbary;
She was in love, and he she loved proved mad
And did forsake her. She had a song of willow;
An old thing 'twas, but it expressed her fortune,
And she died singing it. That song tonight
Will not go from my mind; I have much to do
But to go hang my head all at one side,   30
And sing it like poor Barbary. Prithee, dispatch.

EMILIA   Shall I go fetch your night-gown?

DESDEMONA   No, unpin me here.
This Lodovico is a proper man.

EMILIA   A very handsome man.

DESDEMONA   He speaks well.

EMILIA   I know a lady in Venice would have walked bare-
foot to Palestine for a touch of his nether lip.

DESDEMONA   [Sings]
        The poor soul sat sighing by a sycamore tree,
            Sing all a green willow;
        Her hand on her bosom, her head on her knee,

Desdemona sings the willow song, but cannot remember the words. She dismisses Emilia, asking whether the fact that her eyes are itching is a sign that she will weep. Emilia says it means nothing and Desdemona asks her if women abuse men as men do women. Emilia is sure some do. Desdemona says she would not be unfaithful for all the world. Emilia replies that the whole world is a big reward for a small sin. Desdemona does not believe that Emilia would not do such a thing.

44 **Lay by these:** Desdemona is referring to her clothes; she has paused from her singing
46 **Prithee ... anon:** Please hurry, go; he'll be here soon
47 **garland:** adornment
48 **his scorn I approve:** I accept his scorn
49 **not next:** not what comes next
53 **court:** chase after, woo
   moe: more
   couch with: lie with, sleep with
55 **bode:** mean, foretell
   'Tis ... there: It doesn't mean anything
57 **Dost ... conscience:** Do you really believe
59 **In such ... kind:** in such a disgusting way
   There ... question: There are some like that, without a doubt
61 **by ... light:** Desdemona swears by the sun
62–63 **I might ... dark:** I might easily do it in the dark
67 **In troth:** truly

> • *What is the effect of Desdemona's singing and the difficulties she has with the words?*

	Sing willow, willow, willow.	40

        Sing willow, willow, willow.   40
        The fresh streams ran by her, and murmured her
           moans;
        Sing willow, willow, willow;
        Her salt tears fell from her and softened the stones –
Lay by these –
[*Sings*]
        Sing willow, willow, willow;
Prithee, hie thee; he'll come anon –
[*Sings*]
        Sing all a green willow must be my garland.
        Let nobody blame him; his scorn I approve –
Nay, that's not next. Hark, who is't that knocks?

EMILIA   It's the wind.   50

DESDEMONA   [*Sings*]
        I called my love false love; but what said he then?
         Sing willow, willow, willow;
        If I court moe women, you'll couch with moe men.
So get thee gone, good night. Mine eyes do itch;
Does that bode weeping?

EMILIA   'Tis neither here nor there.

DESDEMONA   I have heard it said so. O these men, these men!
Dost thou in conscience think – tell me, Emilia –
That there be women do abuse their husbands
In such gross kind?

EMILIA   There be some such, no question.

DESDEMONA   Wouldst thou do such a deed for all the world?   60

EMILIA   Why, would not you?

DESDEMONA   No, by this heavenly light.

EMILIA   Nor I neither by this heavenly light. I might do't as
well i'th'dark.

DESDEMONA   Wouldst thou do such a deed for all the world?

EMILIA   The world's a huge thing: it is a great price for a small
vice.

DESDEMONA   In troth I think thou wouldst not.

Emilia wouldn't commit adultery for trinkets, but it might be worth cuckolding her husband to make him a king. Desdemona says she would not do such a wrong thing and Emilia offers the view that if you won the whole world it would be a wrong you could easily put right. Desdemona perseveres in her view. Emilia argues that men's treatment of their wives is often the cause of a woman's 'falling'. Emilia finishes what she's saying, stating that women have desires and weaknesses just as much as men. Men should beware or women will learn from how they are abused to abuse them. Desdemona would prefer to learn to improve from, rather than copy, abuse.

68   **undo't:** swear I hadn't done it

69–70   **joint-ring:** ring made in two separate parts (symbolising a commitment to marriage)
       measures of lawn: pieces of cloth

71   **petty exhibition:** little showy adornment

73–74   **I ... for't:** I would risk purgatory for it (purgatory was the place of punishment between heaven and hell)

77   **the wrong ... th'world:** the wrong is only wrong in the world's eyes

78   **labour:** work

78–79   **'tis ... own world:** it is a wrong in the world which you rule

81–82   **as many ... played for:** and as many in addition as would populate the world they were playing for

84   **slack ... duties:** neglect their role as husband

85   **our ... laps:** give the sexual pleasure due to their wives to other women

86   **peevish:** petty

88   **or scant ... despite:** spitefully take from us what is ours

89   **galls:** the ability to be bitter

91   **sense:** feelings

92   **palates:** tastes

94   **change ... others:** exchange us for other women

95   **affection:** desire

97   **frailty:** weakness
       errs: goes astray

99   **use:** treat
       else: otherwise

100   **The ills ... us so:** the wrongs we do we have learned from the wrongs they have done to us

101–102   **God ... mend:** God grant that I be given such bad experiences, not so that I copy them but learn to do better

- *Why do you think Emilia puts this point of view? How does it affect Desdemona's situation and our response to it?*
- *What tone does Desdemona's final couplet give to the end of the scene?*

EMILIA   In troth I think I should, and undo't when I had
          done it. Marry, I would not do such a thing for a joint-
          ring, nor for measures of lawn, nor for gowns,   70
          petticoats, nor caps, nor any petty exhibition. But for
          all the whole world – why, who would not make her
          husband a cuckold to make him a monarch? I should
          venture purgatory for't.

DESDEMONA   Beshrew me, if I would do such a wrong for the
             whole world.

EMILIA   Why, the wrong is but a wrong i'th'world; and
          having the world for your labour, 'tis a wrong in your
          own world, and you might quickly make it right.

DESDEMONA   I do not think there is any such woman.   80

EMILIA   Yes, a dozen; and as many to th'vantage as would
          store the world they played for.
          But I do think it is their husbands' faults
          If wives do fall. Say that they slack their duties,
          And pour our treasures into foreign laps,
          Or else break out in peevish jealousies,
          Throwing restraint upon us; or say they strike us,
          Or scant our former having in despite;
          Why, we have galls, and though we have some grace,
          Yet have we some revenge. Let husbands know   90
          Their wives have sense like them; they see and smell,
          And have their palates both for sweet and sour
          As husbands have. What is it that they do,
          When they change us for others? Is it sport?
          I think it is; and doth affection breed it?
          I think it doth. Is't frailty that thus errs?
          It is so too. And have not we affections,
          Desires for sport, and frailty, as men have?
          Then let them use us well; else let them know
          The ills we do, their ills instruct us so.   100

DESDEMONA   Good night, good night. God me such uses send,
             Not to pick bad from bad, but by bad mend.
                                              [*Exeunt*

ACTIVITIES

Keeping track

Scene 1

1 What happens while Othello is in a trance?
2 What 'proofs' does Iago give Othello of Desdemona's affair with Cassio, and how?
3 How does Bianca's arrival help Iago's plans?
4 What are Othello's plans for Desdemona by the end of the scene?
5 What is the reason for Lodovico's arrival from Venice? What does he see that shocks him?

Scene 2

1 Why does Othello question Emilia and what answers does he get?
2 What reason does Desdemona suggest for Othello's rage?
3 What explanation does Emilia offer for Othello's suspicion?
4 Whom does Desdemona ask for help?
5 How is Roderigo's appearance a possible threat to Iago?
6 What does Iago want Roderigo to do? What reason does he give for this?

Scene 3

1 What does Othello tell Desdemona to do?
2 What do Emilia and Desdemona discuss?
3 What are Desdemona's feelings as she prepares for bed?
4 Why does Desdemona remember the 'willow' song?
5 What reason does Emilia give for wives 'going bad'?

Discussion

Scene 1

1 How does Iago work on Othello's mind? What sensitive and vulnerable spots does he touch in Othello's character, and how?
2 Discuss the violence of Othello's response to what he believes has taken place between his wife and Cassio. What does it make you think of him? Can his reaction be justified? Is this the outcome Iago had hoped for?
3 How would you stage the exchange between Iago and Cassio while Othello looks on? Continue this work for the section when Bianca is on stage.

Scene 2

1 Discuss the role of Emilia. How does she try to influence Othello about Desdemona? What is Othello's attitude to her and what she tells him? What conclusions has Emilia herself reached about the change in Othello? Why does she express them with such vigour? Do you think she suspects Iago?

2 Look at Othello's little soliloquy at 19–22. What does this reveal about his state of mind? Why, having questioned Emilia, has he ignored what she says? Is he in any doubt about Desdemona's guilt? Does he listen to Desdemona at all?

3 What is your view of Iago at this stage of the play? Has it changed or developed? Does he seem to be in command of the situation? Are there any threats to the success of his plotting?

Scene 3

1 Discuss the effect of the early part of this scene, up to line 19. Why do you think Shakespeare wrote these lines involving Lodovico as a prelude to the intimate scene which follows between Desdemona and Emilia? What views of Othello emerge from the speakers in these few lines?

2 Discuss the female perspective on men and marriage that the rest of the scene offers. Why does it happen at all, since Desdemona, following Othello's command, dismisses Emilia? What are the views of Emilia and Desdemona on men and marriage? Do you think they are each basing their ideas on their own experience?

3 What is the effect of this scene in the context of the play so far? Iago's plotting and Othello's passion have reached a powerful momentum: why do you think Shakespeare has created this scene of reflection? What is the impact of Desdemona's song in this context?

Close study

Scene 1

1 Lines 1–20.
   • What does Othello's use of 'devil' and 'heaven' tell us about him (6–8)?
   • How does Iago's seeming rationality affect Othello?

2 Lines 29–35. Compare Othello's quick questions with Iago's evasions. What is the dramatic effect?

3 Lines 34–44.
   • 'With her? On her. What you will.' What does Iago's use of language tell us about him?
   • What tensions or contradictions in Othello's speech enable us to believe in his collapse when it occurs?

4 Lines 45–209. Look at Othello's language after he recovers. In what
   way has he changed?
   • Look at 'Where, how, how oft, how long ago, and when/He
     hath, and is again to cope your wife.' Look at Iago's detailed,
     almost legal vocabulary when it comes to the most inflammatory
     facts. How does this affect your sense of Iago? Is there any
     potential for humour here? How do you think this might affect
     the audience's responses to him? How do you respond to his
     enjoyment of suggestions for killing Desdemona?
5 Lines 211–277.
   • What is the impact of Lodovico's entrance? Do you echo
     Desdemona's hope that he shall 'make all well' (222)? How is this
     hope dashed or strengthened during the rest of the scene?
   • How does Desdemona's plea to Lodovico for Cassio's
     reinstatement heighten dramatic tension at this point (221–222)?

Scene 2

1 Lines 1–18. Othello and Emilia enter in mid-conversation. Othello
   is questioning her about Desdemona and Cassio.
   • Othello has previously resolved to kill Desdemona. Why is he
     questioning Emilia?
   • Notice how many times 'nothing' and 'never' (or 'nor ever')
     occur in this exchange. What is the effect of this repetition? How
     do Emilia's short negative comments affect our response to the
     dialogue?
2 Lines 19–22. How do you read Othello's tone here – what are his
   views of Emilia and Desdemona?
3 Lines 23–25. What is the dramatic effect of these lines being shared
   between Othello and Desdemona? (Remember that for an actor to
   deliver the verse accurately, there should be no pause between the
   speakers.)
4 Lines 30–63. Othello and Desdemona are alone, and for the first
   time he voices his suspicions to her.
   • What are Othello's motives here? At what point (if at any) do you
     think he is listening to what Desdemona says? If he does not
     believe a word she says, why is he questioning her?
   • Pay attention to the religious imagery in this exchange ('upon my
     knees', 'heaven', etc.). What does this reveal about (a) the
     significance Othello gives to Desdemona's sin and (b) the
     significance she gives to this conversation?
   • If Othello believes Desdemona is 'false as hell' (38), to what is he
     referring when he says she is 'like one of heaven' (35)?

- How does Othello respond to Desdemona's direct questions, 'To whom, my lord? With whom/ How am I false?' (39)? Why does this move him? He has previously accused Desdemona of weeping crocodile tears – where do his tears spring from?
- Look at Othello's speech (46–63), which begins with 'heaven' and ends in 'hell':

(i) To whom is Othello talking here? How do you react to him speaking like this at this point?

(ii) What is Othello saying? Why does he claim at this point that other fates would have been easier to bear? What is it that galls him in lines 52–54?

(iii) Lines 56–61. What is the 'there' that Othello refers to? Does it help you to understand Othello's preceding rage to know that he sees Desdemona as his life's spring? If the word 'discarded' (59) is so central to his feelings, what does that tell you about him and his jealousy?

5 Lines 64–89.
- How do you react to Desdemona's one-line response to Othello's speech? Is it understandable that she may not have grasped what he was saying about her?
- Lines 66–68. Othello seems able to react to Desdemona only as a sensory object. Do you think his love for her has only ever been a thing of senses? Where does he equate her loveliness with virtue?
- Lines 70–71. What does this metaphor tell us about Othello's view of Desdemona?
- Lines 64, 69, 80, 81–84 and 85. Look at the tone of Desdemona's responses to Othello. What sense of her do they convey?

6 Lines 89–108.
- What effect does Desdemona's questioning of Emilia's 'my lord' have? And her 'I have none'?
- What is the tone of Desdemona's "Tis meet I should be used so, very meet'? Pay attention to her following words.
- What is ironic about Desdemona's request to Emilia (105), particularly as it follows mention of her bed and wedding sheets?

7 Lines 109–170.
- What do you make of Iago's treatment of Desdemona in this passage? Does his attitude to her change at any point? If so, where and why?
- Lines 117–118 and lines 160–161. What do you make of Desdemona's inability to say 'whore'? The semi-pun (whore/abhor) seems to suggest that to her even to say the word is to become it.
- Lines 124–126. What does Emilia's reminder of Desdemona's isolation, of all she has left behind, do to our responses to the drama at this point?

(i) Look at the terms Emilia lavishes on the person she believes has abused Othello. How do you account for her vehement outburst?

(ii) How would you play Iago here? Is he at all moved by Desdemona's suffering?

(iii) Compare Desdemona's 'heaven pardon him' with Emilia's 'A halter pardon him'.

• Lines 147–163.

(i) Why does Desdemona choose to speak when she does?

(ii) Look at Desdemona's speech. What elements of a creed or vow does it have? Compare it with Othello's earlier in the scene (46–63). What differences and similarities are there (note particularly their conclusions)?

8 Lines 171–242.

• Look at the division of dialogue between Roderigo and Iago. What does this suggest about the nature of this conflict and the use of language?

• This exchange begins with Roderigo 'wanting out' and ends with him almost persuaded to kill Cassio. What means does Iago use to turn Roderigo from his purpose of seeking satisfaction? What really makes Roderigo stay?

• What is the dramatic effect of the change from verse to prose when Roderigo enters? How do you react to Roderigo's attack?

Scene 3

1 Lines 1–8.

• Compare this passage with that at the end of Scene 1 where Lodovico witnesses Othello's treatment of Desdemona. What do you notice about the way Lodovico speaks to Desdemona here? Compare it with Othello's language in lines 6–8 – note how all three of his sentences begin.

• How would you stage this interaction between Othello, Lodovico and Desdemona? Look carefully at who speaks to whom and when, paying particular attention to the shared lines 4–5.

2 Lines 9–23.

• Lines 9–12. Emilia and Desdemona both refer to Othello as 'he'. What effect does this have?

• Lines 13–19. What is the effect of Desdemona's 'adieu' to Emilia? What is the tone of line 15? How might the actress playing Desdemona deliver it in order that Emilia's response in line 16 makes sense?

• Lines 21–23. How do you read Desdemona's tone here? Here are some suggestions: resignation, fear, foreboding, 'foolishness' or a cry for reassurance that her fears are extreme?

3 Desdemona suggests Emilia should leave a number of times. What dramatic
   tension does this create? Why doesn't Emilia leave?
4 Lines 25–55.
   • 'She was in love, and he she loved proved mad/And did forsake her'. What
     resonance does this have here?
   • Line 33. What effect does Emilia's mention of Lodovico have when neither she
     nor Desdemona has referred to Othello by name? What is poignant in
     Desdemona's 'He speaks well'?
5 Look at the song (37–53) and the interruptions to it.
   • Why have Desdemona sing it here? Should the actress playing Desdemona sing
     beautifully? What are the dramatic implications of your decision?
   • Notice the line Desdemona gets wrong (48) which echoes her earlier 'my love
     doth so approve him'. What is the difference between them? What does it say
     of Desdemona that she is thinking of protecting 'him' from blame at this point?
6 Lines 56–80.
   • Lines 60–67. Emilia responds to Desdemona's figurative language ('by this
     heavenly light'; 'for all the world') literally ('I might do 't as well i'th'dark';
     'The world's a huge thing'). Why? What effect does Emilia's tone here have
     after Desdemona's singing and her line 'Does that bode weeping?'?
   • Lines 68–79. What is Emilia's argument here? How convincing do you find it?
     How does her idea of morality contrast with Othello's? What response from
     Desdemona is she wanting here?
7 Lines 80–102.
   • Emilia moves from prose to verse. What is the effect?
   • In lines 81–88, Emilia blames husbands for their wives' 'falling'. How many of
     the abuses she mentions can be levelled at Othello?
   • Lines 89–100. What hope do Emilia's words, coming at this point, give an
     audience? Is her attitude cynical? Liberating?
   • Lines 95–100. What is the effect of Emilia's questions here?
   • Two couplets end this scene and act. Contrast and compare their tone and
     meaning. Which resonates more strongly? Why does Desdemona choose this
     moment to bid goodnight abruptly to Emilia?
8 What dramatic effect is achieved by Othello's arrival being always expected but
   never happening in this scene?

Imagery

It is revealing to study the language and imagery of Othello during this act. His mind
is in a state of tortured passion – in Act 3 Scene 3 (333), he tells Iago 'Thou hast put
me on the rack' – and his imagination is plagued by images of heaven and hell, love
and lust. In addition, he has to play the role of Venetian general on Lodovico's
arrival, and use the formal language appropriate to this situation.

Study the way his language and imagery fluctuate. How do you respond to it? It might be helpful to return to Act 3 Scene 3 to see the beginning of this process of loss of emotional control.

Key scene

As always, it is impossible to say that one passage in an act is more important than any other. In Act 4, we could, for instance, point to Scene 1 94–166. In Act 3 Scene 3, Othello instructs Iago: 'Give me the ocular proof.' In this passage, Iago delivers, and we watch him manipulate Othello and Cassio so totally that they could be actors in a play written and directed by Iago. It is very useful to explore the staging problems of this passage.

However, the main suggestion for a key section of Act 4, to develop a new perspective on the play, is to look at all the passages involving Desdemona: Scene 1 (211–255); Scene 2 (23–170); and Scene 3. In these passages we see her, first, rejected and humiliated in public by Othello and her response; then we see the only private scene between them so far, when she has to face an obsessively jealous husband; and finally, we see her discussing men, love and marriage with Emilia.

Think about how you have viewed Desdemona so far: her relationship with Othello and her motives for supporting him. Now study these three passages, and assess her character and beliefs, her attitude to being a wife and to the changes in her husband. How you respond to her murder in Act 5 will be greatly affected by how you feel about her in Act 4.

Finally, there is an interesting key moment at the end of Scene 2 at lines 172 and 181–182. Here, Roderigo, so far apparently a victim of Iago's manipulation, becomes the first person in the play to question Iago's honesty and express his sense of injustice. He is the only character to confront Iago until after the tragic effects of his plotting are accomplished. Two questions:
- Does this make you think differently about Roderigo? Perhaps there is more to him than you have so far suspected.
- What effect does this have on the momentum of the whole drama?

Writing

1 Write an essay in which you explain your view of the role of Desdemona in the play up to the end of Act 4.

2 Reread the passage which gives the arrival of Lodovico from Venice (Scene 1, lines 211–277). Explain in detail what impact you think this passage should have and how it affects our view of the play so far.

3 By careful study of the plot of Act 4, show how Shakespeare has brought the play to the point where the final tragic events can be played out. Is Iago in complete control?

Iago sets Roderigo to ambush Cassio. He tells him that this is the critical moment for both of them. Roderigo wants Iago to be near in case he fails. Iago explains to the audience that, whoever dies, it will be to his advantage. Roderigo attacks Cassio.

1 **bulk:** pillar
   straight: immediately
2 **Wear ... home:** carry your sword unsheathed and thrust it in deep
4 **It makes ... mars us:** killing Cassio will either be the making of us or will destroy us
5 **resolution:** determination
6 **miscarry:** make a mess of it
8 **devotion:** commitment
11 **quat:** spot, pustule (i.e. Roderigo)
   to the sense: to the raw flesh
15 **He ... large:** He will call me to repay the large debt I owe him
16 **bobbed:** conned
19 **daily beauty in his life:** a fineness of character that is always apparent
21 **unfold me:** reveal all about my involvement
23 **gait:** footstep
24 **had ... indeed:** would certainly have been fatal

> • *Look at Iago's words about Cassio in lines 19–20. What does he think of him?*

ACT FIVE

Scene  1

Enter IAGO *and* RODERIGO

IAGO   Here, stand behind this bulk; straight will he come.
            Wear thy good rapier bare, and put it home.
            Quick, quick, fear nothing; I'll be at thy elbow;
            It makes us, or it mars us; think on that,
            And fix most firm thy resolution.

RODERIGO   Be near at hand; I may miscarry in't.

IAGO   Here, at thy hand. Be bold, and take thy stand.

                                            [*Retires*

RODERIGO   I have no great devotion to the deed,
            And yet he hath given me satisfying reasons.
            'Tis but a man gone. Forth, my sword. He dies!   10

IAGO   I have rubbed this young quat almost to the sense,
            And he grows angry. Now, whether he kill Cassio,
            Or Cassio him, or each do kill the other,
            Every way makes my gain. Live Roderigo,
            He calls me to a restitution large
            Of gold and jewels that I bobbed from him,
            As gifts to Desdemona.
            It must not be. If Cassio do remain
            He hath a daily beauty in his life
            That makes me ugly; and besides, the Moor   20
            May unfold me to him; there stand I in much peril.
            No, he must die. Be't so. I hear him coming.

            Enter CASSIO

RODERIGO   I know his gait, 'tis he. Villain, thou diest.

                                    [*Thrusts at* CASSIO

CASSIO   That thrust had been mine enemy indeed,

Cassio retaliates, wounding Roderigo. Iago, unseen by either, wounds Cassio and leaves. Othello enters and believes Iago has carried out his promise to kill Cassio. In his mind, he tells Desdemona that her lover is dead and that he is coming to kill her. He goes, not realising Cassio is only wounded. Gratiano and Lodovico enter. They are nervous of going immediately to help whoever is in distress. Iago enters with a light as though having been roused from bed.

25 **coat:** reinforced undercoat
26 **make ... thine:** test the protectiveness of your coat
(by striking it)
29 **It ... so:** It is true (Othello thinks he has heard Cassio calling himself a villain)
33 **Minion:** ironic term of endearment; can have the implication of mistress or paramour (he is referring to Desdemona); literally, a low servant
34 **unblest fate:** unholy destiny
hies: hurries towards you
35 **Forth ... blotted:** the spell your eyes have cast over my heart has now been blotted out
36 **lust's blood:** the blood of your lustful body
37 **watch:** watchman
passage: people passing
38 **mischance:** accident
direful: anguished, agonised
42 **heavy:** very dark
43 **counterfeits:** decoys, deceivers
44 **come ... cry:** join those who need help

> • *This is the third time in the play Othello has entered a scene of conflict. How does he respond this time?*

But that my coat is better than thou know'st.
I will make proof of thine.

[Draws and wounds RODERIGO

RODERIGO   O, I am slain.

*[*IAGO *from behind wounds* CASSIO *in the leg, and exit*

CASSIO   I am maimed for ever. Help, ho! Murder, murder!

[Falls

Enter OTHELLO

OTHELLO   The voice of Cassio: Iago keeps his word.

RODERIGO   O villain that I am!

OTHELLO   It is even so.

CASSIO   O help, ho! Light! A surgeon!   30

OTHELLO   'Tis he. O brave Iago, honest and just,
That hast such noble sense of thy friend's wrong.
Thou teachest me. Minion, your dear lies dead,
And your unblest fate hies. Strumpet, I come.
Forth of my heart those charms, thine eyes, are blotted;
Thy bed lust-stained shall with lust's blood be spotted.

[Exit

Enter LODOVICO *and* GRATIANO

CASSIO   What, ho! No watch? No passage? Murder, murder!

GRATIANO   'Tis some mischance, the cry is very direful.

CASSIO   O help!

LODOVICO   Hark!   40

RODERIGO   O wretched villain!

LODOVICO   Two or three groan. 'Tis heavy night.
These may be counterfeits. Let's think't unsafe
To come in to the cry without more help.

RODERIGO   Nobody come? Then shall I bleed to death.

LODOVICO   Hark!

Enter IAGO *with a light*

Gratiano realises who Iago is and they follow him to Cassio. Cassio tells Iago he has been wounded by villains. He believes one of them is still nearby. Iago calls Lodovico and Gratiano to come and help. Under cover of darkness, Iago stabs Roderigo, and pretends to search for the killers. He asks if Lodovico and Gratiano are to be trusted; Lodovico says he can find out by trusting them. Iago then recognises them.

47 **in his shirt:** i.e. as though he has just got out of bed
54 **spoiled:** wounded
      undone: disabled
58 **make away:** get away
59 **What ... there?** Who's there?
65 **What ... be:** Who are you?
66 **As ... praise us:** approve of us if you think we pass the test
69 **cry you mercy:** beg your pardon

> • *What problems are there in performing this passage?*
> • *What must the audience understand?*
> • *Look at lines 60–69. What exactly happens?*

GRATIANO	Here's one comes in his shirt, with light and weapons.
IAGO	Who's there? Whose noise is this that cries on murder?
LODOVICO	We do not know.
IAGO	Did not you hear a cry?
CASSIO	Here, here; for heaven's sake help me!
IAGO	What's the matter? 50
GRATIANO	This is Othello's ancient, as I take it.
LODOVICO	The same indeed, a very valiant fellow.
IAGO	What are you here, that cry so grievously?
CASSIO	Iago? O I am spoiled, undone by villains. Give me some help.
IAGO	O me, lieutenant! What villains have done this?
CASSIO	I think that one of them is hereabout And cannot make away.
IAGO	O treacherous villains! What are you there? Come in, and give some help. *[To* LODOVICO *and* GRATIANO
RODERIGO	O help me here! 60
CASSIO	That's one of them.
IAGO	O murderous slave! O villain! *[Stabs* RODERIGO
RODERIGO	O damned Iago! O inhuman dog!
IAGO	Kill men i'th'dark? Where be these bloody thieves? How silent is this town. Ho, murder, murder! What may you be? Are you of good or evil?
LODOVICO	As you shall prove us, praise us.
IAGO	Signor Lodovico?
LODOVICO	He sir.
IAGO	I cry you mercy. Here's Cassio hurt by villains.
GRATIANO	Cassio? 70

Cassio cries out that he is seriously wounded and Iago
attends to the wound. Bianca enters and rushes to Cassio's
aid. Iago dismisses her as a well-known whore and asks
Cassio who attacked him. Cassio doesn't know. Iago binds
Cassio's wound and expresses his suspicion that Bianca is
involved. He identifies the corpse as Roderigo, pretends grief
and greets Gratiano. Iago calls for a chair to carry Cassio
away for treatment.

78   **notable:** notorious, infamous
79   **mangled:** wounded
82   **garter:** i.e. to secure the shirt bandage Iago has put on
     Cassio's wound
85   **this trash:** Bianca
88   **this face:** i.e. Roderigo's
94–95 **These ... neglected you:** please excuse the fact that I
     have neglected to be polite to you but this crisis has
     distracted me

- *Why does Iago repeat Bianca's question (75)?*
- *What signs are there that Iago is in control of the
  situation? How does he treat Bianca?*

IAGO	How is't, brother?
CASSIO	My leg is cut in two.
IAGO	Marry, heaven forbid! Light, gentlemen. I'll bind it with my shirt.

Enter BIANCA

BIANCA	What is the matter, ho? Who is't that cried?	
IAGO	Who is't that cried?	
BIANCA	O, my dear Cassio, my sweet Cassio, O Cassio, Cassio, Cassio!	
IAGO	O notable strumpet. Cassio, may you suspect Who they should be that have thus mangled you?	
CASSIO	No.	80
GRATIANO	I am sorry to find you thus. I have been to seek you.	
IAGO	Lend me a garter. So. O for a chair To bear him easily hence.	
BIANCA	Alas he faints! O Cassio, Cassio, Cassio!	
IAGO	Gentlemen all, I do suspect this trash To be a party in this injury. Patience awhile, good Cassio. Come, come; Lend me a light. Know we this face or no? Alas, my friend, and my dear countryman Roderigo? No – yes sure – O heaven, Roderigo!	90
GRATIANO	What, of Venice?	
IAGO	Even he sir. Did you know him?	
GRATIANO	Know him? Ay.	
IAGO	Signor Gratiano? I cry you gentle pardon. These bloody accidents must excuse my manners That so neglected you.	
GRATIANO	I am glad to see you.	
IAGO	How do you, Cassio? O, a chair, a chair!	
GRATIANO	Roderigo!	

Iago says he will fetch a surgeon. He orders Bianca to stand
back and tells Cassio that the dead Roderigo was his close
friend. Cassio doesn't know Roderigo or the cause of the
fight. Iago asks Bianca why she looks pale and orders Cassio
to be carried inside. Iago encourages Lodovico and Gratiano
to see Bianca's behaviour as guilty. Emilia enters and Iago
tells her what has happened – all the result of Cassio's
whoring. He tells Emilia to find out from Cassio where he
dined. Bianca says he dined with her, and denies that she is
nervous. Iago orders her to come with him. Emilia calls
Bianca a whore, which Bianca refutes. Iago calls Lodovico
and Gratiano to help attend to Cassio.

98   **well said:** well done
101 **Save ... labour:** You are wasting your breath
102 **malice:** ill-feeling
104 **out o'th'air:** indoors, inside
105 **Stay you ... gentlemen:** Wait, gentlemen
106 **gastness:** fear
107 **you:** i.e. Bianca
     anon: very soon, immediately
110 **tongues ... use:** words are not being spoken
113 **are scaped:** have escaped
116 **fruits of whoring:** result of womanising
117 **Go know of:** Go and find out from
118 **shake:** shudder with fear
119 **I ... not:** I do not shudder with fear for that reason
120 **charge:** order
124 **dressed:** bandaged
125 **another tale:** a different story (i.e. the truth)

> • *How do you interpret Emilia's behaviour here?*
> • *Bianca's 'but I therefore shake not' (119) could be
>   interpreted as 'I shake for another reason' (presumably
>   emotion at Cassio's injury) or 'there is not reason here to
>   make me shake'. What difference would it make? It is
>   Iago who tells us what her face is doing (staring, pale) –
>   is he to be believed? How would you direct an actress to
>   play her? How do you interpret her response to Emilia –
>   is she upset, defiant, self-possessed?*

IAGO	He, he, 'tis he. [*A chair brought in*] O that's well said; the chair.

IAGO He, he, 'tis he. [*A chair brought in*] O that's well
    said; the chair.
    Some good man bear him carefully from hence;
    I'll fetch the general's surgeon. [*To* BIANCA] For you
      mistress,   100
    Save you your labour. He that lies slain here, Cassio,
    Was my dear friend. What malice was between you?

CASSIO None in the world; nor do I know the man.

IAGO [*To* BIANCA] What, look you pale? O, bear him out
    o'th'air.

       [CASSIO *and* RODERIGO *are borne off*

    Stay you good gentlemen. Look you pale, mistress?
    Do you perceive the gastness of her eye?
    Nay, if you stare, we shall hear more anon.
    Behold her well; I pray you look upon her.
    Do you see, gentlemen? Nay, guiltiness will speak
    Though tongues were out of use.   110

    Enter EMILIA

EMILIA 'Las, what's the matter? What's the matter, husband?

IAGO Cassio hath here been set on in the dark
    By Roderigo, and fellows that are scaped:
    He's almost slain, and Roderigo quite dead.

EMILIA Alas, good gentleman! Alas, good Cassio!

IAGO This is the fruits of whoring. Prithee, Emilia,
    Go know of Cassio where he supped tonight.
    [*To* BIANCA] What, do you shake at that?

BIANCA He supped at my house, but I therefore shake not.

IAGO O did he so? I charge you go with me.   120

EMILIA Fie, fie upon thee strumpet!

BIANCA I am no strumpet, but of life as honest
    As you that thus abuse me.

EMILIA   As I? Foh, fie upon thee!

IAGO Kind gentlemen, let's go see poor Cassio dressed.
    Come mistress, you must tell's another tale.

Iago tells Emilia to inform Othello and Desdemona about what has happened. He tells the audience that this night is make or break for him.

128 afore: ahead
129 fordoes me quite: utterly destroys me

Othello enters with a light, sure that he must kill Desdemona in the name of justice – or she will lure more men into adultery. He can scarcely bring himself to do the deed, since Desdemona is so beautiful in sleep and her lips so intoxicating. He feels his duty is agonising, yet it must be done. Desdemona awakes and asks if it is Othello.

1 It ... cause: adultery is the reason for what I am going to do – but 'cause' means 'offence', and 'legal case' as well as reason. (We have seen and will see that Othello sees himself as carrying out a judicial sentence)
2 Let ... stars: Let me not mention this sin under the light of you, virtuous stars
4 that whiter ... than snow: her skin is whiter than snow
5 monumental alabaster: translucent white stone used for figures on tombs
6 betray: lure into adultery
7 light: the torch or candle he is carrying
and then ... light: i.e. and then kill Desdemona
8 flaming minister: the helpful light of the torch ('minister' implies the idea of giving aid to one in need, as doctors or priests 'minister' to those in need)
10 repent me: regret my action
thy light: i.e. Desdemona's life
11 cunning'st ... nature: most cleverly created example of nature's excellence
12 Promethean heat: fire from the gods (Prometheus was the human, in mythology, who stole fire from the gods)
13 relume: relight
14 vital growth: life
16 balmy: soothing and fragrant
17 Justice ... sword: Othello thinks of himself as the figure of Justice with her sword
One more: i.e. kiss
20 So ... fatal: no kiss was ever so sweet and yet so deadly
21 heavenly: that of divine justice

- *What feelings would you like the actor playing Othello to convey here?*
- *What is the effect of Othello's image of Desdemona's skin in line 5?*

Emilia, run you to the citadel,
And tell my lord and lady what hath happened.
Will you go on afore? [*Aside*] This is the night
That either makes me, or fordoes me quite.

[*Exeunt*

Scene 2

Enter OTHELLO, *with a light,* DESDEMONA *in her bed*

OTHELLO   It is the cause, it is the cause, my soul –
Let me not name it to you, you chaste stars –
It is the cause. Yet I'll not shed her blood,
Nor scar that whiter skin of hers than snow,
And smooth as monumental alabaster:
Yet she must die, else she'll betray more men.
Put out the light, and then put out the light.
If I quench thee, thou flaming minister,
I can again thy former light restore,
Should I repent me; but once put out thy light,   10
Thou cunning'st pattern of excelling nature,
I know not where is that Promethean heat
That can the light relume. When I have plucked thy
    rose,
I cannot give it vital growth again,
It needs must wither. I'll smell it on the tree.

[*Kisses her*

O balmy breath, that dost almost persuade
Justice to break her sword. One more, one more.
Be thus when thou art dead, and I will kill thee,
And love thee after. One more, and that's the last.
So sweet was ne'er so fatal. I must weep,   20
But they are cruel tears. This sorrow's heavenly,
It strikes where it doth love. She wakes.

DESDEMONA   Who's there? Othello?

Desdemona asks Othello to come to bed but he asks her whether she has purged her soul from sin. He explains that he does not want to kill her and send her soul to hell. She is shocked at the talk of killing and prays for mercy. She can see that Othello's eyes are rolling and that his whole body is shaking.

26 **bethink yourself:** remember
27 **Unreconciled ... grace:** that you have not yet confessed and been pardoned for
28 **Solicit:** pray, beg
   straight: immediately
30 **walk by:** give you some privacy
32 **forfend:** forbid
   kill thy soul: send your soul to hell
37 **fatal:** threatening death
40 **They ... you:** Any sins I may have committed were out of love for you
43 **nether:** lower
44 **your very frame:** every part of your body
45 **portents:** ominous signs
47 **so:** be still

> • *What reactions to Othello do you think the actress playing Desdemona should portray here?*

OTHELLO	Ay, Desdemona.
DESDEMONA	Will you come to bed, my lord?
OTHELLO	Have you prayed tonight, Desdemon?
DESDEMONA	Ay my lord.

OTHELLO   If you bethink yourself of any crime
Unreconciled as yet to heaven and grace,
Solicit for it straight.

DESDEMONA   Alack, my lord, what may you mean by that?

OTHELLO   Well, do it, and be brief; I will walk by.   30
I would not kill thy unprepared spirit;
No – heaven forfend! – I would not kill thy soul.

DESDEMONA   Talk you of killing?

OTHELLO   Ay, I do.

DESDEMONA   Then heaven
Have mercy on me.

OTHELLO   Amen, with all my heart.

DESDEMONA   If you say so, I hope you will not kill me.

OTHELLO   Hum!

DESDEMONA   And yet I fear you: for you're fatal then
When your eyes roll so. Why I should fear I know
    not,
Since guiltiness I know not; but yet I feel I fear.

OTHELLO   Think on thy sins.

DESDEMONA   They are loves I bear to you.   40

OTHELLO   Ay, and for that thou diest.

DESDEMONA   That death's unnatural that kills for loving.
Alas, why gnaw you so your nether lip?
Some bloody passion shakes your very frame.
These are portents; but yet I hope, I hope
They do not point on me.

OTHELLO   Peace, and be still.

DESDEMONA   I will so. What's the matter?

Othello accuses Desdemona of giving the handkerchief to Cassio. She denies this and suggests he ask Cassio. Othello warns her against perjury. She prays for mercy. Othello insists he saw Cassio with the handkerchief and urges her to confess. Desdemona says that Cassio must have found the handkerchief by accident and tells Othello to send for Cassio to reveal the truth. He replies that Cassio has already confessed to an affair with her. Desdemona insists that Cassio will speak for her but Othello tells her Cassio is dead.

51 **perjury:** lying under oath
52 **presently:** immediately
53 **confess ... sin:** confess all your sins wholeheartedly
54 **article:** sin of which you are accused
55 **conception:** belief, plan (with the added implication of 'conception' leading to birth)
56 **groan withal:** labour with
60–61 **But ... love:** except with the general love God allows us to feel for others
61 **token:** a gift symbolising love
63 **stone:** turn to stone
64–65 **And ... sacrifice:** your refusal to confess makes me call my killing you murder rather than sacrifice
70 **used thee:** had sex with you
71 **his ... stopped:** he cannot speak because he has been killed

> • *Why do you think Othello doesn't follow Desdemona's suggestion and ask Cassio about the handkerchief (50 and 68)?*
> • *In 53–56, Othello says that Desdemona may as well confess since even a sworn denial of each sin will not change his mind to kill her. What is the effect of the imagery of childbirth, conveyed through the words 'conception' and 'groan'?*

OTHELLO	That handkerchief which I so loved and gave thee, Thou gav'st to Cassio.
DESDEMONA	No by my life and soul! Send for the man and ask him.
OTHELLO	Sweet soul, take heed, 50 Take heed of perjury; thou art on thy death-bed.
DESDEMONA	Ay, but not yet to die.
OTHELLO	Yes, presently. Therefore confess thee freely of thy sin; For to deny each article with oath Cannot remove nor choke the strong conception That I do groan withal. Thou art to die.
DESDEMONA	Then Lord have mercy on me.
OTHELLO	I say, amen.
DESDEMONA	And have you mercy too. I never did Offend you in my life; never loved Cassio But with such general warranty of heaven 60 As I might love; I never gave him token.
OTHELLO	By heaven I saw my handkerchief in's hand. O perjured woman, thou dost stone my heart, And mak'st me call what I intend to do A murder, which I thought a sacrifice. I saw the handkerchief.
DESDEMONA	He found it then; I never gave it him. Send for him hither. Let him confess a truth.
OTHELLO	He hath confessed.
DESDEMONA	What, my lord?
OTHELLO	That he hath used thee.
DESDEMONA	How? Unlawfully?
OTHELLO	Ay. 70
DESDEMONA	He will not say so.
OTHELLO	No, his mouth is stopped.

Desdemona realises that there is no one who can vouch for her innocence. She asks him to banish her rather than kill her, or to give her time at least to pray. Othello cannot hold back and smothers her. Emilia, outside, calls Othello, but he, not wanting Desdemona to linger in pain, perseveres until she is dead. He veers between shock at the death of Desdemona and putting on an act of calm before Emilia enters.

72 **ta'en ... for't:** carried it out
73 **my fear interprets:** I am afraid I understand
74 **Had ... lives:** if he had as many lives as hairs on his head
75 **stomach:** capacity
76 **undone:** finished, destroyed
81 **strive:** struggle
82 **Being ... pause:** now that I have started there can be no delay
89 **So, so:** Othello completes the killing of Desdemona
92 **Yes ... Emilia:** Othello is speaking to himself
   By and by: I will come to you very soon (speaking to Emilia)
   She's dead: Othello speaking to himself
93 **like:** likely, probable
94 **high:** loud (Emilia was shouting)
   Ha ... moving: Othello assures himself that Desdemona is dead
96 **she:** Desdemona
97 **sure:** certainly
99 **insupportable:** unbearable

> • *What is the effect of Othello's line (87) 'I that am cruel am yet merciful'?*

Honest Iago hath ta'en order for't.

DESDEMONA O, my fear interprets. What, is he dead?

OTHELLO Had all his hairs been lives, my great revenge
Had stomach for them all.

DESDEMONA Alas, he is betrayed, and I undone.

OTHELLO Out, strumpet, weep'st thou for him to my face?

DESDEMONA O banish me, my lord, but kill me not.

OTHELLO Down strumpet!

DESDEMONA Kill me tomorrow: let me live tonight!   80

OTHELLO Nay, if you strive –

DESDEMONA But half an hour.

OTHELLO   Being done, there is no pause.

DESDEMONA But while I say one prayer.

OTHELLO   It is too late.

DESDEMONA O Lord, Lord, Lord!   [*He smothers her*

EMILIA [*Within*] My lord, my lord! What, ho! My lord, my
lord!

OTHELLO What noise is this? Not dead? Not yet quite dead?
I that am cruel, am yet merciful;
I would not have thee linger in thy pain.
So, so.

EMILIA [*Within*] What, ho! My lord, my lord!

OTHELLO   Who's there?   90

EMILIA [*Within*] O good my lord, speak a word with you.

OTHELLO Yes, 'tis Emilia – By and by – She's dead.
'Tis like she comes to speak of Cassio's death.
The noise was high. Ha, no more moving?
Still as the grave. Shall she come in? Were't good?
I think she stirs again. No. What's best to do?
If she come in, she'll sure speak to my wife.
My wife? My wife? What wife? I have no wife.
O insupportable! O heavy hour!

Othello feels that Desdemona's death should be attended by violent natural phenomena. He lets Emilia in, and she reports a murder. Othello assumes Cassio is dead, but when Emilia says it is Roderigo not Cassio, Othello realises that his revenge has gone wrong. Desdemona recovers briefly. In her final moments, she tells Emilia that no one has killed her but she herself.

101–102 that … alteration: the terrified world should gape wide open at this change (i.e. Desdemona's death)

105 curtains: curtains round the bed

107 yonder's: out there is

110 error: wandering from its course

111 wont: accustomed

116–117 Then … harsh: The murder plan has gone wrong and the satisfying revenge I planned has turned painful

126 Commend me: give my love

> * *Do you think Othello's lines (110–112) are addressed to Emilia or do they represent his thoughts?*
> * *What is the effect of Shakespeare's device of making Desdemona, apparently already dead, speak again?*

Methinks it should be now a huge eclipse   100
Of sun and moon, and that affrighted globe
Should yawn at alteration.

EMILIA   [*Within*]   I do beseech you
That I may speak with you. O good my lord!

OTHELLO   I had forgot thee. O come in, Emilia.
Soft; by and by. Let me the curtains draw.
Where art thou? [*Unlocks the door*] What's the
    matter with thee now?

Enter EMILIA

EMILIA   O my good lord, yonder's foul murders done.

OTHELLO   What, now?

EMILIA   But now, my lord.

OTHELLO   It is the very error of the moon;   110
She comes more nearer earth than she was wont,
And makes men mad.

EMILIA   Cassio, my lord, hath killed a young Venetian
Called Roderigo.

OTHELLO   Roderigo killed?
And Cassio killed?

EMILIA   No, Cassio is not killed.

OTHELLO   Not Cassio killed? Then murder's out of tune,
And sweet revenge grows harsh.

DESDEMONA   O falsely, falsely murdered!

EMILIA   Alas, what cry is that?

OTHELLO   That? What?

EMILIA   Out, and alas, that was my lady's voice!   120
Help, help, ho, help! O, lady, speak again!
Sweet Desdemona, o sweet mistress, speak.

DESDEMONA   A guiltless death I die.

EMILIA   O who hath done this deed?

DESDEMONA   Nobody. I myself. Farewell.
Commend me to my kind lord. O farewell.

[*Dies*

Othello reminds Emilia that she heard Desdemona deny that he killed her, but then reveals that she was lying and that he did kill her. Emilia damns him as a devil and he replies that Desdemona was a sinner and a whore. Othello says that Iago told him Cassio had sex with Desdemona, and laments that if he has not killed her on just grounds he will be damned in hell. Emilia queries her husband's role in all this. Othello tells Emilia that her honest husband told him of Desdemona's infidelity.

133 **folly:** sin
134 **belie:** tell lies about
135 **false as water:** untrustworthy (because water might move under any influence)
rash as fire: mad (because fire can be uncontrollable and burn in any direction)
138 **were:** would be
139–140 **But ... extremity:** unless I acted justly in bringing about this extreme conclusion
141 **false to wedlock:** unfaithful to her marriage vows
144 **Of ... chrysolite:** of whole, pure topaz (a precious stone)
146 **on her:** about her
147–148 **the slime ... deeds:** the corruption that comes with sin
149 **iterance:** repetition
150 **made mocks with:** made a mockery of

> • *With what tone and intention do you imagine Othello speaks line 127?*

OTHELLO	Why, how should she be murdered?
EMILIA	Alas, who knows?
OTHELLO	You heard her say herself, it was not I.
EMILIA	She said so, I must needs report the truth.
OTHELLO	She's like a liar gone to burning hell, 130 'Twas I that killed her.
EMILIA	O the more angel she, And you the blacker devil.
OTHELLO	She turned to folly; and she was a whore.
EMILIA	Thou dost belie her, and thou art a devil.
OTHELLO	She was false as water.
EMILIA	Thou art rash as fire, to say That she was false. O she was heavenly true.
OTHELLO	Cassio did top her. Ask thy husband else. O, I were damned beneath all depth in hell, But that I did proceed upon just grounds To this extremity. Thy husband knew it all. 140
EMILIA	My husband?
OTHELLO	Thy husband.
EMILIA	That she was false to wedlock?
OTHELLO	Ay, with Cassio. Nay, had she been true, If heaven would make me such another world Of one entire and perfect chrysolite, I'd not have sold her for it.
EMILIA	My husband?
OTHELLO	Ay, twas he that told me on her first. An honest man he is, and hates the slime That sticks on filthy deeds.
EMILIA	My husband?
OTHELLO	What needs this iterance, woman? I say thy husband.
EMILIA	O mistress, villainy hath made mocks with love. 150 My husband say that she was false?

Emilia tells Othello that Iago has been lying and should rot
in hell if he claims that Desdemona has been unfaithful.
Othello doesn't want to hear this. Emilia says that she will
tell the world and that no threat of his can stop her. She
begins to call for help. When Montano, Gratiano and Iago
arrive, Emilia questions Iago and he admits to having told
Othello that Desdemona was unfaithful to him. Emilia tells
everyone that this was a foul lie.

154 **pernicious:** destructive
155 **to th'heart:** absolutely
156 **She ... bargain:** She was too foolishly faithful to the
     corrupt marriage she made
160 **Peace ... best:** It would be best for you to keep silent
161–162 **Thou ... hurt:** You cannot hurt me half as much as
     I can tolerate hurt
     gull: fool
     dolt: idiot
164 **I ... sword:** I don't care if you threaten me with your
     sword
     I'll ... known: I'll tell the world about you
165 **Though:** even if
169 **lay ... neck:** claim they kill on your say-so
171 **this villain:** i.e. Othello
176 **apt:** credible, probable
179 **odious:** hateful

> * *How do you react to Emilia's description of Desdemona's*
>   *marriage as 'her most filthy bargain'?*
> * *From the evidence of Iago's lines on this page, how do you*
>   *think an actor should portray him?*

OTHELLO	He, woman; I say thy husband; dost understand the word? My friend, thy husband, honest, honest Iago.
EMILIA	If he say so, may his pernicious soul Rot half a grain a day. He lies to th'heart. She was too fond of her most filthy bargain.
OTHELLO	Ha!
EMILIA	Do thy worst. This deed of thine is no more worthy heaven Than thou wast worthy her.
OTHELLO	Peace, you were best. 160
EMILIA	Thou hast not half that power to do me harm As I have to be hurt. O gull! O dolt! As ignorant as dirt! Thou hast done a deed – I care not for thy sword – I'll make thee known, Though I lost twenty lives. Help, help, ho, help! The Moor hath killed my mistress. Murder, murder!

Enter MONTANO, GRATIANO, IAGO, *and others*

MONTANO	What is the matter? How now, general?
EMILIA	O, are you come, Iago? You have done well, That men must lay their murders on your neck.
GRATIANO	What is the matter? 170
EMILIA	Disprove this villain, if thou be'st a man. He says thou told'st him that his wife was false. I know thou didst not: thou'rt not such a villain. Speak, for my heart is full.
IAGO	I told him what I thought, and told no more Than what he found himself was apt and true.
EMILIA	But did you ever tell him she was false?
IAGO	I did.
EMILIA	You told a lie, an odious, damned lie: Upon my soul, a lie, a wicked lie. 180 She false with Cassio? Did you say with Cassio?

Everyone is appalled. Emilia is shocked at the extremity of
Iago's evil: it fills her mind; she can smell it. Iago tries to
silence Emilia and send her away, but she defies him. Othello
collapses in anguish, then tries to justify himself to Gratiano
who expresses relief that Brabantio is dead and so cannot be
affected by this present disaster. Othello insists that Iago
knows that Cassio confessed to having sex with Desdemona.

182 **charm:** put a spell on, i.e. control
185 **forfend:** forbid
186 **set ... on:** brought the murder about
193 **charge:** order
195 **'Tis ... him:** as a wife I should obey my husband
197 **roar:** howl and weep
200 **scarce did know:** hardly recognised
       uncle: i.e. Gratiano, Desdemona's uncle
204 **Thy match was mortal:** your marriage was deadly
205 **Shore:** cut
       thread: thread of life
       Did he live: if he were alive
206 **do ... turn:** take desperate action
207 **better angel:** guardian angel
208 **reprobance:** sin, damnation
212 **gratify ... works:** reward his lovemaking

> • *Why do you think Othello collapses at 197 and rises at*
>   *199?*

IAGO	With Cassio, mistress! Go to, charm your tongue.
EMILIA	I will not charm my tongue; I am bound to speak: My mistress here lies murdered in her bed.
ALL	O heavens forfend!
EMILIA	And your reports have set the murder on.
OTHELLO	Nay, stare not masters, it is true indeed.
GRATIANO	'Tis a strange truth.
MONTANO	O monstrous act!
EMILIA	Villainy, villainy, villainy! I think upon't, I think – I smell't. O villainy! 190 I thought so then. I'll kill myself for grief. O villainy, villainy!
IAGO	What, are you mad? I charge you get you home.
EMILIA	Good gentlemen, let me have leave to speak. 'Tis proper I obey him, but not now. Perchance, Iago, I will ne'er go home.
OTHELLO	O, o, o! [*Falls on the bed*
EMILIA	Nay, lay thee down and roar; For thou hast killed the sweetest innocent That e'er did lift up eye.
OTHELLO	[*Rises*] O, she was foul. I scarce did know you uncle; there lies your niece, 200 Whose breath indeed these hands have newly stopped. I know this act shows horrible and grim.
GRATIANO	Poor Desdemon! I am glad thy father's dead: Thy match was mortal to him, and pure grief Shore his old thread in twain. Did he live now, This sight would make him do a desperate turn, Yea, curse his better angel from his side, And fall to reprobance.
OTHELLO	'Tis pitiful; but yet Iago knows That she with Cassio hath the act of shame 210 A thousand times committed. Cassio confessed it. And she did gratify his amorous works

Othello insists he himself saw the handkerchief in Cassio's hand. Emilia now knows what has happened and promises to tell everything. When Emilia refuses to be silent, Iago attacks her but is restrained. Emilia tells Othello how she found the handkerchief and gave it to Iago because he kept asking for it. Iago accuses her of lying and she denies it. Othello tries to attack Iago. Montano disarms him; Iago stabs Emilia and runs out.

213 **recognizance:** token

215 **antique:** time-honoured

217 **Zounds:** an oath (by God's wounds)

    'Twill out: It will come out

    I peace?: the idea that I should be silent is ridiculous

218 **as … north:** as freely and freezingly as the north wind

224 **by fortune:** by accident

226 **belonged … trifle:** was appropriate for such a trivial thing

231 **coxcomb:** fool (the coxcomb was the fool or clown's hat); also, braggart. Emilia is speaking of Othello here.

232–233 **Are … thunder:** Are the stones in heaven used only for thunder? Are there none for thunderbolts to kill villains?

233 **Precious:** fine

With that recognizance and pledge of love
Which I first gave her; I saw it in his hand.
It was a handkerchief, an antique token
My father gave my mother.

EMILIA   O God! O heavenly God!

IAGO   Zounds, hold your peace.

EMILIA   'Twill out, 'twill out. I peace?
No, I will speak as liberal as the north.
Let heaven, and men, and devils, let them all,
All, all cry shame against me, yet I'll speak.   220

IAGO   Be wise, and get you home.

EMILIA   I will not.

[IAGO *thrusts at* EMILIA]

GRATIANO   Fie!
Your sword upon a woman?

EMILIA   O thou dull Moor, that handkerchief thou speak'st of
I found by fortune, and did give my husband;
For often, with a solemn earnestness,
More than indeed belonged to such a trifle,
He begged of me to steal it.

IAGO   Villainous whore!

EMILIA   She give it Cassio? No, alas, I found it
And I did give't my husband.

IAGO   Filth, thou liest.

EMILIA   By heaven, I do not, I do not, gentlemen.   230
O murderous coxcomb, what should such a fool
Do with so good a wife?

OTHELLO   Are there no stones in heaven
But what serve for the thunder? Precious villain!

[*He runs at* IAGO; MONTANO *disarms him;*
IAGO, *from behind, stabs* EMILIA *and exit*

GRATIANO   The woman falls. Sure he hath killed his wife.

EMILIA   Ay, ay – O lay me by my mistress' side.

Montano orders Othello to be locked in the room under guard. He himself will pursue Iago. Othello and Emilia are left alone with Desdemona's body. Othello feels vulnerable and dishonoured as man and soldier. Emilia reminds Othello of Desdemona's virtue and love. She prays for her own soul and dies. Othello produces a hidden sword and asks Gratiano to let him out. Gratiano refuses. He threatens to attack Gratiano if he doesn't comply. Gratiano enters, and Othello shows he has a sword but tells Gratiano not to be afraid. Othello says he has reached the end of his life.

237 **notorious:** obvious, clear
238 **recovered:** removed
239 **without:** outside
241 **I ... neither:** I too lack courage (i.e. Othello sees himself as like Iago)
242 **every ... sword:** every little weakling can take my sword from me
243 **why ... honesty?:** why should one's honour as a fighting man outlive one's virtue as a man
244 **bode:** prophesy
245–246 **play ... music:** play the role of the swan and sing as I die (swans were believed to sing only once, at their death)
248 **So ... bliss:** so may my soul reach heaven
251 **ice-brook's temper:** tempered (the hardening process) in an icy stream
254 **perforce:** inevitably
256 **naked:** unarmed
261 **impediments:** obstacles, defences
262 **your stop:** any attempt of yours to stop me
    vain: empty
264 **weaponed:** armed
265 **butt:** the target I am aiming for

- *What are the implications of Montano calling Iago a 'notorious' villain (237)?*
- *What is the impact of Emilia's recollection of Desdemona's song (246)?*

GRATIANO   He's gone, but his wife's killed.

MONTANO   'Tis a notorious villain. Take you this weapon
Which I have here recovered from the Moor.
Come guard the door without, let him not pass,
But kill him rather. I'll after that same villain,   240
For 'tis a damned slave.

                        [*Exeunt* MONTANO *and* GRATIANO

OTHELLO   I am not valiant neither,
But every puny whipster gets my sword.
But why should honour outlive honesty?
Let it go all.

EMILIA   What did thy song bode, lady?
Hark, canst thou hear me? I will play the swan,
And die in music. [*Sings*] Willow, willow, willow –
Moor, she was chaste. She loved thee, cruel Moor;
So come my soul to bliss, as I speak true;
So speaking as I think, alas, I die.   [*Dies*

OTHELLO   I have another weapon in this chamber;   250
It was a sword of Spain, the ice-brook's temper.
O here it is. Uncle, I must come forth.

GRATIANO   [*Within*] If thou attempt it, it will cost thee dear.
Thou hast no weapon, and perforce must suffer.

OTHELLO   Look in upon me then, and speak with me,
Or naked as I am I will assault thee.

    Enter GRATIANO

GRATIANO   What is the matter?

OTHELLO   Behold, I have a weapon
A better never did itself sustain
Upon a soldier's thigh. I have seen the day
That with this little arm and this good sword,   260
I have made my way through more impediments
Than twenty times your stop. But, o vain boast,
Who can control his fate? – 'Tis not so now.
Be not afraid, though you do see me weaponed;
Here is my journey's end, here is my butt

He tells Gratiano not to fear him. He contemplates
Desdemona's cold body, which reminds him of her chastity.
He believes he will go to hell. When Lodovico, Montano and
Cassio return with Iago as a prisoner, Othello wounds Iago
and is disarmed. Lodovico recalls Othello's goodness, now
destroyed by Iago. Othello claims he acted in honour. Iago
has admitted to plotting Cassio's death with Othello.

266 **sea-mark:** marker-buoy, or landmark by which to steer for
home
utmost sail: last voyage
267 **go back:** retreat
lost: unnecessary
268 **Man but a rush:** aim only a reed
270 **ill-starred:** ill-fated
271 **smock:** shift, slip
at compt: on the Day of Judgement
274 **chastity:** he is admitting her virtue
slave: i.e. himself
276 **possession:** grip
278 **steep-down:** sheer
282 **viper ... villain:** i.e. Iago
283 **fable:** a mere story (that the devil has cloven feet)
287 **in my sense:** the way I see things
289 **practice:** cunning plot
294 **consent in:** plot

> • *Why do you think Shakespeare does not have Othello kill*
> *Iago, only wound him?*

And very sea-mark of my utmost sail.
Do you go back dismayed? 'Tis a lost fear;
Man but a rush against Othello's breast,
And he retires. Where should Othello go?
Now, how dost thou look now? O ill-starred wench,   270
Pale as thy smock. When we shall meet at compt,
This look of thine will hurl my soul from heaven,
And fiends will snatch at it. Cold, cold, my girl,
Even like thy chastity.
O cursed, cursed slave! Whip me, ye devils,
From the possession of this heavenly sight.
Blow me about in winds. Roast me in sulphur.
Wash me in steep-down gulfs of liquid fire.
O Desdemona! Desdemona! Dead!

Enter LODOVICO, MONTANO, CASSIO *carried in a chair,
and his* OFFICERS *with* IAGO, *prisoner*

LODOVICO	Where is this rash and most unfortunate man? 280
OTHELLO	That's he that was Othello here I am.
LODOVICO	Where is that viper? Bring the villain forth.
OTHELLO	I look down towards his feet; but that's a fable. If that you be'st a devil, I cannot kill thee. [*Wounds* IAGO
LODOVICO	Wrench his sword from him.
IAGO	I bleed, sir; but not killed.
OTHELLO	I am not sorry neither: I'd have thee live; For, in my sense, 'tis happiness to die.
LODOVICO	O thou Othello, that wast once so good, Fall'n in the practice of a damned slave, What shall be said to thee?
OTHELLO	Why anything. 290 An honourable murderer, if you will; For naught did I in hate, but all in honour.
LODOVICO	This wretch hath part confessed his villainy. Did you and he consent in Cassio's death?

Othello asks Cassio's pardon. He wants to know Iago's
reason. Iago refuses to explain. Two letters have been found
on Roderigo: one orders Roderigo to kill Cassio; the other,
written by Roderigo, is a complaint to Iago. Othello wants
to know how Cassio acquired the handkerchief. Cassio says
he found it in his room. Cassio explains how Iago has
confessed that he left the handkerchief in Cassio's room and
that Roderigo's letter reveals how he was to provoke Cassio
into a fight.

298 **demand:** ask
    demi-devil: half-devil
299 **ensnared:** trapped
302 **torments:** torture
    ope: open
303 **thou dost best:** you know what's best
304 **befall'n:** happened
307 **imports:** signifies
310 **discontented paper:** letter of complaint
312 **this ... villain:** i.e. Iago
313 **belike:** it is likely
    the nick: i.e. the nick of time
314 **satisfied:** give him satisfaction for his complaints by killing
    him
    pernicious caitiff: destructive villain
319 **wrought ... desire:** worked towards his aims
321 **upbraids:** complains to
322 **Brave:** provoke

> • *With what tone and attitude do you think Othello would
> say line 303 'Well, thou dost best'?*

OTHELLO	Ay.
CASSIO	Dear general, I never gave you cause.
OTHELLO	I do believe it, and I ask your pardon.
	Will you, I pray, demand that demi-devil
	Why he hath thus ensnared my soul and body?
IAGO	Demand me nothing. What you know, you know. 300
	From this time forth I never will speak word.
LODOVICO	What, not to pray?
GRATIANO	Torments will ope your lips.
OTHELLO	Well, thou dost best.
LODOVICO	Sir, you shall understand what hath befall'n,
	Which as I think you know not. Here is a letter
	Found in the pocket of the slain Roderigo,
	And here another: the one of them imports
	The death of Cassio, to be undertook
	By Roderigo.
OTHELLO	O villain!
CASSIO	Most heathenish and most gross.
LODOVICO	Now here's another discontented paper, 310
	Found in his pocket too; and this it seems
	Roderigo meant t' have sent this damned villain
	But that, belike, Iago in the nick,
	Came in and satisfied him.
OTHELLO	O the pernicious caitiff!
	How came you, Cassio, by that handkerchief
	That was my wife's?
CASSIO	I found it in my chamber;
	And he himself confessed but even now
	That there he dropped it for a special purpose
	Which wrought to his desire.
OTHELLO	O fool, fool, fool!
CASSIO	There is besides, in Roderigo's letter, 320
	How he upbraids Iago, that he made him
	Brave me upon the watch; whereon it came

Lodovico orders Othello to come with him under guard, and
leaves Cassio in command of Cyprus. Othello wants to be
remembered with fairness as one who loved too much and was
tricked into extreme jealousy; as one who did not realise the
worth of what he had and who is now weeping. Othello
expresses his desire to be recorded as the man who killed a Turk
who insulted the state of Venice, and kills himself, dying on
Desdemona's bed and kissing her as he does so.

322–323 whereon … cast: as a result of which I was dismissed

323 even but now: just now

325 set him on: provoked him

328 this slave: i.e. Iago

329–331 If … his: if there is any cleverly devised way of inflicting
pain that can torture him a great deal, and keep him alive a
long time, he will have it

331 close … rest: remain a closely guarded prisoner

338 nothing extenuate: do not make excuses

339 Nor … malice: do not record anything out of hatred

341 wrought: provoked

342 Perplexed: confused

343 base Indian: there is some dispute over what this refers to.
Perhaps it refers to the American Indians who were widely
thought not to value precious stones. Othello likens himself to an
Indian because he did not recognise Desdemona's true value.
Another possibility comes from the Folio which has 'Judean',
thought to be a reference to Judas Iscariot, who, in betraying
Christ, threw away the 'pearl of great price' – i.e. the kingdom of
Heaven (Matt 13:46). This would fit with Othello's sense of
himself throughout the play as a Christian, and what he believes
he has done here. (See also line 351 'circumcised dog'.) Other
speculation has suggested that this is a reference to a fable or
story known to Shakespeare, but not to us.

345 Albeit … mood: although not accustomed to breaking down
in tears

347 medicinable gum: i.e. myrrh used in sacrifices, medicinal

349 malignant: malicious

350 traduced: dishonoured, insulted

351 circumcised: as a Muslim

353 period: end, conclusion

354 thee: i.e. Desdemona

> • *How do you think Othello might say line 334? What
> feelings and intentions might he express or hide?*

That I was cast; and even but now he spake
After long seeming dead, Iago hurt him,
Iago set him on.

LODOVICO   You must forsake this room, and go with us.
Your power and your command is taken off,
And Cassio rules in Cyprus. For this slave,
If there be any cunning cruelty
That can torment him much, and hold him long,   330
It shall be his. You shall close prisoner rest,
Till that the nature of your fault be known
To the Venetian state. Come, bring away.

OTHELLO   Soft you; a word or two before you go.
I have done the state some service, and they know't.
No more of that. I pray you in your letters,
When you shall these unlucky deeds relate,
Speak of me as I am; nothing extenuate,
Nor set down aught in malice. Then must you speak
Of one that loved not wisely, but too well;   340
Of one, not easily jealous, but being wrought
Perplexed in the extreme; of one whose hand,
Like the base Indian, threw a pearl away
Richer than all his tribe; of one whose subdued eyes,
Albeit unused to the melting mood,
Drop tears as fast as the Arabian trees
Their medicinable gum. Set you down this;
And say besides, that in Aleppo once,
Where a malignant and a turbaned Turk
Beat a Venetian and traduced the state,   350
I took by th'throat the circumcised dog,
And smote him, thus.

                                        [*Stabs himself*

LODOVICO   O bloody period!

GRATIANO   All that's spoke is marred.

OTHELLO   I kissed thee ere I killed thee. No way but this,
Killing myself, to die upon a kiss.

                        [*Falls on the bed, and dies*

Cassio says he feared this because Othello was courageous. Lodovico tells Iago to contemplate the tragic results of his plots. He leaves Gratiano on guard and gives him Othello's fortune. Cassio is left to deal with Iago, while Lodovico returns to Venice.

357 **Spartan dog:** famous for their savagery (referring to Iago)
358 **fell:** cruel, fatal
361 **keep:** guard
362 **seize upon:** take possession of
363 **succeed on you:** come to you by law
364 **censure:** judgement

CASSIO   This did I fear, but thought he had no weapon,
             For he was great of heart.

LODOVICO   [*To* IAGO]   O Spartan dog,
             More fell than anguish, hunger, or the sea,
             Look on the tragic loading of this bed.
             This is thy work. The object poisons sight;   360
             Let it be hid. Gratiano, keep the house,
             And seize upon the fortunes of the Moor,
             For they succeed on you. To you, Lord Governor,
             Remains the censure of this hellish villain;
             The time, the place, the torture, o enforce it.
             Myself will straight aboard, and to the state
             This heavy act with heavy heart relate.
                                              [*Exeunt*

CTIVITIES

Keeping track

Scene 1

1 What advantages are there for Iago if Cassio dies?
2 What conclusions does Othello draw from what he witnesses (28–36)?
3 What is the importance of Lodovico's and Gratiano's appearance in this scene?
4 Why does Iago implicate Bianca in Cassio's wounding?

Scene 2

1 What seems to be Othello's motive for killing Desdemona? What feelings are in conflict within him? What is he concerned she should do before he kills her, and why?
2 Why does Emilia need to see Othello urgently? What leads Othello to tell her he killed Desdemona? How does he justify the killing? What is Emilia's response?
3 What leads to Iago's attack on Emilia at line 221? How does this lead on to Othello's attempted assault on Iago at line 233?
4 What happens when Othello is left alone? What are his thoughts?
5 When Lodovico arrives, what evidences of Iago's guilt are produced? How does Iago respond?
6 How does Othello wish to be remembered?

Discussion

Scene 1

1 Iago concludes the scene by saying 'This is the night/That either makes me, or fordoes me quite'. Discuss his performance in this scene. Do you feel he is responding urgently to events, in complete control, or somewhere in between? Why doesn't he kill Cassio when he has the chance?
2 No one seems to suspect Iago of anything here. Why not? What are Iago's successful tactics for concealing his actions and intentions?
3 Discuss Shakespeare's handling of this action scene. What do you think are the vital points an audience should see and understand?

Scene 2

1 Discuss the role of Othello in the final scene. What do you think of his motives for killing Desdemona, and are they consistent with his feelings in Acts 3 and 4? Consider his response to seeing his dead wife and reflecting on his errors. Consider, also, his final view of himself and how he wishes to be remembered. Is he a sympathetic figure?

2 In this scene, everything that the audience already knows (through Iago) now comes to light for the other characters. How effectively do you think Shakespeare has plotted all this?

3 In this scene, Iago is exposed. Why does Shakespeare render him determinedly silent? How do you understand the repeated descriptions of him as 'villain'? Is he merely the 'stage villain', 'the bad guy'?

4 What is the effect of bringing in first Montano and Gratiano, then Lodovico? What do these characters contribute to our final experience of the drama?

Close study

Scene 1

1 Consider Othello's brief appearance in this scene (28–30). What is its impact? Look at Othello's speech in lines 31–36. What are the ironies in lines 31–33? What tones, attitudes and feelings do you sense in lines 33–36 ('Minion ... spotted')? How are they conveyed?

2 How many times is the word 'villain' used in this scene? Of whom? What is its impact?

3 Explore Iago's methods of discrediting Bianca from her entrance (line 74) to the end of the scene. What is the impact of line 116 'This is the fruits of whoring'?

Scene 2

1 Lines 1–22. Othello, carrying a light, contemplates killing Desdemona. What does his language reveal about his state of mind? Consider:
 • references to light (real and metaphorical)
 • language which shows how sensually aware he is of Desdemona's sleeping body, and how he feels she is part of 'excelling nature'
 • language which shows how he regards himself and how he feels about his role
 • in what way is he speaking differently from recent scenes?

2 In line 17, Othello refers to justice's sword. As you read the scene, notice other references to swords and the use of swords. In what way is the idea of the sword important to Othello?

3 Lines 24–89. Othello urgently requires Desdemona to confess her sins. He tells her that, in another sense, Cassio has confessed. Desdemona begs for time to pray. Consider the Christian language of sin, confession and prayer, and assess how you interpret it. How do you interpret line 88 when Othello claims he is both 'cruel' and 'merciful'?

4   Lines 90–106. How do Othello's speech and behaviour here, after
    he has killed Desdemona, contrast with his speech in lines 1–22?
    How does Shakespeare reveal Othello's state of mind and the drama
    of the situation? What idea indicates how catastrophic an act he
    thinks he has performed? How is it followed up in lines 110–112?

5   Between lines 118 and 126, Shakespeare gives Desdemona her final
    words. What is the dramatic impact of what she says and when she
    says it? How do these words affect your view of Desdemona and of
    Othello?

6   Lines 127–166.
    • How does Othello react to Emilia in this passage? Consider how
      they are both using the language of religion: 'heaven' and 'hell'.
    • How do you respond to Emilia here? What thoughts seem to
      develop in her mind?

7   Lines 167–240.
    • Iago has prompted and controlled so much of the action so far.
      How do you view him in this passage? What is the effect of his
      claim in lines 175–176? How does he speak to Emilia? Is he in
      control? Which moments reveal most about him?
    • How does Shakespeare use Montano and Gratiano in this passage?
      What fresh aspect do they give the drama?
    • What do you think are Othello's feelings at line 197? How does
      he recover himself in the following speeches?

8   Lines 241–279.
    • What is the impact of Emilia's death? What is the effect of her
      dying speech (244–249)?
    • How is Othello's mind working in this passage? What is the
      significance of his sword/weapon to him? Why does he refer to
      himself by name (268, 269)?
    • How do you respond to the language and feeling of Othello's
      lines 269–279? What are his thoughts and feelings in response to
      Desdemona's body? How does he think of his own fate?

9   Lines 280–333.
    • What is the full impact of line 281? Why are these words so
      significant for an understanding of Othello? How do you respond
      to Othello calling himself 'an honourable murderer' in line 291?
    • Lines 300–301 are Iago's last words in the play. What is their
      impact? How do they make you think about Iago?
    • From 304–333, Lodovico brings Othello face to face with what
      has actually happened and what is to be done. How does Othello
      react?

10 Lines 334–352. What feelings and motives do you sense in this
    speech of Othello's? Consider that he refers to what has happened
    as 'unlucky'. Consider also the ways he thinks he should justly be
    spoken of. Do you have sympathy for him here?

11 Lines 353–367.
- How do you react to the final comments of Gratiano (353) and Cassio (356–357)? How do they affect the tone of the end of the play?
- What do you think of Lodovico's final judgement of Iago and the way he expresses it? Why is Iago, having so often been described as 'honest', now, in this final scene, so often described as 'villain' and 'devil'?

Imagery and poetic language

A strand of language which expresses a central theme in the play comes to a climax in Act 5. It is the vocabulary of judgement about people's value or moral worth:
- honest, honesty, honour, honourable, good, just, true
- villain, villainy, knave, slave, dog, devil, false.

The influence of Iago has resulted in Othello being confused and deluded about other characters. You will probably have noticed how Othello often affirms Iago's honesty, as do others. In this final act, as the truth emerges, this language and its use become intensely important. Reread act 5 with this in mind. Remember: from the moment Iago is exposed, he resolves to speak no more – and doesn't. Words, and the manipulations he can practise with them, are his weapons. Do you think these words of judgement about people are appropriately used by the end of the play?

Key scene

Scene 2 lines 1–84.

Although Brabantio suspects Othello of practising black magic to seduce Desdemona, and Iago views him as an alien black man, Othello is a professed Christian and he takes his Christianity seriously. The language of heaven and hell is much on his lips. In Act 2 Scene 1, Cassio describes Desdemona as divine and, after this passage, Emilia speaks of her as an 'angel' and of Othello as 'blacker devil'. Reread this passage and assess how the Christian concerns of both characters affect your understanding of the final tragedy.

Writing

1 Write a detailed commentary of Othello's opening speech in Scene 2 in which you explain how the language reveals how his mind and senses are working. You will find the first two questions in the Close Study section on Act 5 Scene 2 helpful. You should also pay careful attention to:
   - the conflicts in Othello's mind and how he expresses them
   - the sense he has of himself as bringing justice and how he expresses this

- his awareness of the sleeping Desdemona
- his awareness of the stars.

2 We hear in Scene 2 (320–325) that Roderigo, who seemed dead, was able to give evidence against Iago before actually dying. We have already seen Desdemona seem dead, only to recover sufficiently to claim that she was 'falsely murdered' (118), affirm her innocence (123), and apparently assume responsibility for her own death (125). In the light of these devices, explain your responses to the last act as a whole. Do you think it is exciting melodrama? Or psychologically believable and interesting? Or just a good last act that sorts everything out? Or does Shakespeare use some combination of elements?

3 Write a detailed commentary of Othello's final major speech (334–352). Focus on how he wants to view himself and be viewed. Explain how you react to him at this point and how this end colours your view of him overall.

Explorations

A question of approach

When you study a play, you need to be able to see it from two different perspectives simultaneously. You need to be able to imagine and experience the text line by line, sharing the thoughts and feelings of the characters as they go through the events of the play, but at the same time you need to be able to look down on the play as a whole and see the patterns of character and relationship, of language and imagery, of themes and issues.

A play is essentially an audio-visual experience. No two members of the audience see quite the same 'play' and no two performances are ever exactly the same. Two important lessons should be learned from this. The first is that the printed text is not the play; the play is what you see when you go to the theatre. The text is a set of instructions to be interpreted by the director and the actors, artists and technicians. The second lesson is that there is no one 'right answer' to the play, only a range of possible interpretations. Your view can be just as valid as anyone else's, but only if you can present it clearly and support it with valid arguments derived from the text. For this purpose you need, again, to see it as a whole **and** as a set of details.

Thinking about the play

By the time you have discussed the text carefully you should be beginning to clarify and organize your response to the play as a whole. Most examination questions concentrate on *content* and *form*, and these are useful terms which offer you an approach and a framework within which you can prepare to write successfully.

Your first task is to establish clearly in your mind the broad issues raised by the text and the possible areas for discussion, including major characters. You need to consider and discuss some of the possible views and interpretations of these issues and lay down a sensible framework within which personal responses can be convincing and well considered. You also need to get close to the text and identify the key incidents, scenes or even quotations which will form the basis of any essay. When you come to write essays on the whole text, or even a specified passage, the appropriate textual evidence and illustrations should be noted and easily available.

What is interesting about Othello?

It is not the task of these suggestions for study to tell you what to think about this play. They are entitled **Explorations** deliberately, because they are intended to help you explore the play for yourself. You may already have a strong reaction to it: maybe you think it is moving, or fascinating or frightening or just plain ridiculous.

Whatever your view, clear or unclear, there isn't much dispute that the play deals with a case of extreme jealousy and its fatal consequences. How you react to this drama, and what you find interesting about it, will depend very much on how you react to the plot. By careful study of the language of the play, you will see that Shakespeare is exploring themes which have a significance beyond the particular plot and characters, though they are conveyed through them. However, it is the plot (which the playwright constructs out of the motives and actions of the characters) which should arouse our interest.

Why do events turn out disastrously for Othello and Desdemona? In real life we often speak of 'a chapter of accidents' to describe the causes of a sad, bad or unlucky outcome – whether fatal or far less serious. The expression implies that the events that led up to the bad outcome were mere chances, but, because of this particular combination in this particular order, the bad outcome was inevitable. You may feel that Shakespeare's plot relies on a pretty unlikely 'chapter of accidents':

- characters enter and exit exactly as Iago would wish;
- they seem to trust him and act on his advice or persuasion;

- Desdemona accidentally drops her handkerchief, Othello orders her to leave it where it is, Emilia picks it up and gives it to Iago though she knows how much Desdemona values it;
- although Roderigo has decided that Iago is not to be trusted because none of his advice has worked, he nevertheless undertakes to kill Cassio;
- Othello never questions Cassio on Iago's allegations, and speaks to Desdemona only when he is in the full grip of jealousy.

Isn't Shakespeare asking us to swallow quite a lot of useful 'accidents'? Might he not answer that all plays require the writer to organise the action to ensure the outcome he wants? Might he not answer, too, that we have the expression 'chapter of accidents' because such things do actually occur?

The playwright's task is to convince us that what characters do and say (i.e. the plot) is the outcome of their thoughts, feelings and motives. Are the events of *Othello* in fact accidents? You might be thinking, after studying the play so far, that Roderigo, Othello, Desdemona and Cassio are all easily fooled and that Iago is some kind of evil genius. If this is the case, your response to the fatal conclusion may be amusement: Iago's entertaining cleverness has won the day and the fools got what they deserved. Or you might simply feel sad for their fatal gullibility, but not feel there was much significance in watching this unfair fight.

It would be easy to imagine that, if you took the villain, 'honest Iago', out of this situation, Desdemona and Othello would live happily ever after. However, it is Othello who kills Desdemona – a wife with whom he is infatuated – not Iago. Iago does not kill Othello, though he professes more than once to hate him; Othello kills himself. It is too easy to say that it was all Iago's fault. It is too easy to say that Iago planned it all – he cannot control the thoughts, feelings, motives and actions of the other characters, however clever he is. Are we back with a 'chapter of accidents'?

There is a difference between a play which depends for its plot on a chapter of accidents and one where the action and outcome are inevitable because events could have gone no other way given the characters involved. What is interesting about *Othello*, therefore, is the motives which drive the characters to act in the ways they do. What is interesting is the way Shakespeare has used Iago both as a character in his own right and as a means of creating his plot. What is interesting is how we view Othello himself, because our answer to this question will affect our final response to the whole play.

Until now, the word 'tragedy' has not been used in this discussion. Let me suggest that, if you feel that Othello and the other main characters are serious and credible and have some depth; if you feel that events could not have gone any other way given this combination of characters; if you think that the outcome is horrifying and shocking – then tragedy is probably a useful word to describe this drama.

Character

Characters in plays function in two ways:
1 They have to be written and acted in such a way that the audience (or reader) can imagine them to have a life of their own; the audience wants to make the characters 'live'.
2 They are part of the writer's overall plan, i.e. they do not, in fact, have a life of their own but are the writer's tools for exploring her/his themes in lifelike form.

Note: Questions about character are common in A-level, but they are not best answered by writing a character analysis (however complex) as though she or he were a 'real' human being. The aim should be to explain why this complex creation is essential to the play as a whole; this is the best **literary** writing.

Three lines of approach

Judging a character is not simply a matter of accumulating the evidence of the written word and drawing conclusions.

It is more complicated, and requires some selection and evaluation to allow you to reach a coherent response to the character.

The evidence – 1

Characters are revealed by:
- what they say
- what they do.

Problems

1 Characters are not always consistent. Indeed, it is their 'inconsistency' that is interesting and gives them a 'life of their own'. Major characters are subject to change because the events on which the action is based are significant enough to affect the main protagonists: the more important the character, the closer to the action and the greater the reaction to events. You must always be aware of how, and why, characters are developing and be prepared to explain and trace the changes.
2 Characters might say or do things for effect. They might be seeking to impress or mislead someone else and not mean what they say at all.
   You must always consider whether the character is being sincere or if he or she has an ulterior motive.

The evidence – 2

Characters are also revealed by:
- what others say about them
- how others behave towards them.

Problems

As in life, whether you accept A's opinion of B depends on how you feel about A. If you believe that A is untrustworthy or has a perverted sense of justice, then A's criticism of B might be interpreted as a glowing character reference! Alternatively, an opinion might be based on false information or might be deliberately misleading.

It is essential that you do not simply accept one character's opinion of another at face value. In the case of *Othello*, and Iago specifically, this problem is at the heart of the tragedy.

The evidence – 3

Characters are also revealed by:
* soliloquies
* asides.

These are often the most reliable evidence on which to assess a character since she/he is sharing her/his thoughts with the audience. All pretence is dropped because the soliloquy and the aside are devices which allow characters to express their thoughts and feelings directly, and solely, to the audience.

However, while this advice may apply very well to Othello's major soliloquy at the heart of Act 3, we may feel that Shakespeare is playing a very different game with Iago's soliloquies and asides. How much does he really reveal?

Conclusion

These lines of approach can work very well when studying the central characters in *Othello,* for example, Othello, Roderigo, Brabantio, Iago, Cassio, Desdemona, Emilia.

You have only to notice the ways in which they are **developed** to be immediately aware of Shakespeare exploring his themes.

Most vitally, you must also be imaginatively and sensitively involved in the life and experience of the characters, much as a good actor would be.

However, Iago may seem to be a special case. The above approach to character study can certainly be helpful up to a point, but there are some extraordinary and interesting qualities about Iago as a figure in this drama which make him worthy of special attention. We might, perhaps, say **our knowledge of him** develops during the early scenes, but does **he** actually develop? Does he show inconsistencies? Are his soliloquies reliable? What is his relationship with the audience? How is Shakespeare using him to present the plot?

In the explorations that follow, consideration of Iago and his role will occur at several points because his influence is so crucial. It is never right to 'extract' a character from a play and study him/her as if he or she were real. In Iago's case, this is particularly true.

Critical moments

At critical moments in the play you can begin to gain a better insight into a character by seeking answers to certain questions. Sadly, there is no formula which will apply to every situation, but you need to identify the key scenes and speeches which relate to a particular character and then ask these questions to start you off and perhaps prompt questions of your own.

- What has the character said or done here?
- Why has the character said or done this?
- What will happen as a result of this speech or action?
- How do you feel about the consequences of this speech or action?
- What does this incident tell us about the character?
- How does the character change or develop as a result of it?
- What does each of these critical moments tell us about the character concerned?

Here is a range of references (in order through the play) which could be described as critical moments for each of four characters. These four have been chosen as major contributors to, and victims of, the events the play depicts. Some references are 'speeches', others may be only a line or two, but all show the character revealing himself or herself, and responding to or initiating important events. Together, they will give you a kind of 'map' of each character's journey through the play.

The audience very often knows more than the character – the element of dramatic irony is all-pervading in this play. As we watch these characters facing critical moments (of which they themselves are often unaware), we not only learn more about them but also become painfully aware of their human frailty.

1 Look up each of the references for a character and decide what is 'critical' about that moment in terms of our understanding of the character and his/her situation in the play. What tensions are there

between the way the character views his/her situation and the way the audience sees it?

2 Now look at the whole sequence of references for each character. What do you learn about the character's 'journey' through the play? How are we affected by the way we see characters responding to situations they don't fully understand? How do you view them finally?

3 Collect suitable quotations for essay writing.

Desdemona

Act 1 Scene 3: 180–189; 247–258
Act 3 Scene 3: 19–28; 286
Act 3 Scene 4: 22–26; 94–96; 142–148
Act 4 Scene 1: 234
Act 4 Scene 2: 81–84; 101–105; 106
Act 4 Scene 3: 21–23; 56–59
Act 5 Scene 2: 125–126

Cassio

Act 2 Scene 1: 43–46; 82–87; 95–99
Act 2 Scene 3: 104–110; 182; 255–258; 320–322
Act 3 Scene 3: 30
Act 3 Scene 4: 104–108; 182–185
Act 4 Scene 1: 112
Act 5 Scene 1: 103
Act 5 Scene 2: 309; 356–357

Emilia

Act 2 Scene 1: 107
Act 3 Scene 3: 3–4; 288–297
Act 3 Scene 4: 21; 96–99; 153–156
Act 4 Scene 2: 11–18; 129–132
Act 4 Scene 3: 93–100
Act 5 Scene 2: 161–166; 171–174; 194–196

Roderigo

Act 1 Scene 1: 1–3; 119–139
Act 1 Scene 3: 304; 378
Act 2 Scene 1: 244–245; 276
Act 2 Scene 3: 353–359
Act 4 Scene 2: 174–179; 217; 241
Act 5 Scene 1: 8–10

Character development: Othello

Othello is the focus of this play. In conventional literary and dramatic terms, he is the tragic hero. However you view him, it is the change in him – or, if you prefer, the revelation of an aspect of his nature of which neither he, nor the other characters, nor the audience had previously been aware – which brings about the fatal consequences. How you respond to this development, and how it and its consequences affect you, will determine your response to the play.

The 'critical moments' approach can be used to highlight the key points in the development of a character. However, the proper answer to the question 'Which are the critical moments for Othello?' is 'All of them'. As soon as you try to select 'moments', you realise how important everything is – this is the sign of a good play. What follows, therefore, is one attempt at selecting critical moments in the development or revelation of Othello – but remember, there is much more to look at, discuss and argue about.

This selection uses comments by other characters as well as Othello's own words, because they all help to form the audience's response to this crucial central character. And remember: Othello is only one role in the whole drama, as well as being a central character whom we are invited to use our imaginations (with the help of an actor) to bring alive.

1 **Act 1 Scene 1**
  lines 8–17
  The first view of Othello we receive is Iago's. (At this point we do not even know that it is he who is being referred to

since he has not yet been named.) We are shown an
arrogant and pompous man who seems to have promoted
an unsuitable man to be his deputy. The audience has
nothing to measure this view against.
• What effect do you think this has on the audience?
lines 88–91
Iago presents us (and Brabantio) with a gross sexual image
of 'The Moor'.
• How does this affect the audience's assessment of
Othello?

2 **Act 1 Scene 2**
lines 6 and 17–28
At his first appearance, Othello seems confident and open
– very sure of himself and of his worth to Venice.
• Since Iago has told us he is arrogant, do you think this
view might confirm what he has said?
lines 59–61
Almost immediately we see his utter confidence in his
ability to command a situation.
• How would you describe his tone: arrogant,
contemptuous, authoritative?
lines 83–84
Othello declares his knowledge of when to fight and when
not to.
lines 62–63
Brabantio accuses Othello of being a thief and a
practitioner of black magic.
• What is the audience's view of Othello at this stage in
the play?

3 **Act 1 Scene 3**
lines 49–50
The Duke greets Othello as 'valiant' – the man to lead the
Christian Venetians against the infidel Turks.
lines 77–95, 115–121, 128–170
We hear Othello declare his readiness to tell the senators
everything openly, his trust in Desdemona, and the story
of his life which he believes won her heart. It is important

to 'listen' to his tone and style.
• Is he performing?
• Is he over-confident?
• Is he a great man aware of his greatness?
• Is he humble, open and honest?
• Does he like the sound of his own voice, or does he think of himself as unsophisticated ('rude') in present company and therefore is trying hard to speak in a stately way?

lines 247–253
Consider the way Desdemona speaks of her love.

4 **Act 2 Scene 1**
lines 178–188
Look at Othello's rapturous language here.
• Does he sound as confident as he did in Act 1?
• Is this a 'new' Othello?
• What are his feelings about love as he is experiencing it?

lines 202, 285 and 289–290
Notice Iago's contrasting views of Othello as good husband and adulterer.

5 **Act 2 Scene 3**
line 6
Othello reveals his trust in Iago for the first time ('most honest').

lines 165–171
He shows his sense of 'Christian shame', his concern for the 'propriety' of Cyprus and, again, his trust in Iago.
• Do you think he still seems to be the man who can deal easily and confidently with this kind of riotous situation?

lines 197–200
• Do you think he is using the threat of anger as a deliberate method of investigation, or do you think he does feel that he could lose control of his temper? (Again, it is vital to 'listen' to the tone and style of his words.)

lines 306–307
Notice Iago's view, as offered to Cassio, that Desdemona commands Othello.
• Although we know Iago has his own motives for saying this, might there be any truth in his view?

6 Act 3 Scene 3
   lines 76 and 83
   Othello repeats his utter commitment to Desdemona.
   lines 90–92
   He declares, in extraordinary language, the power and
   fragility of his love.
   • What is the effect of 'Excellent wretch' and the ideas of
     'Perdition' and 'Chaos'?
   lines 118–124
   He reveals the depth of his trust in Iago, whose thoughts
   are frightening.
   • What is happening to his confidence?
   lines 154, 161, 164, 170
   His insistence on knowing Iago's thoughts leads to
   outbursts of almost wordless distress.
   lines 175–191
   • What is the effect of his claim not to be jealous and to
     trust Desdemona?
   line 212
   Iago's declaration of 'too much loving' Othello, leads to
   his powerful commitment to him.
   • What are the implications of his use of the word
     'bound'?
   lines 241–242 and 256–275
   Now, at the heart of this pivotal scene, Othello is given
   two soliloquies in which his love for Desdemona changes
   to loathing and his trust in Iago is absolute. 'Listen' to
   these speeches. They are key revelations of the way his
   mind is working.
   • How do you interpret the change in him?
   lines 333–355
   He is now emotionally tortured and, in this state, claims
   that he would be happier if he were ignorant of her
   infidelity (343–345), before announcing (345–355) the
   loss of the balance of his mind. Look carefully at the way
   he expresses this.
   • What does it tell you about the way he experienced
     tranquillity of mind?

• What also does it tell you about him that he is so certain of this loss?

lines 358, 429, 440–448, 451–460, 467–471 and 473–476

Finally he moves into a new mode of demanding 'ocular' proof, decisively blowing away his love, and committing himself to Desdemona's and Cassio's death, promoting Iago to take the latter's place. 'Listen' again to the way he expresses all these decisive thoughts.

• What is the tone and style?
• What do you understand about him now?

7 **Act 3 Scene 4**
lines 35–41
Notice the 'tortured' language Othello uses in describing Desdemona's hand.

• What do you interpret about the way he views her from this description?

line 92
• What has happened that he should exit so violently? (Earlier, he said he would deny her nothing.)

8 **Act 4 Scene 1**
line 167
Othello has not seen what is actually happening with Cassio and Bianca.

• Is he seeing what he wants to see, what Iago persuades him he is seeing, or is he deluded in some way?

line 206
When Iago has persuaded Othello not to poison Desdemona but to strangle her, Othello is pleased at 'the justice' of this.

• In what way do you think he means 'justice'?

line 235
• Why do you think he strikes Desdemona and calls her 'Devil'?

lines 247–255
• How does his language show how his inner world has disturbed his 'public' role?

9 **Act 4 Scene 2**
   lines 65–68
   • As Othello confronts Desdemona, what conflict in the
     way he sees her do we see tearing him apart?
   lines 88–89
   For the first time he directly accuses her of being a whore.
10 **Act 5 Scene 2**
   lines 1–22
   Othello, looking at the sleeping Desdemona, contemplates
   the fact that he is going to kill her.
   • Is this the language of the Othello who was so sure of
     himself at the start of the play? ('Listen' to the tone,
     style and rhythm.)
   lines 92–102
   • How does he react once he has done the deed and
     Emilia is banging on the door?
   • Does he seem like a man who has done justice?
   lines 232–233
   • When he has discovered that Iago has misled him, he
     attacks him physically rather than resorting to words.
     What do you make of this?
   lines 257–273
   • What do his words tell us about what he now realises
     about himself?
   • What is his tone?
   lines 334–352
   • What do you understand about his final frame of mind
     and the tone and style with which he describes himself?

A key question about Othello is to what extent you regard
him as responsible for what happens. The way you answer
this will affect the way in which you view the play as a whole.
Other questions to ask are:
• Is Othello a tragic figure?
• Is Othello a fool to believe Iago?
• Even if Iago is very convincing, why is Othello's response
  so sudden and so extreme?

- He himself says he will lose control of himself if he falls out of love. So why does he?
- What is Iago's power?
- To Othello it must seem that Iago is simply (honestly?) revealing the truth. But what do we see?

The final question on character: Iago
- What sort of character is Iago?
- Does he develop?

At the start of the play he tells Roderigo that he hates Othello and why. At the end of Act 1, and at the ends of Act 2 Scenes 1 and 3, he repeats and develops these feelings and motives for the audience. Thereafter, he pushes his stated aims until he is exposed.

- Is he merely Shakespeare's 'tool' to make the plot work?
- Is he a character who changes or is revealed in more depth?
- If you were the actor playing Iago, how would you understand him?

Plot: action and dramatic structure

A play is constructed – that is to say the action is ordered and organised – to achieve two principal aims:

- To tell the story in a way that will keep the audience wanting to know more until the writer is ready to deliver the outcome.
- To explore and develop the themes the writer chooses to bring alive through the words, motives, actions and interactions of the characters.

It is important to remember that, in *Othello*, Shakespeare is delivering a tragedy: we need to have a sense that disaster awaits, even if, no matter how many times we see the play, we go on hoping it won't! You might find it useful to consider the action and dramatic structure of *Othello* in three different, but complementary ways.

1 Organisation of the plot

Consider how Shakespeare has organised and developed the action so that the tragic story unfolds clearly and effectively. (Although Shakespeare did not give his plays act and scene numbers, it will be convenient to use these terms here.) Look at the descriptions of Setting, Character and Problem for each act:

Setting

- How has Shakespeare used the setting in order to focus the themes of his drama?

Character

- Look at the way Shakespeare presents Othello in each act: how has he ensured that this character is the main focus of the act and the play overall?

Problem

- By what means and how clearly does Shakespeare present the problems? How does he make us interested in their outcome?

Act 1

Setting: Venice – supposedly a bastion of civilisation and Christian belief; threatened by the Turkish infidels.
Character: Othello is the outsider whose military prowess all Venice looks to for its protection; he seems self-assured in every way; Othello and Desdemona seem genuinely in love.
Problem: Desdemona's father, a leading Venetian, is horrified that his daughter has been seduced by Othello using (he thinks) uncivilised black magic; his complaint is ignored because of the national emergency. Public affairs overrule private problems.

Act 2

Setting: Cyprus – the characters have survived the hazards of the storm at sea which has destroyed the Turkish fleet. Cyprus seems to be at peace, and is invited by Othello to celebrate the Turkish defeat and his own marriage.

Character: Othello seems to have lost his role since there is now no threat to the island; there are hints that he is not as self-assured as he seemed.

Problem: order on the island is threatened from within by the drunken brawling of Othello's lieutenant Cassio. Othello deals with this by dismissing him.

Act 3

Setting: still Cyprus, but this act mostly has the feel of a private rather than a public world.

Character: Othello changes rapidly and violently from commanding officer to jealous husband; he trusts his new lieutenant, Iago, more than his wife; the order of Othello's mind is descending into chaos; the monster of jealousy emerges; love turns to loathing.

Problem: Desdemona has no idea what has happened to Othello. She innocently pursues Cassio's reinstatement.

Act 4

Setting: still Cyprus – the private conflict is exposed to public scrutiny.

Character: Othello suffers physical collapse, fails to see Cassio, Desdemona and others in a true light, and commits himself to the killing of Cassio and Desdemona.

Problem: will Emilia, Roderigo, Lodovico or anyone discover Iago's plots in time?

Act 5

Setting: still Cyprus – the public street and the private bedroom: private plots disturb public order/public concern breaks in on private horror.

Character: Othello discovers his folly only after he has justly (as he sees it) killed his wife. He tries to present an orderly view of himself before taking his own life.

Problem: Iago is not exposed until too late – whereupon he kills his wife. The commander of Cyprus kills first his wife and then himself.

2 Iago and the audience

As Iago plots the destruction of Othello, Desdemona and Cassio, he takes the audience into his confidence. In a way, we are fellow conspirators – fascinated and horrified as we watch the characters struggle in a web of lies they do not know exists. In this way, Shakespeare gives us a strong sense of fate: the characters believe they are acting from choice, but seem to us to be in the grip of a fatal momentum.

Act 1

We learn of Iago's hatred for Othello, and see his ability to manipulate others (e.g. Roderigo). We see that it is his knowledge of others' characters which gives him his power. We are drawn into his appalling plot:

Hell and night
Must bring this monstrous birth to the world's light.
(last words of Act 1)

Act 2

We see Iago observing the others (e.g. Cassio and Desdemona) and plotting his opportunities. He begins to put them into practice (e.g. by getting Cassio drunk).
'Tis here but yet confused:
Knavery's plain face is never seen till used.
(last words of Act 2, Scene 1)

Ay, that's the way!
Dull not device by coldness and delay.
(last words of Act 2, Scene 3)

Act 3

We see Iago go directly to work on Othello, cleverly provoking and playing on his suspicions – and making the most of the opportunity of the handkerchief. He no longer needs to say much directly though he does explain his plans and hopes for the handkerchief. Look at the whole speech at **Act 3 Scene 3 (319–331)**, but note especially the words 'This may do something'. Iago knows he cannot actually control the other characters completely. His final words to Othello to end the scene are heavy with irony in our ears: 'I am your own for ever.'

Act 4

We see Iago as a kind of ringmaster or puppeteer. Cassio and Bianca behave as they choose, but Othello sees and hears as Iago wants him to see and hear. Iago has no need to address us at all – his plot has gained a life of its own. Can he control it?

Act 5

> This is the night
> That either makes me or fordoes me quite.
> (last words of Act 5, Scene 1)

Iago tells us that the outcome of the brawl he is setting up should benefit him whoever is killed. In fact, at last, events turn against him and both Cassio and Roderigo provide evidence against him. When he is finally exposed, he decides to renounce his lethal weapon – words:

> What you know, you know.
> From this time forth I never will speak word.
> (last words of Act 5, Scene 2)

It is important to remember that Iago is not, finally, in control. Just as his plotting depends on his quick thinking and his skill with words, so, in the end, he is at the mercy of events.

Consider the following questions about Iago:

1 To what extent is Iago
  • a character in the play like any other?
  • a device of Shakespeare's to make the plot work?
  • an embodiment of evil and malice?
  • entertaining and exciting?
  • repulsive and a figure of hate?

2 To what extent is the other characters' discovery of Iago's responsibility for the tragedy the end of the plot?

3 Pivotal point

It is too simple to say that a complex play pivots around a turning point because no one point has any dramatic force without what comes before and after. However, you might like to examine the idea that **lines 35–36 of Act 3 Scene 3** are the turning point of this play. Cassio has just left.

> *Iago:* Ha! I like not that.
> *Othello:*   What dost thou say?

Soon after this, Othello and Desdemona bid each other farewell. Up until this point, there has been no hint of suspicion, mistrust or jealousy in Othello. After this, Othello's suspicions become obsessive until he kills her.

Try to decide how you would dramatise lines 29–44 around this turning point. Such an activity will enable you to explore your ideas about the relationship between Othello and Iago and the whole question of responsibility for the tragedy.

Language and imagery

If you have not already done so, it will help you to follow the advice for language study at the end of each act. What follows are some guidelines for looking at the significance of some aspects of the play's language.

1 Vocabulary

There are some words, often quite simple, which Shakespeare uses frequently in ways which give them an increasing significance as the play develops. Here are some examples for you to explore. Consider how they reflect on the person using them and what they reveal about his/her attitude to the person spoken about. Notice how often there is an element of unintended irony in their use.

(a) honest, honesty, honour, honourable, good, true, truly
(b) dishonest, villain, villainy, knave, slave, dog, devil, gross.

You may also notice how often characters refer or appeal to 'heaven' (or 'hell'), and are concerned about 'soul'. The frequency of this simple vocabulary makes it clear how much the play is concerned with human and divine values.

A comparison of a speech of Iago's with one of Othello's will reveal differences in characters' vocabularies.

2 Language and character

One aspect of the playwright's skill is to create a language, or style of speech, for each character according to the dramatic needs of the moment. In Shakespeare, the actor has very little but the language to base his/her interpretation on: the character **is** the language.

(a) Compare Othello's speech in **Act 1 Scene 3** in which he tells his life story (and how he won Desdemona) with Iago's soliloquy at the end of the same scene. Notice how the former has a sense of order – almost as if it were rehearsed – and yet is full of feeling. By contrast, notice how Iago's gives the sense of a mind working things out and arriving at an exciting conclusion.
(b) Consider the range of language of Othello. Use the references given under **Character development: Othello** to see how Shakespeare reveals character through language.
   • In **Act 1**, Othello conveys great self-confidence, trust and

control through the stately style of his speech.
- In **Act 2**, he conveys his utter happiness with Desdemona, coupled with a sense that this cannot last. We are also given a hint of his capacity to lose control of his temper.
- In **Acts 3 and 4**, we hear his speech break up into exclamations and crude outbursts under the pressure of his jealous obsession.
- In **Act 5**, in the final scene, we hear echoes of his early style as first he expresses his sense of the justice of murdering Desdemona, and finally as he tries to retain control of how he will be remembered after he is dead.

(c) Consider in a similar way, the references given for the four characters in **Critical moments**. Note particularly:
- Cassio's elaborate poetry on the arrival of Desdemona at Cyprus, and his sense of shame expressed to Iago in prose after he has been dismissed.
- The utter simplicity of Desdemona's speech throughout the play, but especially in her declarations of love and faith in her husband, and at her death.

3 Poetic language and imagery

In poetic drama, it is the poetic language which conveys the ways in which the writer's imagination is working. Through poetry, he hopes to engage the minds and imaginations of his audience so that they will think and feel more intensely. As with vocabulary (see above), poetic language is often developed through the play by more than one speaker so that it acquires more and more significance and interest. Here are some examples:

Animal lust

At the start of the play (Act 1 Scene 1 88–89), Iago calls up to Brabantio in the dark ' ... an old black ram/Is tupping your white ewe'. At this point, we know very little about the characters involved, or their motives. However the image is very striking in itself: 'black' and 'white' have the connotations of evil and good as well as racial difference, and 'tupping' is a term more usually applied in farming: it implies that sex is something a male does to a female in lust not love. The idea that the ram is 'old' adds to the grotesqueness of the image.

As the play develops, we learn that Iago nearly always speaks of lust not love, and in crude terms. Is Shakespeare implying that Iago is disgusted by sex? Or is he himself frustrated and obsessed? Or is this merely the way soldiers talk?

In Act 2 Scene 3, while Cassio speaks of Desdemona as 'a most exquisite lady' and 'delicate creature', Iago refers to her as 'sport for Jove' and 'full of game'. In mythology, Jove was depicted as taking the form of various animals in order to have sex with beautiful females. The idea that a woman is 'sport' or 'game' (for sex) has little to do with love – and maybe a lot to do with male fantasy.

In Act 3 Scene 3, Othello has insisted Iago provide him with 'ocular proof' of Desdemona's affair with Cassio. In lines 392–394, Iago is asking Othello whether he really wants to see them having sex and echoes his image in Act 1 Scene 1: 'Would you, the supervisor, grossly gape on/Behold her topped?' 'Topped' is very close to 'tupped' and has the same implication. Iago goes on to explain how difficult it would be to watch them, even if they were so rampant as to be completely careless (400–401): 'It is impossible you should see this,/Were they as prime as goats, as hot as monkeys ...'

Even though Othello never sees Desdemona and Cassio having sex, we understand how receptive he is to Iago's image and how deranged he is by it. From the start of Act 4 Othello is tormented by images of nakedness and of a man (Cassio) on top of a woman (Desdemona). Later, after striking Desdemona in front of Lodovico, he politely invites Lodovico to supper, only to exit with a cry of 'Goats and monkeys!' In Act 4 Scene 2, he tells Emilia to 'leave procreants alone'. The term 'procreants' implies that husband and wife are merely breeders.

In Act 5 Scene 2, when Emilia is insisting on Desdemona's innocence, Othello states baldly: 'Cassio did top her' (some texts have 'tup'). Iago's crude image has so infected Othello that, for him, it is the truth.

The sea

In Act 1 Scene 2, Othello explains that, but for the love of Desdemona, he would never give up his freedom to roam 'for the sea's worth'. He speaks of the sea as a huge natural power which he would not wish to have if it meant losing his freedom.

At the start of Act 2, the 'real' sea destroys the Turkish fleet, but, ominously, Cassio says he has 'lost' Othello's ship 'on a dangerous sea'. In the same scene, Cassio expresses confidence that Othello's ship will survive the storm because it is 'stoutly timbered' and has a good pilot; later, when Desdemona comes ashore, he claims that the 'high seas' and 'guttered rocks and congregated sands' have been influenced by 'divine' Desdemona's beauty to keep her safe. (Ironically, it also keeps Iago safe on the same ship.) The sea seems a force for good, destroying enemies and preserving friends.

However, in the first act, we find the storm being used as an image of violent emotional turmoil. Brabantio, shocked at his daughter's seduction by Othello, says:

> For my particular grief
> Is of so floodgate and o'erbearing nature
> That it engluts and swallows other sorrows,
> And yet is still itself.

Later, Desdemona (ironically) speaks of her 'storm' of love.

In Act 3 Scene 3 (451–458), Othello uses an image of the sea to describe his 'bloody thoughts' and the fact that they are so irresistibly powerful that they will not cease until 'a capable and wide revenge' has been achieved. The sea is a force beyond man's power to control – and yet Othello speaks of it here almost as if he had deliberately turned it on.

Suggestions for further exploration of language

1 Iago first speaks the word 'jealousy' and calls it 'the green-eyed monster' (Act 3 Scene 3, 165). Study how the words 'monster' and 'monstrous' are used through the play. What are their implications?

2 Cassio tries to provide music (Act 3 Scene 1) to appeal to Othello after his wedding night. Desdemona sings (Act 4 Scene 3). What musical metaphors can you find in the play? How are they used and to what effect?

3 In Act 3 Scene 3, Othello swears 'by yond marble heaven'. In Act 4 Scene 1, he says his heart is turned to 'stone'. In Act 5 Scene 2, he sees Desdemona's sleeping body as 'smooth as monumental alabaster'. How do you interpret these 'stony' images?

4 Pay attention to all images which embody ideas of control and loss of control, order and chaos.

4 Significance

It may well be that, for a modern audience, the poetic language will not have its full impact after one viewing of the play. Teachers are often told they are reading too much into a text! However, as we study the play on the page, we can become aware that there are patterns in the use of language which convey a developing imaginative significance to which people may react in different ways.

Themes

If a play is to work successfully, its themes will not seem abstract or theoretical because they will be seen in the form of 'real' issues in the 'lives' of the characters, and will be explored through parallel and contrasting experiences.

As has been suggested earlier, the play seems to focus on the tragic consequences of a group of characters coming together in a fatal combination. Perhaps the play does not explore 'universal' themes to the extent to which *Hamlet* or *King Lear* do. What it does offer are extreme human emotions, and a questioning of the idea that a civilised society is orderly and secure.

1 Belief, trust and 'seeming'

The plot depends on characters fatally giving their trust. It also depends on characters believing the way things seem to them, when the audience knows the situation to be otherwise. Consider the following questions –

- Why do Roderigo, Cassio and Othello trust Iago? Why does he seem 'honest' to them?
- Why does Othello believe Iago's stories and innuendoes about Cassio and interpret Cassio's behaviour with Iago and Bianca (Act 4 Scene 1) in the way he does?
- Why does Desdemona continue to trust Othello even after he has struck her?
- Does Emilia trust her husband? What are the implications of your answer to this question?

2 Love and jealousy

It is common in Shakespeare studies to say that *Othello* is a tragedy of jealousy. You should question this. Iago first uses the word, warning Othello to 'beware the green-eyed monster'. Othello says he is not a jealous man. Desdemona says the same. Emilia explains that 'jealous souls' are 'jealous for they're jealous' – there is no cause. Think about these questions:

- What understanding do you have of the love between Othello and Desdemona?
- How can Othello just blow it away?
- Why is he so consumed with desire to kill Desdemona – and to use his own bare hands to do it?
- Is it enough to say, simply, he is a 'jealous soul'?
- What views of love and jealousy is the play offering?

As part of this study, it would be interesting to pursue the question of hate. Iago professes hatred of Othello. Othello believes he must loathe Desdemona.

3 Order and chaos

The play depicts a Venetian state which believes it represents Christian order against the threat of Turkish infidels. At the same time, a senator, Brabantio, believes his idea of Venetian order has been disrupted by the black man – the very man charged with fighting the Turks – who has seduced his daughter by black magic. At Cyprus, natural chaos in the form of the storm at sea destroys the enemy and seems to favour the Venetians. However, their order is threatened from within by a drunken street brawl – but Othello restores order by dismissing his newly appointed lieutenant. There is a hint that Othello may lose his self-control.

In Act 3, we are presented with the sight of Othello, so far the effective and dignified commander and loving husband, thrown into emotional chaos. As Desdemona faithfully sticks to her belief in love and marriage, the consequences of Othello's mental chaos engulf them both. In Acts 1 and 2, Othello quells street brawls. In Act 5 he watches, hoping that Cassio will be killed. In the two scenes of Act 5, public and private situations are the scenes for the coming together of public and private chaos.

• To what extent is order restored?

Brabantio thought that Othello, the black outsider, was the source of disorder. He prophesied that Desdemona had betrayed him and would betray Othello.

• Do you see things this way?
• Or do you think the cause of chaos is the Venetian, Iago?
• How secure is civilised Christian order in the face of powerful individual emotions?

4 Good and evil, heaven and hell

Throughout the play, questions are raised about who is good, honest, true, honourable – and who or what is evil.

At the end of Act 3 Scene 3, Othello, a professed Christian, swears 'by yond marble heaven' that his 'bloody thoughts' will never turn back until a 'wide revenge' has been accomplished. In Act 5 Scene 2, he believes that he is an agent of justice in killing Desdemona. He believes he must resist the distraction of her almost irresistible beauty. From the moment his uncertainties are aroused, he is not sure whether she is angel or whore. The play seems to ask the question: 'If Christian judgement can be perverted so totally by powerful emotions and if evil can work so effectively through vulnerable emotions and insecure characters, how secure is any belief or any sense of good?'

5 Race

In the original preparation of this edition, no consideration of race as a theme was offered – i.e. it was not thought that the play focused on race as an issue, even though Othello's race is the object of Iago's and Brabantio's scorn and disgust. Venetian society – as represented in the play by the Duke, Cassio, Montano, and other leading figures – respects him highly. The play does not depict Othello as a victim of a racist society.

Further consideration, however, led to the idea that race might be a theme for the modern student because we are studying the play with modern perceptions. We live in an age of great sensitivity to matters of race – race is always an issue (like gender). In support of this, we might instance the fact that Othello, when his self-confidence has been undermined, wonders whether the fact that he is black may have been the cause of the infidelity of which he believes Desdemona to be guilty.

What do you think? Is Othello's race the focus of a theme in the play, or is it our modern concern about race that might lead us to see this? Is Shakespeare using Othello's colour contrasted with Desdemona's 'whiteness' symbolically, especially in the death scene? Might Othello's race merely mark him as an outsider in the drama? At the end of the play, do we feel race has been a central issue?

(The aspect of race is considered further in the next section – **Contexts**.)

Contexts

Our understanding of literature is bound to be enriched if we know and understand something about the contexts in which the play was written and performed. Since the time when Shakespeare wrote his plays, readers and performers have been finding them relevant to their own times and others. Productions of the plays have been set in all sorts of historical and social contexts. However, we are better able to understand the texts we have if we know something about their topicality for Shakespeare, his actors and audience.

It is not possible in this book to provide detailed material for the wide range of contexts of a Shakespeare play. We can, however, indicate broad areas where students would benefit from further research. We can break 'contexts' down into four categories.

1 Historical and political

Shakespeare sets *Othello* in a particular historical context. During the sixteenth century, Venice had become the supreme trading state of what we now call Europe; for Shakespeare, it seems to represent an extremely self-confident state, secure in its belief in its own civilisation and Christianity. Venice was very rich, very influential, and saw itself as a leader in the conflict between civilised Christianity and barbarism. Shakespeare uses conflict between Venice (Christian) and the Turks (barbarian) as the 'public' context for his drama. How do the Christian Venetians behave in the play?

Thus, Cyprus becomes the focal point of commercial and religious conflict between Venetians and Turks, and, when the Turkish threat is destroyed, between Venetians themselves as their civilised order breaks down as a result of the uncivilised passions of Iago and Othello.

2 Social and religious

(a) Shakespeare chose to write a tragedy about a black man in a position of power in a white European society. Some people believed myths about black people, including the idea that they were beasts or subhuman, evil, in touch with the devil and the black arts. Brabantio's response to Othello **(Act 1)**, fuelled by Iago's animosity towards him **(Acts 1 and 2)**, is very significant in showing us how racial difference is an easy target for those with hatred in their hearts. Shakespeare, however, does not allow his audience to see Othello as Iago and Brabantio describe him. Othello is given almost excessively 'civilised' language and a commanding presence which he uses to preserve civil order.

(b) Social status and background are important features of the motivation of Iago, the instigator or catalyst of the drama. In Shakespeare's time, order in society was believed to depend on hierarchies which were perceived as part of the order of nature. Iago threatens the hierarchy (the army) of which he is a part by wanting to destroy Othello and remove Cassio. Shakespeare makes this situation far more interesting and problematic by making the top of the hierarchy a black outsider, and the lieutenant a highly educated outsider from Florence – this at a time when Italy did not exist as a single nation, but was a country of competing city states. At various points in **Acts 1 and 2**, Iago gives his reasons for hating 'the Moor'. What are they? In what ways are they focused on race, rank and status? We also learn of his contempt for Cassio. Why does he despise Cassio? What do his reasons have to do with background and education? Answers to these questions will reveal Shakespeare's use of conventional contemporary attitudes and social values.

(c) We have already seen – in (1) above – that Shakespeare uses the Christian/barbarian conflict as part of his broad historical context. However, in **Act 5 Scene 2**, the final dialogue between Othello and Desdemona concerns the fate of Desdemona's soul after death. As he has in *Hamlet*, Shakespeare shows us a contemporary belief that the soul could never rest unless its sins had been forgiven. Othello urges Desdemona to pray because he says he 'would not kill [her] soul'. As the scene continues, we hear Emilia describe Desdemona as 'angel' and Othello as 'devil' – both supernatural entities which contemporary audiences were used to hearing about.

(d) In **Act 4 Scene 3**, we see Desdemona presenting her view of a woman's role in marriage. As we have also seen earlier, she is concerned to explain Othello's treatment of her as the result of some external problem or a fault in herself. She is utterly committed to uncritical faith in her husband. While she expresses, and tries, tragically, to live by, these principles, Emilia takes a much more sceptical view of men, marriage and the fate of women.

(e) Cassio is the character who best represents conventional ideals of honour – he is, perhaps, a character who echoes the knightly ideals of chivalry of a bygone age. In **Act 2 Scene 3**, we see him in a state of utter distress because he has lost his 'reputation'. This is the quality we might call respectability – a concern to be seen and known as trustworthy, polite and chivalrous.

3 Theatrical

(a) Contemporary. – The theatre was not a 'holy' place, treated with respect or reverence. The audience was not quiet, but responsive, enthusiastic and critical. The actors were familiar and had learned very precise skills and mannerisms to convey

the characters' passions. Shakespeare was demanding a
particularly powerful 'play of passions' from the actor
playing Othello, whom he would have known well. Which
would have been the most popular bits? When might
Othello have 'brought the house down'? Which other
characters might have done so? It is a fair bet that
Desdemona's 'return to life' might have done so. We will
never know the answers to such speculations, but it is worth
thinking about this original style of performance and what
kind of experience it was.

- It was the convention of the theatre that plays were about
  people of high status, probably because they were
  perceived to inhabit a more exciting world, just as our
  modern media focus on the rich and powerful, famous and
  infamous.
- Before Othello appears, he is referred to as 'the Moor' –
  i.e. as a racial type. Shakespeare presents the audience with
  the unexpected: a black man as hero and Christian, and a
  white man as villain. It is fascinating to try to imagine the
  impact of this juxtaposition on the Elizabethan stage,
  especially when Othello's jealousy erupts at a point when
  sympathy for him and his marriage have been established.

(b) Modern. – In a modern theatre, the performance of a
tragedy is given an automatic hushed respect – almost a
reverence. Although, in a good production, there is intense
two-way communication between actors and audience, there
is little direct or spontaneous interaction. Modern audiences,
as a generality, are perhaps less attuned to listening intently
to rich language. It is worth thinking about what this says
about our attitudes to theatre, and whether what we now
see as 'Shakespeare' is as his work was originally performed.

- A modern audience may be aware of racial matters in a
  different way from Shakespeare's audience. For instance,
  the Royal Shakespeare Company and the Royal National
  Theatre have decided that only black actors will play the
  part of Othello in future. What do you think might have
  been their reasons for this? Is it racist to say that a good

actor cannot play Othello because he is white? This then becomes a decision about acting, not race. Indeed, the part was written for a white actor. But perhaps, for the modern audience, the issue of racism is more clearly defined by seeing a black actor in the role.

4 The drama of Shakespeare and his contemporaries

(a) The idea of tragedy. Shakespeare was living and writing at a time when the classical civilisations of Greece and Rome were being re-discovered. Tragedy was the high literary form of the Greeks, and Shakespeare was influenced by this. Aristotle's theoretical exploration of tragedy was known in Shakespeare's day, and it is reasonable to assume that Shakespeare would have read or heard about it. However, he was developing his own style of tragedy and the main interest (in this context) of finding out about Aristotle's observations of successful Greek tragedies is to see that Shakespeare's are different.

 • A Greek tragedy, typically, would be given a strong sense of fate (the hero, whatever he does to avoid it, is doomed to die) through the involvement of the gods in the drama. How does Shakespeare give his play a sense of fate? You can develop your ideas about Shakespearean tragedy by looking at how he does this in his other tragedies – especially *Macbeth, King Lear*, and *Hamlet.*

 • Aristotle observed, for instance, that successful tragedies had a 'unity' of time, place and action – i.e. that they took place at one time (about the length of the play), in one place and with a single plot. This would certainly provide focus and intensity. But what does Shakespeare do in *Othello?*

(b) Shakespeare set another play in Venice – the 'comedy' of *The Merchant of Venice* – which focuses on another 'outsider' character, the Jew, Shylock. In this play, the power and prejudice of Christian Venice are ranged against the Jew. Although Shakespeare was again drawing on conventional stereotypical attitudes to Jews, and portrayed Shylock as a bitter and vengeful man, he uses this scenario to question the justice of this Christian society.

Writing an essay

There is rarely a 'right' answer to an A-level essay question. However, there is not an infinite range of sensible responses to a text, and any interpretation must be clearly based on close reading and supporting evidence. This is a fairly typical A-level question:

How do you interpret the character and role of Desdemona in Othello?

The challenge of every exam essay is fourfold:
- to take an intelligent view of the text as a whole
- to show a detailed knowledge of the text, its language and action
- to focus the essay on the question
- to write a clear and purposefully structured essay.

The essay printed below was written under examination conditions – i.e. it had a time limit of 50 minutes and there was no copy of the text or other notes or preparation permitted. It was not written in a 'real' exam, but was exam practice. It attempts to address the four 'challenges' quite well, and would probably obtain around a B grade.

  Read it, and assess its strengths and weaknesses, paying particular attention to the four 'challenges'. What would you add/alter/remove?

If any character in *Othello* embodies goodness, it is Desdemona. In simple terms, she appears to be the antithesis of all the evil and malice that is represented by Iago. Yet she is not a completely 'flat' character – Shakespeare gives to her certain

characteristics and human qualities that
result in her being a far deeper and more
interesting character. Much of the interest in
her is owing to the fact that each character
in the plot appears to have his/her own
impression and opinion of her, and that, in
some cases – not least Othello himself – this
impression is altered as the play unfolds.

It would be natural to think that her own
father, Brabantio, would have the truest and
most accurate opinion of Desdemona. However,
it would be equally natural to think that a
father would have a rose-tinted impression,
his vision coloured by love for his daughter.
The latter is the case with Brabantio. He
describes Desdemona as 'unhappy girl', which
is rather ironic given that she has just
married the man of her choice. Brabantio sees
her as 'a maiden never bold,/Of spirit so
still and quiet that her motion/Blushed at
herself'. Although he claims that she is so
modest that she would blush at her own
passions and desires, he may well here be
indicating unwittingly the strength of these
hitherto suppressed desires.

Brabantio regards his daughter as an
innocent child, who has been stolen by a
'lascivious' Othello, the 'foul thief' who
'hast enchanted her'. He believes that 'she is
abused, stol'n from me, and corrupted/By
spells and medicines'. This view is similar to
that apparently held by Iago – although who
can say what Iago really thought? He describes
Desdemona as the innocent party and Othello as
the 'Barbary horse', the devil incarnate, the
'old black ram (that)/Is tupping your white
ewe'.

Closely linked with Desdemona's innocence –
that is with her moral fairness – is her
physical fairness, described elegantly in
Cassio's courteous verse as 'a maid/That
paragons description and wild fame,/One that
excels the quirks of blazoning pens,/And in
th'essential vesture of creation/Does tire the
ingener'. Even in the light of Cassio's
tendency to speak with copious amounts of
hyperbole, Desdemona's beauty is undeniable.
Ironically, it is her beauty and the praise
she receives for it that eventually leads to
her tragic downfall.

However, Desdemona's character is deeper
than her skin-deep beauty and innocence.
Shakespeare gives her a far more human form,
a form that allows her to be wooed by the
warlike Othello, whose life had been dominated
by 'all quality,/Pride, pomp, and circumstance
of glorious war'. She appears not to be the
innocent girl, blushing at the thought of such
marital activity, but rather 'she'd come again
(i.e. back from her domestic chores), and with
a greedy ear/Devour up my discourse'. By the
very fact that she is prepared against the
wishes of her father to elope with a soldier
– and, moreover, a black soldier – one can
see that she is not simply the 'white ewe'
that Brabantio sees. In fact, Brabantio even
comes to realise Desdemona's potential for
independent action when he warns
prophetically, 'Look at her, Moor, if thou
hast eyes to see,/She has deceived her father,
and may thee'.

This less flat image, this image of a mature
young lady who can act from her own

initiative, is further reinforced when she
shows herself quite capable of presenting
herself in the council chamber, before the Duke
and all the assembled senators, and speaking up
for herself in a direct and yet still elegant
manner. She shows a great sense of duty and
respect towards the two men in her life. She
sees her 'noble father' as 'the lord of duty'
to whom she is 'bound for life and education'.
She goes on to say that she is required to
follow her late mother's example and place her
husband above her father. Therefore, she 'may
profess (her faith)/Due to the Moor my lord'.
An indication of the faith she inspires in
people, not least in Othello, is given in the
Moor's highly ironic words, 'My life upon her
faith'.

Yet, in contrast to these ideas that
Desdemona's character is one of honesty and
clearness, her reputation is constantly being
undermined by the sordid allegations of Iago.
This master of manipulation and malice attempts
to instil in the mind of Roderigo the
impression that Desdemona is simply a common
prostitute who will quickly tire of the Moor
and make herself available for Roderigo. Iago
persuades his companion to 'put money in thy
purse' by convincing him that 'it cannot be
long that Desdemona should continue her love to
the Moor … She must change for youth. When she
is sated with his body, she will find the error
of her choice'. Iago also manages to create a
false impression of Desdemona in the mind of
Othello, convincing him that she is a 'lewd
minx', the 'Devil' and the 'cunning whore of
Venice'.

It is this deception (and misconception) that

causes Othello to murder his wife. However, Desdemona's deathbed bearing, actions and words reveal her true character. Her sense of confusion is apparent; she does not understand why Othello has turned on her in the way he has: 'I understand the fury in your words,/But not the words'. This, perhaps, demonstrates that she is still the innocent ewe of her father's eye, unprepared for life as a soldier's wife. In addition to being innocent in the sense of being naïve, Desdemona is undoubtedly innocent in the sense of being blameless. Her death is not her fault; as her dying words maintain, 'A guiltless death I die'. This demonstrates how Shakespeare intended her character to be that of the embodiment of goodness. This is re-enforced in the very last words she speaks. When asked by Emilia who it was who had murdered her, Desdemona replies, 'Nobody, I myself. Farewell./Commend me to my kind lord. O, farewell!'. These two lines encompass the characteristics that make up Desdemona: innocence, naïvete, a slowness to blame others and a readiness to accept her death as being the result of her own (imagined, non-existent) faults.

Comments

Strengths

1 The big danger in a character question is to treat the character as 'real' rather than as a component in a drama. The first and second sentences of this essay immediately avoid this danger by stating Desdemona's role in the drama – 'embodiment of goodness' and 'antithesis of all the evil … Iago'. You may not agree with this view, and the point should

in any case be taken further, but it is exactly the kind of start an essay needs because it offers a view of the character in the context of the play as a whole which the essay can go on to explore.

2 The rest of the introductory paragraph emphasises that Desdemona not only has a representative function but also is an individual character of whom it is possible to take a range of views which may alter as the play develops. This point is vital, as the character needs depth and individuality to engage the audience's interest and concern.

3 The main body of the essay (paragraphs 2–7) focuses largely on other characters' views of Desdemona. This is an essential aspect of the discussion because it is how Othello's view of her changes, and how the audience is able to see that he is wrong, that produces the tragic effect.

4 The comments in paragraphs 2 and 3 about Brabantio's mistaken view of this daughter's innocence are crucial, because they serve to show that Desdemona is, in fact, a healthily passionate and sexual woman. (This point needs to be spelt out in the essay.)

5 The definition of Desdemona's innocence (paragraph 4) as 'moral fairness', though not explained, is interesting, because it takes away the implication of naïvete. The next point about 'physical fairness' is also interesting, but not fully explained.

6 Paragraphs 5 and 6 develop the view that Desdemona is a figure of some depth and strength. The amount of detail in support of this is impressive, as is the amount and handling of detail throughout. As elsewhere, the concluding sentence of paragraph 6 does well to point out the irony of Othello's expression of absolute faith.

7 The main body of the essay concludes (paragraph 7) by dealing with the crucially destructive view of Desdemona offered by Iago. It is good to point out how Iago develops his malicious and perverse view of her with Roderigo. The vital point is then made about the fact that he poisons Othello's view of her.

8 The concluding paragraph begins well, logically focusing on

Desdemona's dying words. The view taken of Desdemona can be disputed, but it is a sensible conclusion to this essay, because it follows up well the view taken in its introduction.

9 The essay is simply and clearly organised, working towards a reasonable conclusion, and building to its most significant point just before the conclusion.

2 Aspects to question

(To criticise an essay as full of detailed quotation as this for omitting points when written in such restricted circumstances may seem harsh. However, perhaps the writer was too keen to use the quotations he or she knew, at the expense of developing the argument to its full potential.)

1 The introduction should include some consideration of the tragedy of the play so that the essay can consider Desdemona's role in bringing that about.

2 There needs to be more consideration of Desdemona's own words and actions before her death scene – especially her account of her love for Othello, her action on Cassio's behalf, her view of herself as a wife, and the way she tries to handle and account for Othello's jealousy.

3 The point about Cassio's elaborate description of Desdemona's beauty leading to her tragic downfall needs full explanation. It is the change in Othello (induced by Iago?) that makes him see the fact that she is irresistible to him as a sign that other men will also be unable to resist her which is the cause of the tragic ending.

4 In paragraph 7, too much space is given to Iago's view of Desdemona as expressed to Roderigo. Too little time is given to the crucial point about Iago's influencing of Othello.

5 All conclusions are up for discussion. This one is, perhaps, oversimplified. To call Desdemona naïve and innocent make her sound pale and uninteresting. Goodness is not a weak quality, and the essay, at the end, betrays some of its earlier points, and undervalues the character and, therefore, the power of the drama.

Essay titles

The play as drama

1 To what extent do you find the term 'tragedy' useful in describing the dramatic impact of *Othello?*
2 'Iago is a successful villain; Othello and Desdemona are innocent victims. Such characters are too simplistic for interesting drama.' Discuss.
3 Assess Shakespeare's use of a black 'hero' and a white 'villain' for both contemporary and modern audiences.

Themes

1 How important is the historical setting of Venice, Cyprus and the conflict with the Turks to the overall impact of *Othello?*
2 How does Shakespeare question the idea of Christian civilisation in *Othello?*
3 '*Othello* is a tragedy of vulnerable love.' Discuss.
4 'At the heart of *Othello* are passions – love, hate, jealousy – that cannot be controlled.' Do you agree?
5 'It is trust which brings tragedy in *Othello*.' Discuss.

Character

1 'In the theatre, Iago is far more interesting than Othello.' Explore this idea, showing an awareness of its contemporary and modern applications.
2 In what ways might a contemporary and a modern audience respond differently to the character of Othello?
3 Are Desdemona and Emilia anything more than victims? To what extent do they offer different perspectives on marriage?
4 Assess the significance of Cassio in *Othello*. In your answer you should show an understanding of the significance of his cultural background and his concern for 'reputation'.

Glossary

Alliteration: A figure of speech in which a number of words close to each other in a piece of writing begin with the same sound:

> *... you'll have your nephews neigh to you; you'll have coursers for*
> *cousins, and jennets for germans*
> (Act 1 Scene 1 lines 111–113)

Alliteration helps to draw attention to the words and emphasises rhythmical structures.

Antithesis: A figure of speech in which two opposite or contrasting ideas are brought together, often with rhythmical balance:

> *O thou weed,*
> *who art so lovely fair, and smell'st so sweet*
> (Act 4 Scene 2 lines 66–7)

Apostrophe: When a character speaks directly to someone or something who/which is absent.

> *Patience, thou young and rose-lipped cherubin –*
> *Ay, there look grim as hell.*
> (Act 4 Scene 2 lines 62–3)

Assonance: The repetition of vowel sounds, usually stressed, to reinforce rhythm and mood:

> *O the world hath not a sweeter creature;*
> (Act 4 Scene 1 lines 180–181)

Blank verse: Unrhymed verse in which each line has ten syllables, comprising five 'feet', or measures, of two syllables each. The form of the measures, a short (weak) syllable followed by a long (strong) syllable, is known as an iambus. Thus the main form of the play is unrhymed iambic pentameter:

> *Though in the trade of war I have slain men,*
> *Yet do I hold it very stuff o'th'conscience*

To do no contrived murder: I lack iniquity
(Act 1 Scene 2 lines 1–3)

To avoid monotony and to achieve special effects this basic form of blank verse is varied by a change in the pattern of weak and strong syllables, and/or by altering the number of syllables in a line.

Caesura: A pause within a line of verse. Because of the length of the blank verse or heroic couplet line is often a caesura, which may or may not be marked by punctuation:

Her father loved me, oft invited me,
Still questioned me the story of my life
From year to year – the battles, sieges, fortunes,
That I have passed.
(Act 1 Scene 3 lines 128–131)

Conceit: An extended image in which several points of comparison are developed:

... Like to the Pontic Sea,
Whose icy current and compulsive course
Ne'er feels retiring ebb, but keeps due on
To the Propontic and the Hellespont;
Even so my bloody thoughts with violent pace
Shall ne'er look back, ne'er ebb to humble love,
Till that a capable and wide revenge
Swallow them up
(Act 3 Scene 3 lines 451–458)

Dramatic irony: A situation in a play when the audience (and possibly some of the characters) know something that one or more of the characters do not. In a pantomime, for example, young children will shout to tell the heroine that the villain is creeping up behind her.

CASSIO   *She was here even now; she haunts me in every place. I was*
the other day talking on the sea-bank with certain
Venetians, and thither comes the bauble and, by this hand,
falls me thus about my neck –

OTHELLO   *Crying 'o dear Cassio!' as it were. His gesture imports it.*

CASSIO   *So hangs, and lolls, and weeps upon me; so hales, and pulls me. Ha, ha, ha!*

OTHELLO   *Now he tells how she plucked him to my chamber. O, I see that nose of yours, but not that dog I shall throw it to!*

(Act 4 Scene 1 lines 132–142)

In fact, because Iago reveals his plans to the audience in advance, there is much dramatic irony: the audience is always in possession of information ahead of all the other characters until the very end.

Exeunt: A Latin word meaning 'They go away', used for the departure of characters from a scene.

Exit: A Latin word meaning 'S/he goes away', used for the departure of a character from a scene.

Heroic couplet: A pair of rhyming iambic pentameter lines (see *Blank verse*, above):

If consequence do but approve my dream,
My boat sails freely both with wind and stream.
(Act 2 Scene 3 lines 59–60)

Homophone: A word which has the same sound as another but a different meaning or origin; for example

I know not where he lodges, and for me to devise a lodging, and say he lies here, or he lies there, were to lie in mine own throat.
(Act 3 Scene 4 lines 9–11)

Hyperbole: Deliberate exaggeration, for dramatic effect. For example.

Zounds sir, you're robbed; for shame put on your gown;
Your heart is burst, you have lost half your soul.
(Act 1 Scene 1 lines 86–7)

Irony: When someone says one thing and means another, sometimes with the intention of making fun of, teasing, or satirising someone else.

> EMILIA   *I will be hanged if some eternal villian,*
> *Some busy and insinuating rogue,*
> *Some cogging, cozening slave, to get some office,*
> *Have not devised this slander; I'll be hanged else.*
>
> IAGO   *Fie, there is no such man; it is impossible.*
> (Act 4 Scene 2 lines 129–133)

Metaphor: A figure of speech in which one person, or thing, or idea is described as if it were another.

> *... an old black ram*
> *Is tupping your white ewe.*
> (Act 1 Scene 1 lines 88–9)

Oxymoron: A figure of speech in which the writer combines two ideas which are opposites:

> *fair devil*
> (Act 3 Scene 3 line 476)

Personification: Referring to a thing or an idea as if it were a person.

> *The lethargy must have his quiet course,*
> (Act 4 Scene 1 lines 131–132)

Play on words: see *Pun*

Pun: A figure of speech in which the writer uses a word that has more than one meaning. Both meanings of the word are used to make a joke. For example,

> *If she be black, and thereto have a wit,*
> *She'll find a white that shall her blackness fit.*
> (Act 2 Scene 1 lines 131–132)

Rhymed verse: Sometimes Shakespeare uses a pattern of rhymed lines. Rhyming couplet round off a scene or incident within a scene, or provide the exit lines for a character:

> *Come, Desdemona, 'tis the soldiers' life*
> *To have their balmy slumbers waked with strife.*
> (Act 2 Scene 3 lines 250–251)

Simile: A comparison between two things which the writer makes clear by using words such as 'like' or 'as':

> *... indeed my invention*
> *Comes from my pate as birdlime does from frieze –*
> (Act 2 Scene 1 lines 124–125)

Soliloquy: When a character is alone on stage, or separated from the other characters in some way, and speaks apparently to himself or herself.

> *That Cassio loves her, I do well believe it;*
> *... Knavery's plain face is never seen till used.*
> (Act 2 Scene 1 lines 280–306)

Stychomythia: Dialogue in which two characters speak single lines of dialogue alternately. The speakers often play with each other's words and echo each other rhythmically, for example,

DESDEMONA   *Heaven bless us!*

OTHELLO   *Say you?*

DESDEMONA   *It is not lost.*
                    But what an if it were?

OTHELLO   *How?*

DESDEMONA   *I say it is not lost.*

OTHELLO   *Fetch't, let me see't.*
(Act 3 Scene 4 lines 78–80)